Witches

A King's Obsession

Witches

A King's Obsession

STEVEN VEERAPEN

BIRLINN

First published in 2025 by
Birlinn Limited
West Newington House
10 Newington Road
Edinburgh
EH9 1QS

www.birlinn.co.uk

ISBN: 978 1 78027 952 7

British Library Cataloguing-in-Publication Data
A catalogue record for this book is available from the British Library

Designed and typeset by Hewer Text UK Ltd, Edinburgh
Papers used by Birlinn Ltd are from well-managed
forests and other responsible sources

Printed and bound by Clays Ltd, Elcograf S.p.A.

For my mum – a very nice witch!

Contents

Part IV:
Possession

Introduction: That Old Black Magic

In April 1610, a London-based occultist and quack doctor returned to his lodgings following a visit to the Globe Theatre in Southwark. After picking his way through the rutted streets, stinking sewer drains, and overhanging, jettied upper galleries of the city, this colourful character – Simon Forman was his name – took up his quill and made an entry in his extensive catalogue of journals. This one went into the 'Bocke of Plaies' section and it concerned the celebrated playwright – by then he was a King's Man and Groom of the Chamber – William Shakespeare's Scotland-based drama, *Macbeth*: 'In *Macbeth* at the Globe, 1610, the 20 of April, Saturday, there was to be observed, first, how Macbeth and Banquo, two noble men of Scotland, riding through a wood, there stood before them three women fairies or nymphs, and saluted Macbeth, saying three times unto him, "Hail, Macbeth, King [sic] of Cawdor; for thou shall be a King, but shall beget no kings," etc.'[1]

Forman's record of the performance has long been of interest to literary scholars, not least for the rare glimpse it gives us into a definite staging of one of the Bard's plays. Yet it is noteworthy, too, for what it doesn't say. The infamous 'Weird Sisters', the witches, of *Macbeth* are, under Forman's pen, not witches but 'women fairies or nymphs'. We can hardly blame Forman for the confusion; in the play, the three Sybilline figures who prophesy Macbeth's murderous future (or do they merely encourage an ambition already present in the eponymous thane?) are rarely explicitly identified as witches. Given Simon Forman's own engagement with, and apparent belief in, the power of prophecy – and, given he became posthumously embroiled in a case involving accusations of witchcraft – it is both understandable and curiously prescient that he should avoid the word. 'Fairies or nymphs', though replete with their own vibrant histories of wickedness and mischief-making, seem like reasonable alternatives.

Whatever Forman's terminology, the production and success of *Macbeth* tell us something both about the early modern period and our own. Witches, then as now, were crowd-pleasers. They drew, and still draw, our attention. Indeed, the figure of the witch has remained remarkably useful across cultures, both temporal and geographical. They feature in the first nursery stories we hear. They are identified as figures in ancient religious texts and in the writings of antiquity (Circe, for example, occupies a role somewhere between sorceress and witch). Asian and African nations each have their own conceptions of the figure who keeps familiars and uses black or white magic for such goals as revenge or gain. Ancient Rome had its own laws against witchcraft, associated with practices including spell-casting, necromancy (raising the dead), and poisoning. In early modern Britain, these black and white demarcations did not really exist beyond the concept of *maleficia*, or magic intended to cause harm. The witch was generally a practitioner of 'low magic': the stuff of immediate effects, good or ill, achieved by magical words or acts (and even then, the association of it with the explicitly demonic required promotion by witch-hunting theorists).[2] It seems that as long as people have been able to look at the world and ask 'why?' and 'how?', there have been those who believe they could wield supernatural powers – and there have been those who distrust or fear them. The basis and usage of these ostensible powers has always been – and will always be – complex, drawing on tradition, religion, and invention; the means by which 'witches' are identified and treated, whether according to the law, via avoidance, or with fascinated interest has been equally complicated.

Every 31 October, millions of children across the western world, pointed hats perched on their heads and the straws of their broomsticks scraping along the ground, troop up to strangers' doors to earn

treats (or to have the occupants studiously pretend not to be home). On television and in film, the witch is useful: she – and it is usually but not always a she – can be good; a feminist symbol of resistance and power; or, as in *The Wizard of Oz*, a beautiful counterpoint to the ugliness of evil. She can be villainous, hook-nosed, green-skinned, and eager to destroy; beautiful and dangerously seductive; an empowered and relatable outcast; or, as in 2015's *The Witch: A New England Folktale* and the iconic *The Blair Witch Project* of 1999, she can provide pure psychological terror.

The frightening possibility of demonic cults or covens, the idea of which came to prominence in the course of the Scottish trials, has proven attractive to modern audiences and writers too – witness *The Witches* (1966), in which Joan Fontaine faces an imaginary rural witch cult in an English village, or Ira Levin's *Rosemary's Baby* (1967), which sees an elderly cult active in New York City. It is small wonder that the silly notion, held by some modern-day practitioners of witchcraft, that today's subcultural covens are the natural or even direct successors of imaginary ancient cults remains popular. Nor is it surprising that anthropologists and sociologists have, in seeking to counter these claims, identified far bigger patterns of persecution and recurring narratives of otherness in societies across the ages (and across the globe), of which the witch panics are simply a serious and sobering example – and one which drew on tropes of prejudice, fear and disgust that predated the dark age of hunts and trials. Witch hunts have thus proven to be of as much interest to social scientists seeking to explain wide-scale social phenomena as to writers and filmmakers.

As well as spooky thrills, witches can provide harmless wish fulfil-ment: what child wouldn't envy the fantasy life of Sabrina Spellman, who can freeze time and turn her high school bully into a pineapple merely by pointing her finger? The witch can therefore be a sanitised figure whose powers come from no particular source – and which might thus be depicted as natural ability – and who might use them for good or ill, born of a sense of fun or fury. The stuff of conflict – of drama – is born. A witch can as easily be an internally conflicted villain or reluctant anti-hero, who derives power directly from Satan or any other outré source (as does, for example, Netflix's more adult 2018 version of Sabrina the eternally teenage witch). As generations of children raised on *Hocus Pocus* (1993) can attest, the witch might move easily between comedy, fantasy, and horror.

Thus, the usefulness of the witch as a pop culture figure lies in her elasticity. As shall be seen, this malleability has always been part of the mythos: contrary to the idea, for example, that a witch was always a social outcast marked by stereotypical costume or physical defects, her danger lay in the fact that she could be anyone, of any rank – a friend, an enemy, a neighbour. Notable figures who found themselves suspected or accused of witchcraft at various times and in various ways included the 3rd Lord Ruthven, the preacher John Knox, two earls of Bothwell, the countess of Somerset, and the 1st Duke of Buckingham. At one point Henry VIII might even have toyed with the idea of blackening Anne Boleyn's name by associating her with sorcery (an activity then loosely associated with *maleficia* under the not-explicitly-demonic umbrella of witchcraft), before abandoning the idea – with the probable connivance of Thomas Cromwell – in favour of purely sexual, equably treasonable slurs. Yet it is still surely notable that it was predominantly the lower and middle classes who fed the gallows at the height of witchcraft mania, with seemingly ordinary or respectable people facing accusation by others of their ilk. Hence, there arose a number of invasive – and often ritually humiliating – means of trying to find physical evidence and, later, the production of identifiable outfits and exaggerated attributes which would reveal her for what she was. It was true also that doubts about the source and efficacy of her powers have always been subject to debate and academic interrogation. Shakespeare saw this and, the Bard being the Bard, he made his memorable Weird Sisters only ambiguously powerful, as liable to be accused of simply telling people what they wanted to hear – and letting those people cause their own problems – as they were of being genuine seeresses or active agents in the play.

We have, in a sense, made witches 'safe' by making them either good-natured – one thinks of the inherently likeable Elizabeth

Montgomery as nose-twitching witch-turned-housewife Samantha Stephens – or cinematic monsters, no more real than the less malleable zombie or vampire. Historically, the name of 'witch' has been more loaded. What might now be thought of as a 'good witch' didn't and couldn't exist, and those who believed themselves to be performing benevolent white magic were increasingly caught up in the general obloquy and legal proscription of all forms of sorcery (or the illicit usage of magic by artful, physical processes). For those who believed in the efficacy of witchcraft, its power had to come from somewhere ungodly. Conversely, those who indulged in what would now be thought of as supernatural endeavours by then-licit means – astrology, scrying, divination, or angelic writing – were keen to distance themselves from folksy cunning arts or devilish dark ones; they were, rather, rational and sceptical thinkers, interested in natural sciences and acting according to existing and developing academic practices. Believers in various forms of magical thinking (or practices) could, then, differ: the educated believer in the 'high magic' of divination via crystals or pentacles could consider himself quite different from the humble village seeress, who might in turn consider herself different from the milk-curdling witch.

This naturally raised questions about how one might sort one from the other. Witches were thought to have, like the poor, always been with us – but men of science wanted no association with their unnatural arts other than to denounce them. This sense of the natural and unnatural would have meant much to those in the early modern period. Educated men sought to lift the veil to learn the godly secrets of the natural world. In doing so, they might test the limits of man's knowledge and abilities within a godly cosmos. Witches were by contrast motivated and powered by the unnatural and the devilish. To complicate matters further, the majority of people believed the universe operated according to certain – generally religious, and in Britain generally Christian – principles. They might therefore differ only in how much and by which means human control of operations could be exerted. It is here worth remembering Jeffrey Burton Russell's accurate summation of medieval witchcraft as 'a composite phenomenon drawing from folklore, sorcery, demonology, heresy, and Christian theology'.[3] The witches of the sixteenth, seventeenth, and eighteenth centuries were the heirs to this complex brew. So were those who made it their business to catch them.

If the witch has been ubiquitous across time and place, then so too has her opposite number: the witch-hunter. The term conjures up a number of figures, from the buckle-hatted, Geneva-cloaked Puritan (epitomised by opportunistic Matthew Hopkins, self-proclaimed Witch-Finder General, of whom we will hear much more) to the twentieth-century politician declaring ideological warfare on anyone suspected of being a fifth columnist. Like the witch, the witch-hunter is something of a shapeshifter, and each might have his own (and it was usually a male) dark motivations: greed, ignorance, paranoia, religious zeal, or political gain. In Britain, the unenviable title of witch-hunter-in-chief has long belonged to one man: James VI and I, whose posterity is stained by his active involvement in some of the worst mass witch hunts Scotland has ever seen, and whose accession to the English throne ensured that what began in Scotland had grisly sequels south of the border.

Yet James seems an unlikely witch-hunter. He has, historically, suffered a poor reputation, not only for his participation in witch hunts but for a welter of much-exaggerated (if not outright invented) physical and mental abnormalities, and, to scholars of less liberal generations, for his unashamed liaisons with a host of predominantly male lovers (the major issue with which, in James's own day, was his tendency to allow them to wield extensive political influence). In truth, he was an effective monarch who, after a hard-won fight, became master of his house in Scotland and proved – when the mood struck him – a diamond-encrusted, glittering sun-king in England, his reign there seeing no major noble rebellions and overseeing a cultural renaissance that produced some of Shakespeare's best works, the flowering of the baroque in architecture, and some of the wildest fashions and most delicious scandals in English history. Although he concerned himself mainly with lofty and idealistic pet projects, he managed religious divisions neatly and, unlike his son, had the charisma and force of personality to defuse constitutional confrontations with Parliament that had been brewing even in the reign of his predecessor, Elizabeth I. The hallmark of his reigns, certainly after acquiring stewardship of England, was peace and cooperation – wherever possible – in both religious and political matters. He was a man who increasingly eschewed conflict and who, by natural inclination and upbringing, was an intellectual and a sceptic. Moreover, his personality was generally affable; one admittedly apocryphal story has him, in 1622, experiencing a fit of royal rage and kicking an unfortunate servant, John Gibb, for losing some state papers; on being informed that he himself had been responsible, James supposedly called for the mortified man and, on his knees, apologised profusely. His belief in witchcraft and his desire to promote wide-scale, terror-filled witch hunts thus seems an aberration, as do his actions in personally overseeing gruesome interrogations. It seems inconceivable that a man who was rarely bloodthirsty and frequently merciful could give rise to the following chilling account:

Upon great consideration therefore taken by the Kings maiestie and his Councell, as well for the due execution of iustice vppon such detestable malefactors, as also for example sake, to remayne a terrour to all others heereafter, that shall attempt to deale in the lyke wicked and vngodlye actions, as witchcraft, sorcery, cuniuration, & such lyke, the sayde Doctor Fian [executed for witchcraft in 1591] was soone after araigned, condemned, and adiudged by the law to die, and then to bee burned according to the lawe of that lande, prouided in that behalfe. Wherevpon hee was put into a carte, and beeing first strangled, hee was immediatly put into a great fire, being readie prouided for that purpose, and there burned in the Castle hill of Edenbrough.[4]

James, however, child of a perforce-absent mother and a repressive, didactic education at the hands of a classical republican and

Calvinist, was a product of his time. If he generally refrained from sending thousands of young men to die of starvation, disease, and injury in Europe's seemingly endless continental wars of religion and territorial aggression, he did not shrink from mounting a spiritual battle against the demonic armies of Satan – as real to him and many of his era as any European belligerent – at home. There was in fact no contradiction between his academic leanings and his belief in witchcraft – quite the contrary. In Britain, witch-hunting was, as leading expert on Scottish witch trials Julian Goodare notes, a Protestant pursuit (though, as will be seen, this was not always the case on the continent). James was nurtured in a nation which, like others of the period, held the possibility of witchcraft as a real and present danger, and at least one trial took place during his minority and in the environs of his childhood home at Stirling Castle. Although the Catholic Church had long had an ambivalent attitude to the idea that witches could really harness demonic powers – some medieval theologians wholeheartedly endorsed the idea and encouraged sanctifying persecutions, whilst others rejected it as the product of devil-sent delusions – it was one that increasing numbers of Protestant thinkers came to believe.

There is therefore no real contradiction in James's dual positions as intellectual man of reason and credulous believer in crimes we know the accused 'witches' couldn't possibly have committed (or at least not in their more fantastical aspects). Rationality and reason in this period did not preclude – far from it – the role and presence of a visible, active God. To subscribe to reason meant to accept this, and to appreciate and assess the limits of the divine order which supposedly followed from it. That meant, to many, the role and presence of a visible, active devil or devils. And an active devil could, and often did, mean devilish acolytes. Educated opinion thus largely centred on whether the devil really did have sufficient power to manifest on earth and whether he could bestow supernatural powers on followers, or whether humans simply deluded themselves that he could. James himself, steeped in Calvinism, was in no doubt: 'Although man in his Creation was made to the Image of the Creator, yet through his fall having once lost it, it is but restored againe in a part by grace onelie to the elect: So all the rest falling away from God, are given over in the handes of the Devill that enemie, to beare his Image: and being once so given over, the greatest and the grossest impietie, is the pleasantest, and most delytefull vnto them.'[5]

Rationally, bad things – plagues, storms, and unexpected deaths – happened for a reason, and an appropriately rational man might discover that reason within the framework of Christian theology. This James believed he had done. Scotland, at least in the king's mind, was a disorderly realm in which Satan found rich pickings. Although he was not always explicitly mentioned in witchcraft cases, the role of the devil as the source of witches' supposed powers was increasingly assumed and accepted by the learned. As the king was, throughout his time in his home nation, ever striving to cement his role as head of his Church (or Kirk), it followed that he believed himself best placed to stand up against God's fallen angel. Naturally, he became Satan and his acolytes' favoured target. James was not a stupid or gullible man but one who was, by his lights, at the cutting edge of what was considered new continental thinking about the problem and presence of evil in the world, and how it might best be dealt with in its physical manifestations. He bequeathed to his realm both a belief in and the machinery to prosecute witchcraft on an almost industrial scale. Scotland, sadly, thus saw some of the highest numbers of executions for witchcraft in Europe, beaten only by the German Protestant states. It serves as a sobering reminder that history is not always a progressive march towards enlightenment but frequently one which sees many stumbles, wrong turns, and reactionary waves of violence and brutality.

Nor was there a contradiction in James's own mix of magical beliefs. He had a strong interest, for example, in numerology as endorsed by the polymath and occult writer Heinrich Cornelius Agrippa, particularly when it came to the supposedly providential value of dates (the 19th being both his and his eldest son, Prince Henry's birthdays, and thus of quasi-magical significance to him). Yet he counted himself an enemy of superstition and witchcraft, and contemporaries would have discerned no double standards. Likewise, Simon Forman, the Shakespeare afficionado, could with equanimity relegate *Macbeth*'s witches to the realm of wicked, mischievous fairies and nymphs (sometimes equated with lesser demons) quite distinct from his own prophesying and pretensions to the serious esoteric sciences explored by such luminaries as Pico della Mirandola and his successors. Educated magical thinking, often based, sometimes dubiously, on ancient knowledge and thus taken as seriously as science, could coexist alongside beliefs in the grubby harnessing of magical powers for gratification, harm, or help. None of this should be surprising or even alien to us – today, a person might visit a fully qualified, medically trained GP in the morning and consult a psychic medium in the evening without spending much thought on the apparent contradiction between scientific and magical thinking.

Given his much-vaunted attitudes when in Scotland and the trials he oversaw there, it is natural to question whether the king modified his beliefs when he gained power in England – a nation which had already long boasted influential believers, not least Sir Francis Drake (who accused, tried, and executed Thomas Doughty for witchcraft and treason) as well as doubters of the real-life, nature-bending power of witches, such as Reginald Scot. In some ways, it is an academic question; as will be seen, James's beliefs, once codified in his *Daemonologie* (1597) and given force of law in England via the 1604 Act Against Conjuration, Witchcraft and Dealing with Evil and Wicked Spirits, set the stage for the horrors that unfolded over the coming centuries. The king certainly did not invent witchcraft as a phenomenon (either in Scotland or England), but he did lead the charge against it as a crime worthy of condign punishment regardless of its apparent results (England having historically only prosecuted witches when alleged harm caused by their craft could be proven). Following his death in 1625, others picked up the mantle of the godly and led persecutions for their own ends. King James had left, probably without intending to, not only a set of persuasive and pervasive beliefs (and given the ongoing popularity of witches, it's not hard to see why people were so interested in the phenomenon), but a model by which other enterprising witch-hunters could follow: one comprising a sufficiently credulous populace able to provide victims; a legal system willing to swing into operation whenever accusations were levelled; and a charismatic, forceful leader willing to endorse or even push trials from the usual scattering of local anomalies into wider-scale hunts. Thereby, authority, legitimacy, and legal rectitude were bestowed. These mass trials, though they deserve attention and explanation, were, however, never the norm. Witchcraft accusations and trials more generally were always relatively unusual and newsworthy. The general approach appears to have been that witches, whatever their origin and the usage of their ostensible powers, existed, but only infrequently were they punished, either singularly or in rare clampdowns (which invariably provided hideous spectacle).

Given the popularity of the figures of witch and witch-hunter, it is not surprising that a vast number of academic and popular texts have been penned, either focusing on particular case studies (usually of mass trials) or looking at the phenomenon more widely. Since Christina Larner's seminal *Enemies of God* (1981), scholars, writers, and novelists have picked up the cudgels and attempted to explain why so-called witches began to be hunted in such numbers, why mass trials erupted at certain times and not others, and why the law eventually ceased to take such matters seriously (even if, as will be argued, popular belief persisted and, in some subcultures, persists). In Great Britain – but, curiously, not in Ireland, which largely escaped the worst of the terror – mass witch trials spanned the late sixteenth to the early eighteenth centuries. Those seeking to explain why have produced a number of explanations and theories. Was the dark age of witch trials a conspiracy against women, given how much more women were affected by and judicially killed following accusations? Given witches were sometimes thought to be sterile and able to cause sterility and impotence (to say nothing of the ritual stripping and prurient examinations), was there a sexual element to the craze? Was the whole thing evidence of a class war resulting from social unrest, whereby the elite sought to divide and control the lower orders? Or did it represent the reclassification of some ancient folkloric beliefs and practices and the stamping out of others? Perhaps it was all the product of the wars of religion and the concomitant fear that others, even in the same hamlet or town or locality, might hold the wrong beliefs and could therefore not be trusted. Punishing witches – in early modern Britain, at least – might have been an acceptable replacement for the wide-scale killing of 'heretics', itself made unfashionable following various European massacres. Or were psychoactive agents – or natural psychological disorders – responsible for provoking delusions and false confessions, with herbal drugs administered sometimes unwittingly and sometimes deliberately? Here, it will be argued that whilst all of these might – might – have played a role in some cases, the underlying causes of the centuries-long witch craze were messier, more complex, and more scattered to ever be answered by a single theory.

Scholars have, too, sought to identify and categorise different elements of historical belief: sorcery, early science, *maleficia*, and religion. Yet it is not always clear how much these categories were shared across early modern society, nor even how much one individual's attitudes to any of them might be fluid over time. Did the wise woman who murmured healing words whilst proffering a herbal potion to a sick neighbour's lips, or a jealous man cursing his colleague's better fortune, think of themselves as witches? Sorcerers? Magicians? Natural philosophers? Did the elite court scryer ever dabble in magical quick fixes? In this sense, witchcraft existed in that certain people did – as some still do – attempt sorcery and curses, and some might well have believed themselves to be serving the devil or demons rather than Christ. All presumed to some degree a human ability to control aspects of the world, whether the course of sickness, fate, or the elements. All accepted that arcane, ancient or specialist knowledge existed and could be accessed – and perhaps updated – with the right tools or words. As witch-hunting authorities repeatedly lent legitimacy to the bizarre and ludicrous powers ascribed to witches, it is interesting to ponder, too, how many poor souls felt themselves ostracised by society and thus drawn to the illusory powers of witchcraft and demonism, if only to see if it could achieve results. Any and all such people, if accused and punished, deserve the same sympathy as others killed or maimed by the state for committing acts that were then illegal but since recognised as acceptable: writing against political leaders, privately engaging in proscribed but consensual sex acts, or believing in alternative faiths (the latter of which could easily overlap with some witches' beliefs).

Alongside the harmless, hapless would-be witches, many more individuals were undoubtedly innocent even of these quasi-religious delusions and simply got caught up in a general, ballooning persecution against anyone thought not to conform to Christian orthodoxy (and thus considered capable of the vilest acts and inverted anti-Christian practices that God-fearing Christians could concoct or pluck from the late-medieval historical record). To understand how various figures thought of themselves at different times – and to recognise how they were thought of – it is necessary to look at accusations of witchcraft across the social spectrum and to see how shifts and developments in attitudes shaped, created, and ultimately disregarded them.

In doing so, it will become apparent that not all accusations of witchcraft were born equal. Some, as we will see, were dismissed; others were so nakedly political in intent that they got no further than weak accusations thrown against powerful figures and quickly denied, downplayed, or suppressed. In order to understand how and why this mania for the supernatural affected – and sometimes didn't affect – those living in Britain during the darkest period for witchcraft, it is necessary to understand the people whose lives were touched by accusations, the legal systems which developed to serve (or punish) them, the local and national leaders who held the whip hand over all, and the beliefs all three held in common.

This is the history, told through its key cases and personalities, of a centuries-long conflict fought on a spiritual, theological, academic, and legal battleground. It is the history of a conflict between hunters and hunted, between sceptics and believers, and between truth and justice. It is the history of fear – of the other, of natural disasters, and of authoritarian reprisals for refusing to believe the right thing – versus developing scientific knowledge and assurance in natural laws, a time during which trials proliferated when a climate of terror prevailed or could be whipped up. And this conflict, though it had long been present in Great Britain (albeit downplayed and frequently stalling), was blown into a long-running war, rising and falling in the frequency of its battles, by one man.

PART I

Infestation

'First, the initiation of the witches and their profession of sacrilege'
— Sprenger and Kramer, 1496, *Malleus Maleficarum*

I

The Origins of Evil

Witches were a persistent problem to Heinrich Kramer. Trained as a Dominican, having risen to Prior of his local order in Sélestat, and having achieved the title of Master of Sacred Theology for his scholarly endeavours, he found himself elevated to the position of Catholic Inquisitor – not in his native France but instead with responsibility over considerable Holy Roman territories, including the County of Tyrol, Salzburg, Moravia, and Bohemia. Given his fiery nature and obvious ambition – he attached himself to the influential Archbishop of Salzburg and through him had a connection to the Holy See – it was a role he relished and intended to make use of. Kramer was a man determined to make a name for himself, and he sought to do it by entering a battle against those antithetical to the Catholic orthodoxy. There were, Kramer believed, devilish creatures in the world who formed themselves into sects and held assemblies; they were flagrantly worshipping Satan and, in return, wielding fantastical powers. The Church had been too preoccupied debating these people's existence and the reality of their powers to do anything useful about them. What was needed was a purge. In short, he wished for a new, active belligerence against witches. As an Inquisitor and a scholar, he was well placed to encourage just that.

Heinrich Kramer (also known by the more ominous name of Heinrich Institoris) was, however, not an original mind – indeed, the definition of invention was, and continued for centuries to be, more akin to breathing fresh life into what was old, lapsed, and worthy of vigorous revival. The concept of witchcraft and witches was ancient, drawn from a conglomeration of primitive, pagan, and traditional beliefs (such as the night-riding, blood-sucking female *striga*). Even the diabolic pact, which became such a feature of early modern beliefs, had found expression via St Augustine who, though he denied the ability of humans to shapeshift, nevertheless acknowledged the delusive power of demons: 'All arts of this sort [he was speaking of prophesying or divination] . . . are therefore nullities, or are part of a guilty superstition, springing out of a baleful fellowship between men and demons and are to be utterly repudiated and avoided by the Christian as the covenants [pacta] of a false and treacherous fellowship.'[1]

Demons, evidently, were thought to be at work on the weak, sparking in them false notions of their own power. Just prior to the high medieval period, in the tenth century, the Benedictine chronicler Regino of Prüm had voiced scepticism not in the existence of witches as people who attempted magical acts but of their actual power to do harm. His *Canon Episcopi* stated:

Bishops and their officials must labour with all their strength so that the pernicious art of *sortilegium* [sorcery, or physical acts – brewing potions or uttering incantations – with the aim of producing magical results] and *maleficium* [the broader form of evil magic intended to harm, whether by thought or deed], which was invented by the devil, is eradicated from their districts, and if they find a man or woman follower of this wicked sect to eject them foully disgraced from the parishes.

It is also not to be omitted that some wicked women, who have given themselves back to Satan and been seduced by illusions and phantasms of demons, believe and openly profess that, in the hours of night, they ride upon certain beasts with Diana, the goddess of pagans, and an innumerable multitude of women, and in the silence of the dead of the night to fly over vast spaces of earth, and obey her commands as of their lady, and are summoned to her service on certain nights . . . An innumerable multitude, deceived by this false opinion, believe this to be true, and so believing, wander from the right faith and return to the error of the pagans when they think that there is any of divinity or power except the one God. Because of this, the priests in all their churches should preach with all insistence to the people that they may know this to be in every way false, and that such phantasms are sent by the devil who deludes them in dreams.[2]

It was an attitude of scepticism – and a call for non-draconian correction of errors – responding, apparently, to a vexatious problem: fantasy-driven paganistic women deluding themselves into believing they possessed supernatural powers and might harness them to do harm. According to the *Canon Episcopi*, they were wrong, as was anyone who lent credulous ears to their 'infidel' claims: 'Whoever therefore believes that anything can be made, or that any creature can be changed or transformed to better or worse, or be transformed into another species or likeness, except by God Himself who made everything and through whom all things were made, is beyond a doubt an infidel.'[3] Yet the rather reasonable – if one can overlook the misogyny – approach was not, and would not be, universally shared. The Roman Catholic medieval world was not born in a vacuum. The people who lived under its considerable territories inherited a vast, colourful array of superstitions, mythic figures, and religious customs from the cultures and belief systems which preceded Christianity. And the Catholic Church, much as it might have liked to, could not wipe out centuries of lingering beliefs and practices, some of them tailored over time and place to fit a Christian framework, others more nakedly belonging to pre-Christian tradition. It could, though, engage in the same kind of process, repackaging some beliefs as its own (an obvious example being the overlaying of Christian holidays onto former pagan festival days) and proscribing others as either demonic or delusional. What once might have appeared to be useful pagan spirits might, over time, be transmuted into witches' familiars.

The Church had reason to worry. If the Christian God didn't appear to be answering prayers, an individual might, for example,

try their luck with a pagan deity or some other folkloric sprite. The
Church might then encourage them back into the fold by providing
ritualistic alternatives – appeals to the saints, for example – or otherwise denounce the un-Christian deities and sprites as demons.
Depending on time, location, and the perceived spread of anti-
Christian practices – and depending on the perceived numbers of
people betraying God – the Church and its more militant leaders
and agents might, of course, turn to more severe measures of control
and repression.

By the late fifteenth century, when Heinrich Kramer was active
(having been born in around 1430), witchcraft was largely understood as a form of heresy: a belief or set of beliefs contrary to established, orthodox Catholic doctrine. It is notable that Pope Lucius III
issued the decretal bull Ad abolendam ('To Abolish') in 1184, with
a view to 'abolishing divers malignant heresies' such as the anti-papal
and anti-Catholic Waldensian movement. In time, this led to a
formal, episcopal Inquisition (which laid the groundwork for future
medieval Inquisitions, empowered to torture and kill). As ever, the
desire to discover wickedness invariably found it and spurred on
further suspicions and searches. This was certainly the case with
Pope Innocent III's Albigensian Crusade (so-called due to the appellation pertaining to the southern French heretics) against the Cathars
in Languedoc in the early thirteenth century. The murky episode of
the Cathars – identified and ruthlessly hunted by the Catholic
Church – can itself be seen as a step forward in advancing both
beliefs about the evils of witchcraft and in devising means of eliminating it.

The Cathars, if they ever even existed as a unified, theologically
coherent sect (and scholars have long recognised the lack of evidence
for a single Catharistic faith, as opposed to a smattering of theologically disparate non-conformists across southern France), were of
interest to the established Church. Over the course of the thirteenth
and early fourteenth centuries, strenuous efforts were made to identify, label, denounce, and punish these heretical anti-Christians. Not
only Innocent III but his successors attributed to this supposed sect

a slew of dark beliefs and practices. Via Crusades and Inquisitions, the plan was to wash Christendom clean of them, although in practice this led to variation in efficacy amongst Inquisitions, often according to the personal beliefs of Inquisitors (some of whom were far more active than others, and some of whom showed themselves believers in demonic witchcraft whilst others were more dubious). Whatever the enigmatic Cathars believed (and popularly this has been thought to include female participation in religious practices, a rejection of materialism, and an overarching Manichaean view of the cosmos as being composed of a duality between good – the human – and evil – the material world), the Holy Fathers were in no doubt. To them, the Cathars existed, were a threat, and were engaged in heretical, anti-Christian acts. These people were Satanists and must be crushed. Thus the campaign of armed persecution and suppression wore on, with one anti-Cathar papal legate – in response to being asked how the Catholic soldiery might sort Cathars from the innocent – supposedly uttering the horrifying words '*Caedite eos. Novit enim Dominus qui sunt eius*' (popularly translated as 'Kill them all. Let God sort them out').[4]

It is due to the Cathar threat (or the enflaming of it) that institutional organisation against evil practices gained ground. This had implications for the future of witchcraft persecution both in its processes and its tendency to synthesise unorthodox beliefs with religion and the profane. The Cathars, it was claimed by Church authorities, were not just Satanists, nor even just heretics deserving of correction, but monstrous and devilish. This was not merely a dominant Catholic Church attempting to stamp out an inferior potential rival, but a genuine question of theology. The Church believed that a powerful sect of Cathars existed and formed a stable and dangerous bloc. It believed, too, that if these heretics rejected the Church and the material world, and if they viewed God as occupying a separate realm from the world, they must view the world as the devil's territory. As earth-bound humans, must they not then worship Satan? It is even possible – and probably likely – that some people denounced as Cathars, who had doubts about the powerful

Roman Church and its glittering hierarchy of wealthy clergymen, did think this way, whilst others subscribed to equally heretical beliefs about Christ being, as God was, pure spirit and thus unable to have suffered on the cross (which should therefore not be venerated).

The militant Catholic Church went further. These people were apparently sexual libertines who indulged in orgies, the better to abuse and degrade the physical bodies they held in contempt. They met in secret, dark places – caves, for example – and offered sacrifices to the devil. They could use inanimate objects to fly through the air with the aid of demonic forces. They assembled in 'synagogues' (the anti-Semitic sentiment being impossible to ignore). These were, in short, what future generations would recognise as outright witches; common, existing tropes about anti-Christian evil-doing (the sucking of blood and the eating of infants) would cross over with these stereotypes and a host of others in producing what became the traditional witch figure.

It was a figure already taking shape, as noted by the Welsh writer Walter Map, who also, typically, collapsed witchcraft, heresy, and anti-Semitism. To Map, writing in around 1182, families of heretics worshipped Satan, who might take on animalistic corporeal forms, with their bodies: 'The families sit in silence, each in their synagogue, and wait. And in the middle of them, hanging by a rope, a black cat of marvellous size climbs down a rope. On seeing it, they put out the lights. They do not sing hymns or repeat them distinctly but hum through clenched teeth and pantingly feel their way towards the place where they saw their lord. When they have found him they kiss him, each the more humbly as he is the more inflamed with frenzy – some the feet more under the tail, most the private parts.'[5] This description gives us an early association of devilry with black cats, but it also again reveals the obsession with bestiality – and sexuality more generally – that became such a feature of witchcraft accusations and trials.

The Cathars were wiped out by the mid fourteenth century, but the problem of heresy was not. Neither was an interest in exactly what kind of evil and perverse acts might be ascribed to heretics, or the associations between heretics and witchcraft, devil-worship, the invocation of servile demons, and sorcery. Nor were the active Inquisitions.

So it is that we find, in this period, people caught up in the net who were not thought to be part of any major heretical traditions. In 1384, in Italy, Sibilla Zanni and Pierina de Bugatis were investigated by the Inquisition, where they revealed a tale of a mystical cult which met with and worshipped a quasi-divine woman, Madonna Oriente, who had the power to kill and, with a magic wand, reanimate animals, the flesh of which the women would eat (excluding the donkey, due to its association with Jesus Christ). According to Pierina, at least in her later accounts, both the living and the dead attended such pagan-flavoured meetings. Both women were ordered to do penance by wearing red crosses, with the Inquisition evidently believing them to be fantasists. Yet six years later the Church was less forgiving of their tall tales and charged both with devil worship, rewriting their more or less pagan claims with anti-demonic pens. Their tale – under the Inquisitors' gaze having developed to include raising the devil in human form and signing a blood pact with him – saw them both sentenced to death. So did confessions (often obtained under torture from people who had probably attempted no more than simple curses, oaths, or harmless rituals) of summoning devils and begging favours of them elsewhere in Europe at this time – as, for example, Jeanne de Brigue, burnt at the stake in 1390 in Paris for alleged divination and invocation of a demon called Haussibut.

During this period, sorcery and *maleficia* – traditional 'low magic' practices still in the process of being aligned with demoniacal activity to produce classic witchcraft – were thriving. Here, Church figures were not immune from accusations themselves. In the sphere of high politics, then inextricable from religion, Bishop Peter of Bayeux was accused of resorting to sorcery against Philip III of France in 1278. Kings were, indeed, susceptible to *maleficia*; Louis X of France investigated claims that the sorcerers Jacques Dulot and his wife had been hired by the royal minister and Grand Chamberlain, Enguerrand de

Marigny, and his wife, Alips de Mons. Their magic had aimed at the crown. All four were executed in 1315. The means of sorcery – and one which recurs throughout the early modern period and which exists today – was the use of wax dolls, manipulated with the intent of causing actual harm to the person whose likeness they captured. Political witchcraft – or political *maleficia* and the hiring of sorcerers for political ends – remained a potent accusation across the centuries (with a curious lull in the mid fourteenth century), carrying on alongside the more infamous mass trials of those thought to have engaged in diabolic pacts. The two strands might even collide in spectacular fashion, as in the case of the disgraced one-time French military hero Gilles de Rais, who was sentenced to be hanged and burned in 1440 following an *inquisitio infamiae* (a secret ecclesiastical investigation) and trial which saw him accused of summoning demons, consulting magic books, engaging in sodomy, and – gruesomely – murdering several children.

It is, however, undeniable that the high medieval period was predominantly concerned with shaping a narrative which denounced heretics as witches, and witches as heretics. Their focus, however, was very much on the heresy. As Goodare has pointed out, the Inquisitors were doing nothing as blunt – or as intellectually dishonest – as calling Jews (or Waldensians, or for that matter Cathars or any other emerging sects) witches; but certain tropes were historically anti-Christian and thus easily reused and further exaggerated. Not all heretics were witches, but all witches were heretics. The category of 'witch' would take time to come into its own, especially among those leaders and lawmen who took it seriously as a threat. Accordingly, as the late medieval era bloomed, so too did a flowering of scholarly discussion and debate on the issue of witchcraft, often in response to the findings of the Inquisitions, the trials held in various territories, or those curious cases of sorcery and *maleficia* which continued to flourish.

As Brian P. Levack has noted, 'Prior to the 1420s, the concept of witchcraft as a crime involving both harmful magic and devil-worship was in the process of formation: therefore, it is problematic to speak of the prosecutions that took place during those years as witchcraft trials.'[6] In other words, most 'witches' were persecuted not as full-blown devil-worshipping, demon-pact-signing, black-magic-casting classic witches; they were predominantly on trial either for anti-Catholic heresies (such as paganistic devil- or demon-worship), for causing harm (or intending to cause harm) via *maleficia* or sorcery (without consistent interest in outright diabolism), or for political reasons (either due to bad faith accusations by opponents or due to the accused having genuinely attempted harm against rivals by magical means). It was in the fifteenth century that these accusations began to converge to form what we might confidently call the 'classic witch'. This period also, not coincidentally, began seeing the first 'classic witch hunts', as reports out of Switzerland indicated shocking outbreaks of demonic activity on the part of suspected heretics.

It is curious – and prescient for the patterns to be followed in Britain – that the Swiss hunts signalled what would be features of mass hunts across Europe: paranoia, contagion, and the involvement of the secular authorities in prosecution. Switzerland had experience of witchcraft tried secularly, notably in the case of one Stedelen, a man burned in the early fifteenth century (with the judge, Peter von Greyerz, affirming his own belief in the reality of *maleficia*, sorcery, and the demonic pact). The Valais region (then part of Savoy but today a Swiss Canton) had been troubled by Inquisitorial interest in rooting out heretical Waldensians in Fribourg (to the north). It is likely that, as with the Cathars, fear of witchcraft and demonic practices had been enflamed in the process. At any rate, according to contemporary chronicler Johannes (or Hans) Fründ, what began as a small number of complaints – neighbour against neighbour – snowballed, with a medley of accusations (including heresy, lycanthropy, sorcery, invocation and worship of Satan, *maleficia*, flying on enchanted chairs, invisibility, and demonic pacts) spreading across the entire region. Authorities swooped. In August 1428, the use of torture was authorised, provided sufficient accusations against a person were secured.

Unsurprisingly, barbaric methods apparently worked. According to Fründ (who, it should be noted, might have embroidered what was originally a series of accusations of simple *maleficia* in order to sensationalise the phenomenon), lurid confessions emerged, involving the murder and cannibalism of children, mass-meetings (nocturnal gatherings which, like similar meetings in previous Inquisitorial trials, were prototypical 'sabbats', though that word was centuries away), and the casting on of illness, impotence, and injury. Fründ claimed hundreds were burned, the idea being that the flames separated the soul from the body, provided a double execution (both secular and spiritual), and proved a deterrent to others. As a method of final punishment, this grisly act found favour in Scotland, France, Denmark, and Spain – though not in England or North America, where hanging alone would be considered sufficient.

One sees in the Valais affair – and its many Swiss sequels (and it is worth noting that the last individual 'witch' executed in Switzerland was Anna Göldi in 1782) – many of the Inquisitorial and secular fears of heresy, dark magic, and devilry combining under a secular hammer, whether through Johannes Fründ's elaboration or not. Whether the trials were mainly for *maleficia* or if they did indeed produce the more extreme, demonic accounts the author claimed, it is apparent that they progressed in number as the community became embroiled in its own terrors and suspicions, which in turn affected neighbouring communities.

What caused the Valais affair in Switzerland? What caused neighbour to turn on neighbour? Certainly, they had the example of the Inquisition, which was doing much to cement the image of the witch. But it is worth noting that the duchy of Savoy had fairly recently witnessed high-profile witchcraft accusations against the enemies of its leader, Amadeus VIII. In 1417, Jean Lageret, the duke's former councillor, and a physician called Michael Dishypotis, had attempted to conjure demons using statuettes (a form of both sorcery and invocation) to gain influence at the ducal court.[7] Witchcraft worries were in the air – and that air was blowing down from the top. It is difficult in this case – given the sparseness of material – to blame any individual figure as a leader, but it is clear that both the Inquisition and the secular ruler had been active in matters involving witchcraft. The problem was that a climate of fear and suspicion, once created (deliberately or accidentally, whether by high politics or general political instability, or a combination of both) could not necessarily be curtailed if the people began availing themselves of the legal machinery to vent their fears, or even to escalate local disputes. Amadeus himself, elected by a rump of the troubled Council of Basel in 1437 as anti-pope, was denounced by the pontiff, Eugenius IV, as

> the first-born son of Satan, the most unfortunate Amadeus, once duke and prince of Savoy. He meditated this scheme for long. Several years ago, as is widely said, he was seduced by the trickery, soothsayings and phantoms of certain unfortunate men and women of low reputation (commonly called wizards or witches or Waldensians and said to be very numerous in his country), who had forsaken their Saviour to turn backwards to Satan and be deceived by demonic illusions, to have himself raised up to be a monstrous head in God's church.[8]

Dispute and accusation were rife, from the top to the bottom – and dispute and accusation begged victims and scapegoats. The beleaguered Eugenius found one in Amadeus (who would outlive the pope and continue his own Church career). Yet the mass trials which began in Valais indicated that witchcraft was not just a spiritual crime but one which, given its apparent power to endanger life and property, interested secular authorities who could, like the Inquisitions (but not the normal ecclesiastical courts, which lacked the power of arrest), authorise torture and execution. Legal systems and jurisdictions across Europe were still developing and sometimes competing, and laws were still being written to deal with crimes of all kinds. The Catholic Church, or the pope at least, was unwilling to relinquish its role as chief accuser.

This was made clear in the Inquisitorial mass trials which took place at Arras in 1459. There, the focus was, again, on heresy, with witchcraft – in particular the Waldensians (known also as the Vaudois) – an easy target. The most energetic persecutor was the fanatical Inquisitor Pierre le Broussard, whose attentions were brought to a young woman, reputedly a sex worker, called Deniselle (or Demiselle) Grenieres, who was arrested and thrown in the bishop's palace. There, she was asked if she knew a hermit named Robinet de Vaulx. It was an ominous question. Robinet had recently been burnt for sorcery at Langres, claiming during his trial that a number of Frenchwomen, including Deniselle, were sorcerers. The unfortunate woman was repeatedly tortured and confessed, naming an elderly painter, Jehan la Vitte, known colloquially as Abbot Little Sense. La Vitte was arrested and, in a terror of what he might say – or be induced to say – mutilated his own tongue. It did him little good. He, in turn, was tortured into confessing that he had indeed been a heretical Waldensian – and he, too, told the Inquisitors what they wanted to hear: there had been many others. Further, he named names.

The hunt was on, taking in barbers, sex workers, sergeants, and business owners. When the vicars at Arras began expressing doubts – or rather fears that the affair was getting out of hand – the Dean of Arras, Jacques Dubois, as dedicated to the cause as Broussard, regrouped with the more active Inquisitors to double down on proceedings. The whole thing threatened scandal, as battle lines were drawn between those leading the charge against heretical witchcraft and those who opposed what was becoming an embarrassing explosion of torture and accusation. The fever pitch of spectacle was reached when the accused were brought to the scaffold wearing mitres with the devil painted on them (his appearance resembling that found in their confessions: he was a goat with a monkey's tail and a human face). Publicly, they confessed to using devil-procured salves which they rubbed on sticks, thus giving them the power of flight. On their enchanted sticks they had flown to meetings with Satan, where they had drunk wine, sold their souls, and kissed his backside whilst holding flaming torches. With la Vitte presiding as master of ceremonies, they had trod and spat on the cross, and engaged in sex with their shapeshifting, gender-fluid new master. This was the crux of the Inquisitors' fears: conspiratorial meetings of the ungodly, which they alleged took the form of illicit, often sexually charged assemblies. After affirming the confession, the self-congratulatory ecclesiastical authorities handed the accused over to the secular ones for execution. Immediately, the terrified victims began recanting and claiming that Dubois had promised the accused their lives if they confessed to the pre-written litany of evil. Dubois and his cronies had an answer. The devil was making them obstinate. Twelve people were led to the stakes at various locations.

The horrors continued and increased, the first flames setting light to a terror that threatened to engulf local dignitaries and senior burghers. Arras began to get a dark name. Trade was threatened. The wealthy began to decamp, sometimes being chased in their flight from potential accusation. Towards the end of 1460, such luminaries as the Lord Colard de Beaufort had been taken up and confessed to flying on sticks and attending woodland assemblies. At the intervention of the Duke of Burgundy, who was invited to assess matters and who consulted academic opinion (which was typically divided), the latest batch of prisoners were found guilty but merely imprisoned. This proved to be a mistake on the authorities' part. Beaufort, at least, was capable of independent action in response to his treatment, and he undertook to sue his tormentors in the Parliament of Paris. The Parliament, examining what had been going on in detail, loudly denounced affairs at Arras as an abuse of power on the part of the Inquisitors. Beaufort was freed, as were the others. Dubois, who had been one of the most duplicitous and tyrannical ecclesiastics involved, was spared embarrassment: he suffered a stroke and died without regaining the power of speech in early 1461.

Arras, then, was freed from the grip of suspicion – and there was even condemnation of its religious excesses as an unusually abhorrent anomaly. It is here worth noting that these multiple-accused affairs were, both in the 1400s and later, never normal. Indeed, wide-scale persecutions (as against the Waldensians, the Cathars – or even the Knights Templar, who faced the typical accusations of blasphemy, heresy, devilish cross-denying, and cat's bottom-kissing in the course of their suppression) resulted from the desires of particularly active leaders who took their beliefs seriously enough to pursue them to extremes. This sense of intense hunting being the exception would set the pattern for centuries to come.

But what, then, was a witch? A heretic of the wrong opinions whose activities smacked of the demonic and were patched together from a melange of ancient or traditional practices? A separate category of anti-Christian felon? And, depending on the answer, who should be hunting them – the Inquisitions (which were hardly spread fairly across Europe, with some nations, such as England and Scotland, untouched by them) or the secular authorities? These questions needed answers.

Medieval and early modern scholars disliked nebulous origins; they liked to be right, and they liked to argue (ideally about how right they were). Above all, they liked order. Witches, constructed from a variety of sources welded and melded together by different institutions at different times and in different places, had to have a clear origin, purpose, and definition. It wasn't good enough to conflate or confuse witchcraft with the disparate heretical sects which seemed to be popping up across Europe. The question of the veracity of their supernatural abilities, too, had to be settled. They were either really possessed of powers (with demonic intervention) or deluded by the devil into thinking they were. Happily, they could fit into the established order. The universe, it was believed, was fixed, with God ruling heaven and the earth from the apex of the cosmos. The earth, fixed and immovable, was surrounded by rotating celestial spheres, on whose axes the sun, moon, and other planetary bodies moved. Above and outside them, under the guiding hands of the good angels, rotated the sphere of stars, and above and outside that was the kingdom of heaven. It therefore stood to learned reason that the devil and his demons dwelt as far from God's celestial kingdom as possible: in hell, at the centre of the earth. The question was whether witches could act as his earthly servants and bring him topside.

It was probably in response to the various secular and Inquisitorial trials that academics and writers sought to codify witches as representative of something newly identified and distinct. Johannes Fründ, who documented the Valais affair, called this new category of evildoer the *Hexsen* (which would catch on in Germany). Nicolas Jacquiers was unusual in connecting demonic witchcraft with the harmful low magic of *maleficia*; his ideas are particularly notorious as a potential trigger of the Arras trials. Other writers followed, including amongst their ranks poets, Dominicans, Franciscans, and secular authorities, each arguing their case for or against the reality of witchcraft. Particularly influential was Johannes Nider's *Formicarius* (1475) which, though sceptical of some claims arising from heresy trials, did much to promote the idea of female susceptibility to diabolical witchcraft and thereby link the idea of the village witch engaged in *maleficia* or sorcery to a source every bit as demonic as that from which the heretical magic wielder derived their powers. In this way, trials fed academic belief, and academic legitimacy fed trials. Cases would recur throughout the late fifteenth century (with the periods 1455–60 and 1480–85 seeing spikes).[9] Some, however, failed entirely. It was the failure to ignite an assault on witches – in the Tyrol – that prompted Heinrich Kramer to take up his pen and write a book which would have more influence on witchcraft, even if not immediately, than any other until King James's own *Daemonologie*.

2

This Twilight and Evening of the World

The *Malleus Maleficarum* (popularly translated as *The Hammer of the Witches*), published in 1486, was originally attributed to Heinrich Kramer, though from 1519 Dominican Inquisitor Jacob Sprenger (whose level of involvement in the authorship is disputed) was co-credited. It has gone down in history as the springboard for the wider acceptance of witchcraft and witches as real, at least in terms of their actual abilities and demonic associations. So too has it the dubious honour of cementing the idea of witches as female. It can therefore be said to have met its goals. Having failed to spark a mass persecution at Innsbruck in the Tyrol, Kramer was determined to end the decades, indeed the centuries, of doubts, uncertainty, and debate on the nature of witchcraft.

In truth, the book has certainly been influential and deserves its infamy; but it was, at least initially, a failure in that it appears not to have unleashed a wave of witch-hunting across Europe. The *Malleus* was, if anything, a sleeper hit rather than an immediate success; it instituted no immediate cultural (or religious) revolution. The text's misogyny is typical, albeit illustrative of the codification of a trend which was already apparent: the idea that women were more likely to be witches. According to Kramer, the reason why 'a greater number of witches is found in the fragile feminine sex . . . is accredited by actual experience, apart from the verbal testimony of credible witnesses'. Further, 'there are three things in nature, the Tongue, the Ecclesiastic, and a Woman, which know no moderation in goodness or vice'. The Bible supported him. Ecclesiasticus XXV acknowledged that 'there was no wrath above the wrath of a woman', and women were popularly considered (in a reversal of modern attitudes) to be the gender more inclined to carnal lust. The preoccupation with women as a threat to masculine virtue is typical if unedifying. Two chapters of the *Malleus* are dedicated to fears of women enchanting (or stealing) male virility. In addition to concerning herself with causing impotence in men and abortions in women, the witch might go further: 'In the town of Ratisbon a certain young man who had an intrigue with a girl, wishing to leave her, lost his member; that is to say, some glamour was cast over it so that he could see or touch nothing but his smooth body.'[1]

Understandably, the afflicted young man, 'in his worry over this went to a tavern to drink wine'. There, he learnt the maleficent cause of his missing member from a friendly woman and returned to the young witch, whom he half-strangled with a towel until she put her hand between his thighs and restored his manhood. If not made up out of whole cloth, the mind reels at the actual event on which this bizarre episode was based. Equally strange is another tale recounted by the *Malleus*, in which another man, similarly afflicted, confessed his malady to a priest, removing his breeches to prove that he had been unmanned not in the literal sense, apparently, but via 'some prestidigitatory art' or convincing illusion. Mercifully, he was supposedly able to convince the witch to remove the enchantment. Other witches, however, would be less generous: some of them 'collect male organs in great numbers, as many as twenty or thirty members altogether, and put them in a bird's nest, or shut them up in a box, where they move themselves like living members, [and] eat oats and corn . . . it is all done by the devil's work and illusion'.[2] One fellow, climbing a tree with the permission of a witch to retrieve his penis, apparently got greedy. According to Kramer's report, 'when he tried to take a big one, the witch said, "You must not take that one . . . because it belonged to a parish priest."'

These fantastical tales – always carefully glossed to emphasise the delusive nature of the diabolical phenomena, as were accounts of transformation and shape-shifting – are the stuff of sheer misogynistic anxiety, as many other stories recounted reveal male fears about women who show themselves the antithesis of the good, nurturing wife and mother.

Less illusionary was the ability of witches – borrowed from demons, who had been permitted the power by God – to 'raise up winds, and make fire fall from heaven [lightning]', causing damage to crops and property. As the devil and his minions dwelt within the earth, and as weather phenomena were held to be caused by 'vapours released from the earth and water', this made good sense. A witch might 'dip a twig in water and sprinkle the air to make it rain' or cause sheep to fly up into the air repeatedly before dropping dead. A number of means, from the otiose to the downright sadistic, existed to test whether witchcraft was indeed to blame for calamities; if an animal was suspected to have been killed by witchcraft, its intestines could be removed and dragged home, carried through the back door (but not the front), and burned on a hurdle. If witchcraft had indeed caused the death, the witch would feel the burning agony in her own gut and attempt to gain entry to the house to retrieve a coal from the fire with which to end her misery. Such superstitions, to Kramer, were hardly ideal, but they were tolerable. Less tolerable were lay attempts – mostly by superstitious means – to relieve victims of the effects of witchcraft. Though the *Malleus* acknowledges that, when it comes to the spells and sorceries of witches, like must be met with like, it is clear that healing magic by non-witches must be carefully administered by ecclesiastical experts. The ideal remedy, of course, is the intervention of the Catholic Church, its ministers, its sacraments, and its pilgrimages.

On the question of how witches ought to be treated, Kramer was unequivocal. Whilst those who engaged such creatures as sorcerers – he names princes – might be shriven if penitent, the witch was less lucky:

Let the accused be stripped; or, if she is a woman, let her first be led to the penal cells and there stripped by honest women of good reputation. And the reason for this is that they should search for any instrument of witchcraft sewn into her clothes; for they often make such instruments, at the instruction of devils, out of the limbs of unbaptised children ... the Judge shall use his own persuasions to induce her to confess the truth voluntarily; and if she will not, let him order the officers to bind her with cords, and apply her to some engine of torture; and let them obey at once but not joyfully, rather appearing to be disturbed by their duty. Then let her be released again at someone's earnest request, and taken on one side, and let her again be persuaded; and in persuading her, let her be told that she can escape the death penalty.[3]

As cruelly manipulative as this sounds – and was – the goal was to produce a confession. If torture was required, torture was to be applied. If false promises were required, they might be delivered. If the witch had a reasonable reputation, she might be confined for some time, the aim being to procure from her the names of other witches. Ideally, the confession would be upheld later, when the immediate threat of torture had ceased. This might be arrived at if the witch had given her service to Satan with her words but not her heart, in which case a divine angel might inspirit her to reveal the truth of her devilish antics. If she held her peace even under torture, she was likely to have given both her heart and soul to the devil, denying the Catholic faith with her lips and her soul. It is difficult to see how the accused could win.

Why, one might wonder – not unreasonably – did these supposed witches not simply call upon their demonic powers to smite their tormentors and fly to safety? Kramer had an answer. Such godly men as those who interrogated and imprisoned witches were specially blessed with immunity against the dark arts. If it seems inconceivable why any woman (or man) would allow herself to fall into the vice of witchcraft, the answer was simple. Satan preyed on those who had been laid low – 'weariness' in life bred dissatisfaction, and that opened the door to the devil. Satan was, after all, both seducer and tempter (as the Bible indicated) and he might speak through the mouths of others. Witches might thus, fairly easily, be found amongst the marginalised, downtrodden, and outcast.[4] Especially troubling was the sense of conspiracy and illicit assembly thus created (always a source of anxiety to authorities). Having seduced one person into witchcraft, the devil would naturally encourage that person to indoctrinate others into making the pact and receiving demonic powers.

Their new master might allow them to cure but not injure, to injure but not cure, or to do both (this last being the most powerful and dangerous kind of witch – the kind who devoured children, drove horses mad, terrified or mesmerised magistrates, and flew). All, however, were demonic. All copulated with the devil. The old heretical trope of travelling great distances to be inducted into the Satanic faith via a pact was asserted, in the teeth of sceptics such as Ambrosius de Vignate (who doubted confessions involving magical travels, animal transformations, and carnal intercourse with Satan, and insisted on a more cautious approach to understanding true malicious witchcraft). But witches, to Kramer, were 'not simple heretics but apostates . . . they must not be punished like other here- tics with lifelong imprisonment [a fate allowable to penitent here- tics], but must suffer the extreme penalty'.[5] Catholic thinkers could only understand non-Christian faiths, non-Christian beliefs (whether pagan or popular), and otherwise inexplicable harmless phenomenon as anti-Christian, anti-order, and therefore demonic. Witches were all of these things – or they could be acknowledged as such. A public enemy – a new, clearly identifiable public enemy who might cause injury, serve a master who delighted in destroying good people's fortunes, or disturb the weather – was being born.

The *Malleus Maleficarum* is fascinating to the student of history for its codification of beliefs which played so important a role in later developments. In parts it is impossible not to see it as a source of morbid, absurdist humour (nests of bewitched, oat-eating penises seldom cropping up in serious works of Catholic theology). Yet it is horrifying in that those beliefs – and those developments – cost so many innocent lives. Perhaps most insidious is its opening delibera- tion: 'Whether the belief that there are such beings as witches is so essential a part of the Catholic faith that obstinacy to maintain the opposite opinion manifestly savours of heresy.'[6] In this chilling line, opposition is threatened. To deny the reality of witches and witchcraft is to risk accusation of heresy at least. In the future, the risk became even greater.

Given this extensive scholarly investigation into the truth of witchcraft and its practitioners, and given that the text was read widely (it was republished with Pope Innocent VIII's bull *Summis desiderantes affectibus*, which had originally empowered Kramer to investigate witchcraft in his Inquisitorial bishoprics, proudly printed as front matter), it is perhaps worth asking not what effect it had but rather why it didn't result in an immediate blossoming of trials. The answer is that Heinrich Kramer was ahead of his time. Though he died in 1505, having seen few successful mass trials, the storm was coming. And his book, so sensational and thought-provoking amongst those with the time and skill to read and respond, would achieve success in ways – and in alien politico-religious climates – its author could never have imagined.

3

A Continent Cursed

On 31 October 1517, Martin Luther, a disaffected Augustinian Friar and professor of moral theology, sent his 'Ninety-five Theses' to Albert of Brandenburg, Archbishop of Mainz. It is likely he also, as tradition attests, nailed copies to the doors of the Schlosskirche and various other Wittenberg churches, as was the custom in kick-starting learned disputes. Luther's aim was to wake up the Catholic world to the corruption within, and the false doctrines emanating from, the Roman Church. He not only woke up significant sections of society – high and low, ecclesiastical and secular – with a start; he introduced complicated new rules to the never-ending chess game played out on the board of Europe. The *Theses* expounded his views on Indulgences (often paid-for remissions of sins purchased from the clergy), and these were his primary concern. Yet Luther's concomitant views on sin and forgiveness, and on the relationships between humans, God, and the Catholic hierarchy, were as radical. His views on witches were not. Though he showed little interest in driving persecutions, on hearing reports of witches near Wittenberg, he said, 'One must show no compassion. I myself wish to see them burned according to the law.'¹ Europe was about to be shaken, and the religious identities of its nations challenged or turned upside down, but the belief in witches was only going to strengthen. This was the world into which James VI of Scotland and I of England was born in the middle of the century.

Great Britain – Scotland, England, and Wales – had its own colour-ful history of magical beliefs, embracing wicked fairies, local healers, cunning folk, political sorcerers and necromancers, and woodland sprites. It also had its own history of prosecuting heresy: the English Lollards, for example, remained a lurking source of anxiety to the government throughout the early sixteenth century. But Britain was to come to the new thinking about witches, as developed by such texts as the *Malleus Maleficarum*, slowly. So too was its acceptance of a new dominant religion to be reached by fits and starts.

King Henry VIII was, in the late 1510s, an avowed enemy of Luther and his newfangled doctrines. Supported by passionate Catholics such as Thomas More and Cardinal Thomas Wolsey, the king won plaudits from Pope Leo X for writing his *Assertio septem sacramentorum adversus Martinum Lutherum* (*The Declaration of the Seven Sacraments Against Martin Luther*). More than that, he won a papal title: Defender of the Faith (something Henry had long coveted, having cast jealous eyes at the French monarchs' 'Most Christian King' and the Spanish sovereigns' 'Most Catholic Majesty'). He became, in effect, the secular ruler of a typical Roman Catholic state, with all that that entailed – and, in the early part of the sixteenth century, that entailed blatantly politically motivated whispers of witchcraft; his chief minister Cardinal Wolsey, for example, was spoken of as possessing a magic ring and a familiar spirit, whilst his friend Suffolk was rumoured to have cast diseases on his political rivals. If this was believed – and it might well have been by some, though clearly it was only valuable scurrility to others – it was not taken seriously as indicating the genuine use of witchcraft (on the part of either man) by the government. Indeed, the claims were taken less seriously than had been those against Jacquetta of Luxembourg, Duchess of Bedford, who stood trial in 1469 for making maleficent wax images of the royal family in 1469–70 (albeit the charges were dropped and only ineffectually resurrected by Richard III after her death). Clearly, by the early 1500s, rumours of witchcraft against powerful politicians in western Catholic nations was a fact of political life; if the authorities chose to ignore them, they did their targets little real damage.

Henry's love affair with the papacy, however, did not last. As early as 1515, he had claimed, 'We are, by the sufferance of God, king of England, and the kings of England in times past never had any superior but God.'[2] At that time, he had had no thought of actually breaking with Rome but was rather performing a piece of political theatre (or preening) in response to a scandal involving the murder, in custody, of a suspected Lollard. His real trouble came later, when he began to seriously consider nullifying his first marriage – which had produced only one living child, a daughter – to Katherine of Aragon. Politics and religion collided. For the first time, Henry met serious and sustained opposition to his will, not least from a temporising papacy then in the pocket of Katherine's nephew, the Holy Roman Emperor Charles V. Henry, infatuated with one of Katherine's ladies, Anne Boleyn, would have his way. In the early 1530s, the king announced himself Supreme Head of the Church of England under God – a title he doggedly insisted was no innovation but a resurgence of ancient English monarchical liberties. The Aragon marriage was ruled invalid by Henry's tame, passionately reformist Archbishop of Canterbury, Thomas Cranmer, and he swiftly wed Anne Boleyn. Appeals to Rome were outlawed. In time, the monasteries were sacked and their inhabitants turned out (with pensions, if they cooperated). Clergymen and politicians who resisted were executed as traitors. Henry's new faith – or, as he would have it, the old faith restored – was an idiosyncratic one: not quite Catholicism without the pope (given the literal changing of the medieval Catholic landscape) but not quite hard reform along Lutheran lines. Anne, a sharp political operator in her own right, showed herself sympathetic to early reform, encouraging Henry's move away from adherence to the Church which had refused to recognise her queenship.

The Boleyn marriage did not last. Despite the intelligent new queen providing Henry with a living daughter (the Princess Elizabeth), she did not produce the longed-for male heir. It seems clear to us – and it must have seemed clearer to Anne – that by early 1536, her former hold over her husband was weakening. Gone were the days of the late 1520s, when she had been the Lady Anne and Henry had played the part of the besotted suitor (and was a fairly convincing human being, for once, when doing so). Unfortunately, what Anne did in response to her husband's wandering eye was engage in the entirely innocent – indeed, the expected and widely played – game of courtly love. In doing so, she appears to have been determined to reclaim the role of unattainable but much sought-after mistress. Her means of doing so included accusing the courtly gentleman (and her husband's Groom of the Stool) Henry Norris of being in love with her, saying, 'You look for dead men's shoes, for if aught came to the king but good, you would look to have me.'[3] She pointedly asked Francis Weston, a gentleman of the Privy Chamber, why he had not yet married, only for him to indulge in the game by replying that he was too much in love with his royal mistress. A general air of forced frivolity and courtly flirtation abounded, with even a lowly musician, Mark Smeaton, attempting to get in on the act (which was too much for Anne, who pointed to his status as debarring him from attempts at high-ranking flirtation). It was all conventional stuff, and it was probably calculated to get Henry's attention. It did, but not in the way Anne expected. Rather than reigniting his passion by reminding him of his wife's charms, it gave his minister Thomas Cromwell the means to accuse her of manifold adulteries. The queen had, like many, misjudged Henry VIII.

Shortly after Anne had miscarried a premature son, in early 1536, it was reported by Katherine of Aragon's friend Gertrude Courtenay, the marchioness of Exeter, that she 'had heard from the lips of one of the principal courtiers that this king had said to one of them in great secrecy, and as if in confession, that he had been seduced and forced into this second marriage by means of sortileges and charms, and that, owing to that, he held it as null. God (he said) had well shown his displeasure at it by denying him male children. He, there-fore, considered that he could take a third wife, which he said he wished much to do.'[4]

If Henry truly made the comment, it seems that he was consider-ing dissolving the Boleyn marriage on the grounds that it had been brought about by bewitchment (and 'witchcraft' is even used in one contemporary version of the report). Yet there was a problem.

Witchcraft was not yet clearly codified as a secular crime in the English legal system. It remained a matter of canon law for the ecclesiastical courts to administer. Although it is possible Henry was toying with the idea of an annulment on the grounds of the marriage having been founded on sinful practices, he did not pursue this course, favouring instead more drastic steps that would rid him of his wife permanently. In the event, Anne was never charged with witchcraft (and thus the many pop culture portrayals of Anne being demonised as a witch arise only from this brief, otherwise baffling attempt by the king – again, if he really made the comment – to blacken her name and raise doubts about the marriage).

Nevertheless, Henry was resolved to be rid of his wife. With Cromwell's efficient aid, he was able to remain aloof as a tissue of dubious stories of Anne's treasonable adulteries was weaved. The important thing was that the king not be ridiculed as a cuckold. The solution alighted on was to make Anne, and not her royal husband, the story. Rather than being simply an unfaithful wife to a dupe, she was turned into something every bit as monstrous as a witch: an insatiable, incestuous Messalina who did not scruple to seduce her own brother. It was all nonsense – but it worked. Anne went to the scaffold in May 1536, freeing Henry to wed her lady-in-waiting, Jane Seymour, who provided him with male issue (though she did not live to see the child, the future Edward VI, grow, dying as she did from postnatal complications).

Henry VIII's interest in witchcraft was not dead, however. In 1537, he considered – and then erased from the letter of instruction – punishing one 'witch of York' for alleged involvement in the Pilgrimage of Grace (the Catholic rising intended to remove the reformist Cromwell and undo the religious changes Henry had instigated). His son, Prince Edward, was, moreover, apparently directly threatened by witchcraft, at least according to the word of one Richard Guercey, who in in late 1538 'told Sir Martyall in the kitchen of Corpus Christi College [Oxford], that one of Peckwaters Inn called Osmond had informed him there was a wax image found in London . . . with a knife sticking through his head or his heart representing the Prince, and as that did consume so likewise should the Prince'.[5]

Osmond's fate is unclear, but in 1541 Henry's Parliament passed an Act against Conjurations, Witchcrafts, Sorcery and Inchantments. This Act was not a mobilisation against witches. Instead, it focused attention on those who 'unlawfully have devised and practised Invocations and conjurations of Sprites, Pretendyng by suche meanes to understande and get Knowlege for their owne lucre in what place treasure of golde and Silver shulde or mought be founde or had in the earthe or other secrete places, and also have used and occupied wichecraftes inchauntements and sorceries to the distruction of their neighbours persones and goodes.'[6]

The penalties were made clear (and a new charge – of making love potions – added, as if only just recalled):

yf any persone or persones, after the first daye of Maye next comyng, use devise practise or exercise . . . any Invocations or conjurations of Sprites wichecraftes enchauntmentes or sorceries, to the intent to get or fynde money or treasure, or to waste consume or destroy any persone in his bodie membres or goodes, or to provoke any persone to unlawfull love, or for any other unlawfull intente or purpose . . . or for dispite of Cryste, or for lucre of money, dygge up or pull downe any Crosse or Crosses, or by suche Invocations or conjuracions of Sprites wichecraftes enchauntementes or sorcerie or any of them take upon them to tell or declare where goodes stollen or lost shall become, that then all and every suche Offence and Offences . . . shall be demyde accepted and adjuged Felonye; And that all and every persone and persones offendyng as is abovesaide their Councellors Abettors and Procurers shall be demyde accepted and adjuged a Felon and Felones

Those convicted were warned they 'shall have and suffre suche paynes of deathe losse and forfaytures of their landes tentes goodes and Catalles as in cases of felonie by the course of the Comon lawes of this Realme'. Yet it seems very few, if any, were convicted under the Act. Henry (and his government) was never an active persecutor of witches, and he set the tone for the rest of the Tudor period in condemning those who used their alleged magical powers to commit actionable crimes (such as theft, injury, or property damage). The demonic pact, already looming large in continental cases, was not mentioned. The Act was, simply, bad legislation, reacting (as English law frequently did) to events and activities rather than pre-empting them (it is worth noting that it was passed – with its condemnation of love magic – on the same day Henry's fifth wife, Katherine Howard, was attained for treason, some months after the revelation of her alleged infidelities). Further, it was ill-thought-out, in that it provided the death penalty for all manner of magical acts according to the common law. Given that the legislation was new and common law precedents for execution (or even loss and forfeiture of property) for, for example, popular activities such as using magic to make love potions or find treasure, were difficult to find, it was functionally toothless. In intent, it wavered between an assault on popular practices and a safeguard against religious disturbance (the idea being then popular that monastics had, in various spots about the countryside, hidden portions of their treasure from looters and the government). It appears to have excited no one.

In the 1530s and '40s, the king was far more concerned with rooting out heretics (the definition of which extended to both papalists and overly zealous reformers), traitors, 'ill-conditioned' wives, and politicians who flew too close to the sun than he was with witches. It is perhaps for this reason that the Act appears not to have resulted in any great flap. England was in a ferment, but the public enemies demonised by the government were not witches. The Act was repealed by Edward VI; and his successor, Mary I, again preferred to focus her government's ire against heretics (not Catholics, in her counter-Reformation, but reformers). It was not until 1562, under the moderate Protestant rule of Anne Boleyn's daughter, Elizabeth I, that the Act against Conjurations, Inchantments and Witchcrafts was passed. It focused on witchcraft as a criminal offence when it could be proven to have resulted in harm – and it had far greater impact.

Why did Henry's Act against witchcraft not yield noticeable results? The answer is that it was never driven by anyone with any particular passion to enforce it. It might, if anything, be read as an attempt to bring England up to date with continental thinking. Charles V's Lex Carolina (1532) had involved the secular authorities with the persecution of witches in his dominions, prescribing as it did torture and the death penalty. The Inquisitions, too, remained active in Europe. In 1529, experienced Inquisitor Jean Boin had, for example, gathered scraps of local gossip in the French village of Anjeux. This brought his attention to one Desle la Mansenée who, it was reported by a forty-year-old informer, had – thirty years before – been renowned as a witch and sorceress. According to the same muck-raker, even her son had confessed that she could fly backwards on twisted willow sticks. Others stepped forward with their own tales. Desle was thus arrested and interrogated but remained stead-fast in her denials. Jean Boin had her surrendered to the secular authorities, who subjected her to an extreme form of torture called the 'strappado' (retroactively named 'squassation' in subsequent centuries). This horrific process involved the suspect's arms being tied behind her back before she was hoisted into the air. Weights of up to several hundred pounds would then be attached to her feet. She would then be jerked up and down, like a human marionette. The agony of broken joints is scarcely imaginable. Unsurprisingly, Desle confessed to making a pact with Satan (in return for great wealth, which he had not made good on), sealed with intercourse. The devil, she confessed – significantly for future Scottish cases – was icy cold. She was induced also to admit to the usual offences of poisoning cattle and raising bad weather. For this litany of sins, she was condemned and burnt – not, interestingly, for witchcraft but for murder and heresy.

England was, in a sense, behind the times. Still it – and its people – clung to ancient ideas of cunning folk, political sorcery, and simple *maleficia*. There was no great appetite, at the top or the bottom, to engage in active persecution against magical treasure-hunters (who remained popular for decades), magical thief-hunting, or love magic – or to punish the users of these services as felons. Further, the emerging reformed Church (at least under Henry VIII and Edward VI), with Henry as its Supreme Head, had not established its own position on witchcraft beyond this. The ecclesiastical courts (or 'bawdy courts') continued to thrive in England (albeit under clergymen who conformed to the new, post-Roman Catholic faith), and it is likely that their jurisdiction over spiritual crimes, including witchcraft, was adequate enough in doling out penances and excommunications.

What that reformed Church – and its originator, Henry VIII – did, however, was attempt to influence Scottish affairs and Scottish religion. The English king had long viewed the northern kingdom as rightly pertaining to his Crown, with (this without convincing historical evidence) the Scottish kings his feudal inferiors. He was determined, much against the taste of his nephew James V of Scotland (son of Henry's sister Margaret by her marriage to James IV), that the Scots should be induced to see the religious light and follow him in breaking with Rome. When James V died after the disastrous (from the Scottish perspective) battle of Solway Moss, leaving the infant Mary Stuart as Queen of Scots, Henry saw his chance. A marriage between Mary and the future Edward VI would bring Scotland under the English yoke. Better still, cartloads of 'English Bibles, primers, and psalters' could be rolled north, the better to encourage a groundswell of anti-papal feeling north of the border. This was the Coverdale version of the Bible, issued in 1535, which, like the Tyndale version, contained the infamous line in Exodus 22:18: 'Thou shalt not suffre a witch to lyue.'

*

Witchcraft itself was not unknown in Scotland, but the country was largely medieval – and certainly Catholic – in its attitudes to it. Attempts had been made to discover *maleficia* in the Borders 1518; in the summer of 1536, one Agnes Scot was actually convicted (though her fate is uncertain); in 1542 three female witches were certainly burned in St Andrews for heretical witchcraft; and in 1560 Elgin paid a supplier for ropes with which to bind accused witches (whose fates and the nature of whose alleged crimes are unknown).[7] Probably these people were viewed, continental-style, as heretics or felons who engaged in witchcraft in addition to their secular crimes.

It is here worth noting that England and Scotland – much to Henry's chagrin, given he had incorporated Wales with ease in 1536, and in 1542 raised Ireland from a lordship to a kingdom pertaining to the English Crown – retained (and still retain) separate legal systems. The English system was primarily concerned with the common law (built on legal precedents established by previous cases); but so too did it involve canon law, civil law, statutory law (constructed from parliamentary Acts), and the royal prerogative. Each of these meant laws established, developed, and administered in different ways and by different institutions: the English Parliament, the prerogative courts, the ecclesiastical courts, magistrate courts, and manorial courts. Scots Law was a similarly hybrid system, built of feudal law, statutory law, civil law, canon law, and Roman law. The institutions engaged in administering it were the Scottish Parliament, the College of Justice and Court of Session (established in the early 1530s), the king's Council, ecclesiastical courts (or Kirk Sessions, which gradually gained a role following the Reformation), specialist commissions of justiciary, and sheriff courts. Henry VIII never achieved suzerainty over Scotland, and neither did he succeed in bringing the northern kingdom under his rule by force or marriage (or forced marriage). Yet his encouragement of reformist thought had significant ramifications north of the border and laid the groundwork for a Reformation which saw witchcraft as a greater danger than Henry ever had.

To escape marriage to Edward Tudor, Mary Queen of Scots was sent to France to be raised in security as the future wife of the Dauphin Francis. In her absence, her mother, Marie of Guise, fought a pitched battle against the rising tide of Scottish reformers (fuelled in part by the preacher John Knox). Her decision to flood Scotland with French Catholic troops did not succeed but bred resentment against the interlopers. Reformers – including Mary Queen of Scots's illegitimate half-brother, who defected from Marie's camp – could present themselves as Scottish patriots chafing against foreign domination. When Marie died in 1560, the Reformist allies (calling themselves the Lords of the Congregation) took advantage of the situation. No longer were they rebels against their queen or her mother, the late regent of Scotland. Now, they were the 'State of Scotland', and in that guise they summoned a Parliament without Mary's approval and banned the Mass, denied papal authority, abolished the Catholic ecclesiastical courts (which, as in England, had dealt with witchcraft as a spiritual crime), and declared a Protestant confession of faith. Scotland, at the instigation of this elite cabal but with support from a significant body of the middle classes (which had been swayed by reformist preachers), became a Protestant country.

It was to this country that the Catholic Mary returned in the summer of 1561, having become both dauphiness and then Queen of France until the sickly Francis II died in December 1560. She announced her religious intentions from the beginning of her personal rule: there was to be no return to the papal fold (though she would not give firm royal assent to the parliamentary Acts of 1560).

Although Scotland must have seemed alien to Mary, who had last seen the country when she was five, there are things she would have recognised. For one, the belief in witches as active agents was lively, even if there were no Inquisitions torturing them (as had been happening outside the purview of the Parliament of Paris, in the outlying areas of France). Scotland, like England, was still much divided in attitudes towards high-level political sorcery and low-level instances of *maleficia*. The latter was to be dealt with on 4 June 1563, with the passing of a parliamentary Act, Anentis Witchcraftis:

ITEM: Forasmuch as the Queen's Majesty and the Three Estates in this present Parliament being informed that the heavy and abominable superstition used by diverse of the lieges of this realm, by using of witchcraft, sorcery, and necromancy, and credence given thereto in times bygone against the law of God: And for avoiding and away-putting of all such vain superstitions in times to come: It is statute and ordained . . . that no manner of person nor persons of whatsoever estate, degree, or condition . . . take in hand in any times hereafter to use any manner of witchcrafts, sorcery, or necromancy, nor give themselves forth to have any such craft or knowledge thereof, therethrough abusing the people; Nor that [any] person seek any help, response, or consultation [from] any such users or abusers foresaid of witchcrafts, sorceries, or necromancy under pain of death, [this law also] to be executed against the user, abuser, as the seeker of the response or consultation. And this to be put to execution by the justice, sheriffs, stewards, baillies, lords of the regalities, and royalties, their deputes, and other ordinary judges competent within this realm, with all rigour, having power to execute the same.[8]

This was largely the Act of a Protestant Parliament (with, as Goodare suggests, amendments suggesting it had been modified so as not to offend the queen by linking witchcraft with Catholicism), with Mary's seemingly unflappable half-brother James (known to history as the 1st Earl of Moray) playing a key role, though the Protestants were hardly united on the question of how witchcraft should be punished (or, rather, how severely). Given the close contact between Scottish and English Protestants in 1563, it is likely that an attempt was made to bring Scotland into closer alignment with the southern kingdom (whose Parliament had recently outlawed witchcraft, at least when it could be seen to cause harm). At any rate, all manner of magical acts were deemed punishable by death, whether 'witchcrafts' (the plural is suggestive), necromancy, and sorcery. As Goodare has pointed out in his exhaustive and illuminating study of the Act, merely being a witch was not proscribed; the activities which witches were supposed to undertake, and those who availed themselves of such services, were. The desire to punish those who consulted witches was so nakedly political – numerous high-ranking figures in Scotland and across Europe had been rumoured to consult supposed sorcerers, and probably they did – that it failed. The Act certainly did not cast politicians and their families wholesale into gaol (or onto the gallows) for seeking advice from diviners and necromancers.

But the key element of the legislation lies in its empowering of the secular Scottish courts in investigating and punishing witchcraft. What it left implicit – at least in developing the Scottish Protestant position on the phenomenon – was the role of the devil. This would, in time, have to be clarified by those (like Mary's son, James) who cared to do so. For the moment, the ambiguity might be useful. Scotland was not England, and Scotland's Reformation was, if the firebrands had their way, to be far more extensive in its purification of the old Church and rooting out of its superstitions (and closet partisans). At this stage, Scotland was still forming its new religious identity. If its Protestant politicians looked to their new spiritual guide, John Calvin, for help in shaping new positions, they will have likewise found a lack of clarity, on witchcraft at least. Calvin, in his *Avertissement contre l'astrologie judiciaire* (*A Warning Against Judicial Astrology*) of 1560 criticised those who tried to seek God's secrets through astrology as having been deluded by Satan. Divination and necromancy, in short, ought to be prohibited, whilst true astronomy was acceptable to the moral order. Though he typically denounced Catholics as witches and wizards (the latter word coming to mean male diviners and magicians), Calvin himself oversaw Consistory Courts in Geneva which were lenient on those who engaged in folk healing.

This somewhat confused, unsatisfactory position continued in Scotland following the passage of the 1563 Act. Two years following it, the Kirk's General Assembly felt the need to appeal to Mary over 'such horrible crimes as now abound in this realm without correction, to the great contempt of God and his holy word, as idolatry, blaspheming of God's name, manifest breach of the Sabbath day, witchcraft, sorcery, and enchantment, adultery, incest, whoredom, maintenance of brothels, murder, slaughter, reaving . . .'[9] The indication was that the previous Act was not being upheld. Suggested implicitly was that the Catholic queen was not doing her job – or was incapable of creating a godly Protestant kingdom. Demands for reform – for stricter enforcement of moral and criminal laws, including against witches – continued.

So too did the time-honoured use of folk magic and political sorcery (or at least accusations of it). When the young and elegant Queen Mary, after a careful and prolonged campaign to get her cousin Elizabeth I of England to give approval to a marriage – any marriage – finally grew vexed with the English monarch's delaying tactics, she elected to marry their mutual cousin (descended also from Margaret Tudor), Henry Lord Darnley. This was spun as a fairytale romance, the better to hide Mary's political goals. Darnley was a Stuart; he had claims to the thrones of England and Scotland; and he was young and might be mastered. Mary might, by marrying him, turn a potential political rival into a subordinate husband. Yet the political reality was downplayed by the English ambassador, Thomas Randolph, who saw witchcraft at work:

> This queen is so much altered from what she was that who beholds does not think her the same. Her majesty is laid aside; her wits not such as they were; her beauty another than it was; her cheer and countenance changed . . . A woman more to be pitied than any that he ever saw. Such one now as neither her own regards, nor she takes count of any that are virtuous or good. The saying is that she is bewitched, the parties named to be the doers; the tokens, the rings and bracelets, are found and daily worn that contain the sacred mysteries.[10]

The supposed agent behind the magical enchantment was Darnley's mother, the ambitious Margaret, Countess of Lennox, whom Elizabeth clapped in the Tower of London in an attempt to blackmail Darnley into returning to England and calling off the mooted marriage (it being Elizabeth's goal to keep Mary single).

These accusations went nowhere. Mary wed Darnley and, when the hapless youth realised he had been duped (by Mary and, in truth, by the patriarchal order of the time) into believing he could exercise political dominance over his wife, the marriage soured. Chafing against being a mere consort, he plotted, schemed, and drank – though, to his credit, he managed to impregnate the queen and thereby serve his primary dynastic function. He joined forces with other malcontents (among them the Earl of Morton and the sinister Patrick Lord Ruthven, the latter reputed by his enemies as having consorted with incantation-uttering wizards) who decided, as a group, to surprise Mary at supper and kill her French secretary, the Savoyard David Riccio – this when the queen was heavily pregnant. Mary, with skill, recovered from the brutal ordeal (forever afterwards declaring that the first dagger blow thrust against Riccio had been done in her presence) and managed to win the frightened young Darnley back to her side, loath though she was to actually reconcile with him. The anti-Riccio faction scattered, some fleeing to England, leaving Mary to establish a stable government with Darnley as *persona non grata* and James Hepburn, 4th Earl of Bothwell, as her chief minister.

Mary's queenship, however, was destined to unravel. Her policy – which she had generally but not always stuck to – of conciliating the Protestant regime and denying any desire to reconvert Scotland to the Catholic faith could not last. Her son was born in June 1566 after a long and difficult labour, during which the Catholic Countess of Atholl resorted to witchcraft by attempting to magically transfer the queen's pains to the stout and presumably game Lady Reres. The healthy baby, the future James VI and I, was born with a caul over his face, which was again widely interpreted magically: it would make him safe from drowning, indicate that he might travel widely without danger, and protect him from magical attacks. The problem with this happy event was one Elizabeth I, the famous Virgin Queen, would have anticipated. Mary was now disposable.

The need to dispose of her was, further, quickly underlined. In December 1566, she had James christened a Catholic (which she could hardly fail to do, given her personal beliefs and her sense of community amongst the Catholic sovereigns of Europe). In swift succession, Darnley was murdered (by Bothwell, Morton, and very likely with the connivance of Mary's disgruntled former secretary, William Maitland of Lethington); Bothwell seized, ravished, and married the queen; and a rebellion was raised which chased the newlyweds about, separated them at Carberry Hill, and allowed Mary to be imprisoned by her rebels for a year. Though she escaped and rallied her supporters in 1568, her counterattack at Langside failed and she fled to England, where her possible involvement in Darnley's death (which, in reality, was probably the haziest sense of foreknowledge, if that) was subjected to a formal inquiry by Elizabeth I (acting, with a kind of exasperated glee, as impartial arbitrator between the Scottish queen and her rebels). Nothing was proved either way, but Mary remained in English captivity for the rest of her life. Moray, by contrast, was not found to have unlawfully rebelled (despite this being impossible if Mary were not judged guilty), given enough money to see him comfortably on his way, and encouraged to return to Scotland to take up the reins of government.

The infant James, meanwhile, was rescued from being turned into a faithful son of Rome by his new Protestant protectors, who were delighted at the prospect of a fresh start without a woman – and a Catholic woman – at the helm. The Earl of Moray served as regent of Scotland (until his assassination in 1570) and the boy-king was raised behind the thick, protective walls of Stirling Castle.

The fallout from these events – remarkable and tumultuous as they'd been – did not settle quickly. Nor did the potential role of witchcraft in inflaming what was manifestly disorderly conduct on the part of Scotland's politicians (of all stripes). Bothwell, who fled to Denmark after Carberry Hill and found captivity there, was said to have confessed that 'all the frendship which he had of [with] the queene, he gatt alwayes by witchcraft, and the inventions belanginge thereunto, especially by the use of sweete water'.[11] The 4th Earl of Bothwell had many and varied faults – not least misogyny and an ambition stronger than any sense of morality or loyalty – but we can be sure he did not use magical water to get his way. Superficial charm, manipulation, and force were his tools – and all failed him in the end.

That architect of the Reformation, John Knox, Mary's one-time bête noire, was not immune from scurrilous, politically motivated accusations of witchery. Though he long predeceased Mary (dying in 1572), he was posthumously accused by his enemy Nicol Burne of having won his much younger wife, Margaret Stuart of Ochiltree (a relation of his hated sovereign, Mary) by means of sorcery. More strangely, it was claimed by one John Low that the old preacher had been banished from St Andrews 'because in his yard he had raisit some *Sanctis*, amangis whome their came up the devill with hornes, which when his servant Richart saw he ran wud, and so deid'.[12] It is significant that these claims were recorded by Kirkcaldy of Grange, a former enemy of Mary who changed sides after her flight to England, becoming an energetic Marian (the Marian cause rumbling on until the early 1570s, when it died with Grange and Maitland of Lethington, who had likewise gone over from the anti-Mary faction).

Witchcraft in Scotland, then, was multiple things when James became, as he later put it, a 'cradle king'. It was illegal, as per the 1563 Act. It was incredibly useful as an ongoing part of political discourse. It was still practised in the form of healing (or at least superstitious pain-reducing) magic. And it was in need of a clear definition in terms of what it really was, and how it ought to be treated, under the new, emerging Protestant polity. That resulted, on the part of the coming regime, in a belief in, opposition to, and persecution of witchcraft. But how should it be done? How might these newly empowered authorities administer the new law?

During the regency of Moray, these questions were tested but not answered. If Mary Queen of Scots had failed to be a hammer of the witches, her half-brother, during his short regency, would attempt to lead a government which might. In 1568, a six-month commission was issued by the 5th Earl of Argyll (probably at the instigation of the reformist friend of Moray's, John Erskine of Dun) to try thirty-eight accused witches (and only witches) in Forfarshire in Angus – a surprising number for this early period, and notable for its attempt to solidify the centrality of the demonic pact.[13] Probably, as Michael Wasser suggests, divisions amongst the commissioners (the time period of the commission covered Queen Mary's escape from captivity and flight from Scotland, which shook loyalties) simply interrupted its course. Equally possible is that politicians and religious figures (sometimes embodied in the same individual, as in Erskine of Dun) were still finding their way in terms of evidence, proof, and the treatment – or levels of torture – they might mete out to the accused. Still political witchcraft was a crime, and still it was associated with the inarguably secular crime of treason; the Lord Lyon, Sir William Stewart, was accused of both and executed in August.

As his sister had done during her personal rule, Moray also held justice ayres (travelling courts), his aim being to cement his authority (given Queen Mary still had considerable support) and put down disaffection to his regime. In 1569 he travelled up the east coast in an attempt to personally dole out justice to political and religious dissidents. He attempted a catch-all distribution of justice, encompassing witches, adulterers, and heretics – all crimes which now fell under the shared purview of religious and secular authorities (if the two could be fully separated in the woolly post-Reformation years). His attempt was largely a failure in that, although it resulted in ten executions for witchcraft (although sadly only the name of one, Niknevin, has been preserved), dozens had been accused, probably locally (there being no indication of torture, confession, or the naming of names by victims, as had been seen in, for example, France's Inquisitions). Moray himself complained that there had been a lack of evidence; but it is worth noting that, at least most of the time, and in both Scotland and England, an accusation was not, contrary to popular belief, itself a death penalty.

What had probably happened was that local parishes had gathered names and scraps of gossip (small towns being especially prone to neighbourly disputes and rumours) and done little in the way of evidence-gathering, it being as-yet unclear what constituted evidence sufficient for this relatively new category of once-spiritual-now-secular crime. Argyll similarly embarked on a western justice eyre in

July 1574, and again it was only reported that a number of persons had been executed (this being a frustratingly common method of reportage, which makes wider calculation of the numbers of indicted witches difficult), with an aside on the 'treatment of those suspected of witchcraft, etc'.

Though officially these attempts to cleanse the country of witchery were failures – and they were, as far as being godly crusades went – they probably represent the majority of witchcraft cases when no great panics were in train: witchcraft was one of several crimes to be punished when those in charge could prove the allegations against those accused. Although this was the norm as far as prosecutions went, it never satisfied ardent witch-hunters, and the Scottish people were probably bemused by this dawning interest on the part of their justices. Scotland had no experience of the Catholic Inquisitions by which to measure its handling of this new felony (a crime serious enough to warrant the death penalty); torture required Privy Council warrants; and it is hardly likely that parish leaders (nor even many reformist national or regional figures) were avid readers of fifteenth-century Catholic polemics such as the *Malleus Maleficarum*. If the government wished to prosecute witches successfully and widely, the people (whether peasant, innkeeper, minister, or local bailie) had to be educated into knowing what was expected of them in terms of belief, accusation, and evidence. In short, if there were ever to be a more systematic approach to the perceived problem of witches – by new Protestant states, at least – there was still work to be done.

A Europe-wide competition was arising, with some Protestant leaders seeking to outdo the Catholics, and some Catholic leaders seeking to outdo the Protestants in their destruction of this common anti-Christian enemy. The Reformation in northern Europe would prove a key battleground area for this rivalry of faith and belief. Moreover, the child crowned amid the turmoil of Mary Queen of Scots's deposition and established by his mother's enemies as a Protestant prince would not shirk his duty, as he saw it. And the childhood and youth he was shortly to endure would make him an ideal candidate for Britain's chief Protestant persecutor.

PART II

Oppression

'Our ecclesiastical punishment is too slender for so griev-
ous offences'

–Edmund Grindal, 1561

4

Birth of a Mania

It is something of a cliché to note that the childhood of James VI and I was one lacking in warmth or love – but that doesn't make it any less true. The upbringing and education of the king were of enormous importance to his keepers and the various regents who governed Scotland in his name, but none of them can be said to have held him in any great affection. Rather, attitudes towards the precocious, flaxen-haired child varied according to the political biases of those around him. To his lady keeper, Annabella, Countess of Mar, he was to be held in awe as the Lord's anointed (an attitude of deference of which King James would always approve). She provided an early model subject for the boy, who viewed her as a faithful, reverential servant (rather than the 'foster mother' sometimes suggested; only a favoured few in James's later life would be 'adopted' into the royal family and thereafter addressed as his 'children'). To those, like his chief educator, George Buchanan, under whose tutelage he arrived when he was out of skirts, he was to be rigorously taught his own lack of importance, and any lofty, absolutist fancies about the divinity of his position were to be beaten out of him.

Buchanan was a classical republican and his scholarship was respected throughout Europe. But he was nevertheless a man of his time. His magnum opus was his *Rerum Scoticarum Historia* (*The History of Scotland*), in the sixth book of which he recounted the story of King Duff (or Duffus), who was afflicted with a frightful and unusual disease. A conspiracy was soon discovered. A young 'harlot', whose mother was reputed a 'wizard' (the word evidently being gender fluid to the earliest translators), revealed all under torture.[1] The mother and sundry others were found roasting a wax image of the king. The authorities apparently put an end to this sorcery and punished the witch, freeing Duff from his agonies. Buchanan was hard at work on his book during his time teaching James.

The scholar was as interested in events – and politically motivated sorcery – closer to his own time. Having been turned from enjoying the deposed Mary Queen of Scots's patronage during the earlier years of her personal rule, Buchanan became one of her most virulent detractors. His poisonous pen – he had an eye for the salacious, even if his attacks sometimes spilled into such obloquy that they verged on satire – had been put to good use by the Protestant regime via the production of his 1571 *Ane detectioun of the duinges of Marie Quene of Scottes thouchand the murder of hir husband, and hir conspiracie, adulterie, and pretensed mariage with the Erle Bothwell* (the early modern period not being noted for its pithy titles). The book was intended to besmirch Mary by accusing her – with the evidence of the ambiguous (and, it seems probably, deliberately and calculatedly ambiguous) Casket Letters used at the inconclusive English inquiry – of direct involvement in Darnley's murder. But it went further. According to Buchanan, the queen 'partly compareth herself to Medea, a bloody Woman, and a poisoning Witch'.[2] She was, further, susceptible to witchcraft: 'the Committers of [the murder] were the Earl Bothwell, Master Iames Balfoure, the Parson of Flisk, Mr. David Chambers, Black Mr. Iohn Spence [all men who had fallen foul of the winning side], who was principal deviser of the Murther, and the queen assenting thereto through the perswasion of the Earl Bothwell, and the Witchcraft of the Lady Bucklough [the much-married Janet Beaton, Lady Buccleuch, with whom Bothwell had an affair]'.

One of Buchanan's motivations, at least in educating James, was to demonise his Catholic mother. Another was to stifle any nascent sense the young king might have of the divinity which, Shakespeare later noted, was incorrectly thought to hedge sovereigns. James was a man, like any other, and susceptible to the corrupt blood of his royal race and the malign practices of sorcery. Given that the old preceptor (he was in his seventies when teaching the king) did not refrain from punctuating his lessons with violent blows rained down on the royal person, it seems inevitable that his lessons, whether James believed them or not, would have remained in his memory. To Buchanan, political witchcraft (and accusations of it) merely existed as a phenomenon like any other crime to which bad rulers were susceptible: murder, poisoning, or adultery. The devil might well be behind it, as he was behind all evil acts, but that was not necessarily worth pointing out. James would, in time, seek to advance beyond this kind of – from his perspective – lazy and old-fashioned thinking.

More to the young king's tastes were the more deferential attentions of his lady keeper, the Countess of Mar. On entering the schoolroom in the Prince's Tower at Stirling to find Buchanan beating his charge, she is said to have voiced shock that the schoolmaster would lay hands on the Lord's anointed. Yet Lady Mar was no shrinking violet, and certainly not in political matters. She, too, had an interest in witchcraft, and one more direct than simply an academic or vituperative one.

By 1577, the Regent Moray was long dead. His successor, the Regent Lennox, had likewise been killed in an affray by supporters of the exiled and imprisoned Queen of Scots. The Regent Mar, who followed him, had died after dining with the Anglophile Earl of Morton (and despite rumours of poisoning, this probably was a coincidence), and Morton himself had attained the regency. Yet he was not universally popular, particularly with the hotter sort of reformers, whom he suspected would go too far if encouraged. He was also, by either disinclination or due to the pressures of state, unable to build much of a relationship with the young king in whose name he governed (this despite James being canny enough to address him in suitably respectful terms). The king, however, would almost certainly have heard – and perhaps been frightened of – events beginning in October 1577.

Thanks to the letter of the Countess of Mar to her brother-in-law Robert Murray of Abercairney, we have surviving information on the matter. It seems that one Violet Mar (whose station in life is unrecorded, but whose surname indicates perhaps a junior relationship or kinship to the noble family) was accused of 'treasonable undertaking to put down my Lord Regent's Grace by witchcraft'. Prior to Violet's trial, the countess wrote to Abercairney asking him to keep the accused woman confined, as Morton was busy dealing with state affairs. She further instructed him to send to her, the countess, the accusers with their depositions in writing, whilst ensuring that Violet herself 'renew the speaking she deposed before [that is, repeat her own deposition]' in the presence of ministers. The Kirk and the secular authorities were thus both seen to have a stake in the affair. Nothing was to be left to chance, and all was to be done formally, legally, and in writing.

By her own confession, Violet had used 'sorcerie, libbis [a lib being a potion or magical compound], and charmes' in her attempt to destroy Morton and was thus an 'abuser of the people against the laws of God and man': the last was a suitable legal construction.[3] The unfortunate woman was thus found guilty; though she was probably executed, there is no record of it. What had happened, though, was classic – and somewhat archaic-looking – political sorcery. Whether Violet really had attempted some futile magical means of ending Morton's life (and many, certainly of the old Marian camp, would have thanked her for it), whether she had been hired to do so, or whether she was wholly innocent (which seems unlikely, given her trial apparently involved genuine thought and acknowledgement of the need for evidence) is unknowable. No discussion of any demonic pact survives; instead, the shop-worn idea of witches attacking the great personages of the realm was still very much alive. It seems unlikely that this latest example did not filter down to the young James in the relatively enclosed world of Stirling Castle.

The presence and agency of the devil in the lives of witches was, however, beginning to be acknowledged elsewhere. Communities were generally focused on the local parish church as meeting place, forum for local gossip and political issues, and developing religious tastes (which could be thundered from the pulpits). Large towns near the centre of power were particularly likely to be up to date with legal and religious developments. Thus, near Edinburgh, in 1579 – the year James made his triumphal entry into his capital – Christine Douglas (the wife of a Leith innkeeper) was accused, found guilty, and strangled (before her body was burnt) for conversing with Satan and causing illness. Still, the issue of *maleficia* was central; Jonet Fultoun, the wife of a farrier who apparently already had a reputation for dabbling in the illicit arts (the fact of which had caused her to flee Prestonpans for Leith), was also accused of causing harm by witchcraft. This was typical. In close-knit communities, reputations were currency. The outré member – the vaguely scandalous, the distrusted, the loudmouthed, or the feared individual about whom everyone whispered, or whom children had been taught to avoid, and whom the occasional adult might secretly visit for illicit advice or help – was always vulnerable. Ecclesiastical censure might have come calling at such people's doors in the past – but they generally survived, their reputations a little darker and their appeal further seasoned, until allegations grew loud enough and the law experienced enough.

In the same year, a local healer named Jonet Carswell (or Caldwell) was tried for the same crime in the local courts. Her offence appears to have been the use of a plaster (compounded of 'blak snailles upoun ane pece blak mantillone yairin') to cure a bad leg.[4] It is tempting here to imagine that this demonisation of folk healing represented the beginnings of a larger conspiracy on the part of the growing body of male medical professionals, but the evidence is slim and conjectural. Though it is certainly possible that some medics – such as they were – occasionally seized the opportunity to rid communities of rival folk healers (whom they might well have genuinely thought were using evil magic), any sustained conspiracy to destroy female healers seems unlikely. For one thing, such women only ever made up a minority – albeit a significant minority – of those accused in Scotland. Across Great Britain, moreover, every town, village, and hamlet boasted its own healer or healers, and probably every household had its own preferred folk remedies for, and harmless charms against, common ills; there was never any hope of eliminating healers wholesale, even if such a thing were to have been attempted. Further, people – in urban areas, generally living cheek-by-jowl and prey to all manner of private suspicions, jealousies, dislikes, and fears – weren't necessarily passive dupes to whom authoritarian punishment just happened. They could be active agents in providing accusations and depositions against anyone they distrusted or disliked. It is often said that all politics is local – but, in these scattered cases of witchcraft, so was a great deal of justice, despite the increasing attempts of authorities to exert centralised control.

None of this – horrific as it is – can constitute a witch hunt in the sense the term is usually understood. Rather, what was happening was what one might expect. The government had identified a crime which most people understood – at least in the sense of it involving magical acts (whether they be intended to heal or harm). The centrality of Satan was not always a significant part of matters, and this haphazard recognition of his role would continue. Essentially, people were being encouraged to recognise that witches and witchcraft were now proscribed, and that they were at liberty to pursue fiercer forms of justice than the old Catholic ecclesiastical courts and the fledgeling Kirk Sessions allowed. This resulted not in a rush of people accusing one another but a trickle of accusations, examinations, and executions; witchcraft was, as Buchanan appears to have viewed it, simply a crime like any other crime.

Into this environment came the young King James, chafing against the ascendancy of the Regent Morton and buoyed by a new figure in his life: his cousin, the dashing, ambitious, predatory Esmé Stuart, who was swiftly elevated to the position of 1st Duke of Lennox. Working with his fair-weather friend and colleague Captain James Stewart, Lennox succeeded not only in ousting Morton from government but resurrecting the quondam regent's role in James's father's death. Morton lost his head in 1581. Lennox, however, did not profit for long. Soon, a faction built against him, led by the son of that alleged wizard-keeper Lord Ruthven, who had conspired with Darnley to butcher Mary Queen of Scots's secretary, David Riccio. James was kidnapped – with Kirk approval – by this faction and held in custody for nearly a year, finally seeing his chance and escaping. On gaining liberty, he denounced his recent captors, demanded their penance, and punished those he could not bring himself to forgive (with William Ruthven, 1st Earl of Gowrie, son of the much-maligned Ruthven, losing his head as a traitor in 1584 following an investigation that saw witchcraft accusations dropped whilst treason charges went forward).

Lennox, having groomed James – probably sexually, given the king's burgeoning and barely concealed sexuality, which always leant towards males, particularly in terms of romantic attachment – was forced to abjure the realm. In his place, the young, nervous, rather haughty king formed a government with Captain James Stewart, by this time ennobled as Earl of Arran. Seizing the chance of being in power – or at least at the head of it – the king pushed his 'Black Acts' through Parliament, these abolishing the presbyteries so beloved of the up-and-coming Kirk elders and establishing himself as the power broker in religious affairs. But James's new consigliere, Arran, also paid for his arrogance and arrogation of the lion's share of power, being ousted from office – by opponents with English backing – and forced into obscurity in 1585–86.

By anyone's measure, this all represented quite an ordeal for the young King James VI – particularly the loss of Lennox, who died shortly after leaving Scotland and whom the king would always mourn as a lost love (this despite the man having never had much more than superficial charm and an eye for the main chance). Yet, even in his captivity, he could show strength of character and was already proud of his incipient skills in playing off one faction against the other whilst holding himself aloof. Even in his youth, James was forming a monarchical identity for himself, which proved every bit as fluid as his sexuality. In Scotland, at least, he coveted the role of the universal king, above divisions and above lesser mortals. He wished to be absolute master of what was self-evidently a deeply disturbed, disorderly realm and a seditiously militant Kirk staffed by uncivilised, irreverent ministers every bit as lacking in respect for royal authority as his old schoolmaster had been.

What was a king – and a rather self-aggrandising and already deeply learned king – to do? James, in time, would find an answer. He would prove himself an intellectual innovator, the fount of Scottish justice, and the supreme enemy of a threat that Kirk ministers – and the law courts – had shown themselves barely capable of tackling with any force or consistency: Satan and his minions, the witches.

5

Elizabeth's Witches

Only three years into the reign of Elizabeth I, her Bishop of London, Edmund Grindal, who had been a Protestant exile during the late reign of Mary I, took up his pen to write. He had a problem. The problem's name was John Coxe (alias Devon). The man had confessed to 'magic and conjuration', yet Bishop Grindal found the ecclesiastical remedy for such offences 'too slender' – as many others already had and would, he wrote to William Cecil, who was already making a name for himself as Elizabeth's most trusted (and most powerful) adviser. Grindal claimed that the Lord Chief Justice (Sir Robert Catlyn) had told him 'the temporal law will not meddle with' witches.[1] So, according to the bishop, secular law was in need of an update.

Already, two malefactors had been fruitlessly accused in Essex because of the legal system's sluggishness. Scant months before, a Danbury beer-brewer named John Samond (who would, in time, prove a serial offender) had been acquitted by the assizes (the central courts on their summer circuit in the localities, preceded by fanfare, fluttering banners, and public excitement) in that same county on charges of being a 'common enchanter and witch' and for fatally bewitching John Graunte and Bridget Pecocke.[2] Even earlier, in around 1559, John Jewel, Bishop of Salisbury, had preached before the queen, warning her that 'witches and sorcerers, within these last few years are marvellously increased within this your Grace's realm. These eyes have seen most evident and manifest marks of their wickedness. Your grace's subjects pine away even unto the death, their colour fadeth, their flesh rotteth, their senses are bereft.'[3]

Things had to change if such people were to be treated as men like Grindal believed they should be treated. He would soon be working on his *Apology* [Defence] *of the Church of England* (1562) and was, like several of the queen's reformist bishops and politicians, interested in defining and defending the legitimacy and theology of the English Church – including its position on witchcraft. Cecil duly set to work but was unable to find a precedent for the temporal punishment of a conjurer in the fourteenth century. This was now a problem for the country's lawmen.

The law did indeed respond, if not directly, to Grindal's plea. In 1562, the Act against Conjurations, Inchantments and Witchcraft lamented that since the repeal of the old (and ineffective) Henrician Act, many 'fantasticall and devilishe persons have devised and practised Invocacions and Conjuracions of evill and wicked Spirites, and have used and practised Wytchecraftes Enchantementes Charms and Sorceries, to the Destruccioon of the Persons and Goodes of their Neighebours and other Subjectes of this Realme'.[4] The new Act sought to remedy this by ensuring that 'all maner of practise use or exercise of Witchecrafte Enchantement Charme or Sorcerye shoulde bee from hensforthe utterly avoyded abolished and taken away'. The death sentence was to be passed on those found guilty of causing death by witchcraft or conjuring evil spirits. Yet this was not quite a call-to-arms. Due process was still to be followed; it was noted, for example, that if the offender was a peer then his 'Triall [was] thereyn to be hadd by hys Peeres, as yt ys used in cases of Felonye or Treason and not otherwyse'. For non-aristocratic witches who either didn't provably cause death or who merely injured, sought treasure, provoked others to unlawful love, or simply intended to do mischief, the penalties were less severe, ranging from year-long imprisonment to execution only for repeat offences.

The Elizabethans, unlike the more ardent Scottish reformers, were not terribly interested in purifying society by purging it of witches, despite the regime setting up – via Elizabeth's 1559 Act of Uniformity – a moderate Protestant state. Rather, they were concerned with political sorcery. Elizabeth's parents' marriage had been annulled days before Anne Boleyn's execution, and although Parliament had willingly endorsed her accession, she remained in an anomalous position: a legally crowned and anointed bastard queen. Her position, to the minds of her politicians, would remain parlous as long as she was unmarried (and thus, despite Elizabeth announcing at the time of her accession her disinclination to wed, she was harangued by her ministers and parliamentarians for decades on the subject). This inherent instability at the heart of the Elizabethan government – the risk that the sovereign might be deposed or might die without issue at any moment – made it vulnerable and open to attack.

In England, those attacks often come from prophecies, sorcery, and the divinations of conjurers. The Tudor dynasty's founder, Henry VII, had supposedly been attacked by John Kendall and Bernard de Vignolles, who had sought his death by means of a magic-practising friar. Henry VIII had been plagued during the Pilgrimage of Grace not just by a 'witch of York' but by the ancient 'Mouldwarp' prophecies which forecast a tyrannical monarch and found identification (not unfairly) in Henry. Indeed, in addition to his 1542 Witchcraft Act, that sovereign's Parliament – in that same year – used the Lords (which suggests a skittishness on the part of the nobility concerning their own activities) to pass an Act Concerning Prophecies upon declaration of names, arms, badges, &c, which saw any prophesiers and their clients declared felons without benefit of clergy (that is, the ability to claim ecclesiastical immunity) unless they were peers.[5] Anne Boleyn, certainly, was reported as having been touched by prophecies concerning the burning of a queen, and she showed an interest in the 'prophetic interpretations of François Lambert', who published *On Prophecy, Learning, and Languages, and on the Letter and the Spirit* in 1525.[6] The radical reformer and medical man Thomas Gybson, however, saw the value in prophecy – he wrote to Henry's minister Thomas Cromwell offering to gather in those prognostications which might glorify the king. Prophesying was, and continued to be, a part of the political and legal discourse of the Tudor era, and there was a lack of certainty as to how its practitioners should be treated depending on their credentials and what they were divining.

Edward VI's reign saw the Countess of Sussex, a clerk of the Duke of Norfolk, and an alleged necromancer called Richard Hartlepool imprisoned in the Tower for using magic to treasonably prophesy against the young king. Mary I likewise endured a blossoming of conjuring in London, most of it presumably inimical to her regime. She had, indeed, imprisoned the polymath John Dee, whose interests crossed deeply into the esoteric, for treasonably calculating her horoscope and that of her half-sister (who later showed faith in Dee's practical magical abilities). In short, the England of the early 1560s was one in which conjuring and political sorcery were a long-standing problem, and the new Elizabethan government – exposed on various flanks in being new, untested, Protestant in the wake of a counter-Reformation, and led by a single woman – intended to do something about it.

The actual nature of those punishments deemed worthy of death – conjuring spirits and causing death by magical means – if the perpetrator was found guilty in the first instance, indicates a hardening of attitudes towards both *maleficia* and prophesying. Although the new Act outlawed both (along with technically outlawing other acts of witchcraft), it did so by treating them as interlinked phenomena, probably because so many prophecies touched on the monarch's demise. This was a development of thought from the days of the *Malleus Maleficarum*, in which Heinrich Kramer had noted that certain forms of divination ('geomancy, which is concerned with terrene matters, such as iron, crystal, and polished stone; hydromancy, which deals with water and crystals, aeromancy, which is concerned with the air; pyromancy, which is concerned with fire; soothsaying, which has to do with the entrails of an animal sacrificed on the devil's altars') were all done by the invocation of devils, they were aimed only at achieving 'foreknowledge of the future' rather than causing harm.[7] By the early Elizabethan period, in England, witchcraft and the invocation of spirits – commonly thought to be done with an eye to the future – were equally worthy of condign punishment.

Thus, if Elizabeth's 1562 Act was less harsh in its penalties than her father's failed one had been, it was not because Parliament was any more friendly towards witches but because it was less concerned with finding its way towards a godly society than were the more passionate Scottish reformers. The main aim of the queen's movement against witchcraft was stemming the flow of false prophecies and asserting secular authority over what was, essentially, a weapon – witchcraft – which might be wielded in the enactment of an existing crime: murder. At heart, Elizabeth was not concerned with purging England of witches (whether folk healers or cattle-botherers). She was concerned with preserving her own life, legitimising and entrenching her regime, and stilling the tongues of those who would speak against her. In Scotland, James VI was likewise troubled by slanderers – witness his 1584 Act Anent Slanderers of the King, his Progenitors, Estate, and Realm, followed by his 1594 move against 'the Authors of Slanders') – but his route to establishing his regime and authority combined with a far more active interest in witches.

It is worth noting, too, that the Elizabethan government was also largely unwilling, following the burnings witnessed in Henry VIII's and Mary I's reigns, to crack down on heresy. It became a point of pride that Queen Elizabeth could declare that non-conformists would be punished in England only if they engaged in active treason. She might have said the same about witches, and, as we will see, her justices largely refrained from doling out the full penalty for witchcraft unless either treasonable action or actual harm could be proved on the part of the accused.

The queen and her people as a rule believed in genuine seers, magicians, and masters of esoteric natural philosophy, and such men – if they were suitably educated or appeared to be – were coming into fashion. Elizabeth also, naturally, believed in frauds, troublemakers, and traitors who used magic falsely for political ends. In the middle, it was axiomatic that she would believe in those who were possessed of genuine powers but wished – or were hired – to use them for nefarious or political purposes: witches. This credulity is not surprising. This was a world and a society still in the process of understanding the cosmos and its workings, still a distance from discovering the human body's mechanisms, and still building knowledge (much of it classical or medieval) based on erroneous assumptions and theories.

And so the Witchcraft Act passed and, unlike Henry VIII's less considered and less thoughtful one, it would bear gruesome fruit, with the 1565 execution of Elizabeth Lowys in Chelmsford – famously the first hanging for murderous witchcraft under the Act – being only a prelude.

*

In 1566, an anonymous writer (with the aid of a London publisher) issued a little news pamphlet titled *The Examination and Confession of Certain Witches at Chelmsford in the County of Essex, before the Queen Majesty's Judges, the 26th day of July Anno 1566*. This was shocking stuff: an early example of what we would now call true crime. Like much true crime of future centuries, it gave a sexed-up version of events, providing a supposed eyewitness account of the trial and confessions of one Agnes Waterhouse (tellingly referred to as 'Mother Waterhouse', in a still-developing convention of naming female witches by a disconcertingly maternal appellation) and her fellow witches. The trial itself would have been typical: the accused were often unable to afford defence counsel, and the only lawyers present might be those assisting the justices. Before a jury, witnesses and the accused would be called on to speak, with the courtroom frequently descending into voluble arguments between those on trial and the witnesses called by the Crown to aid in prosecuting them. It is small wonder that the dramatic scenes – and the arrival of the assizes – generally represented cheap entertainment, on which writers and publishers were eager to capitalise.

Before Dr Cole and Master Foscue of the Essex assizes, Elizabeth Fraunces confessed to having been bequeathed a white-spotted cat called Satan by her grandmother, who inducted her into witchcraft (in the seductive manner warned about by the *Malleus*) when she was twelve. This cat was well named by its new owner, because it was a devilish creature, promising its mistress she should have her heart's desire. Elizabeth wanted wealth, and sought it via the acquisition of sheep. The cat 'spake to her, as she confessed, in a strange hollow voice (but such as she understood by use), and this Cat forthwith brought sheep into her pasture to the number of twenty-eight black and white, which continued with her for a time, but in the end did all wear away she knew not how'.[8] Not satisfied, she asked for a wealthy husband. The cat again provided, with the caveat that she must let her new husband abuse her (presumably have sex with her) before marriage – which she did. Yet after the act, he would not marry her. In retaliation, Elizabeth asked Satan the cat to despoil his goods and kill him. This he did, in addition to killing the unborn child of her abuser to prevent her disgrace. For each act, Elizabeth was required to relinquish a drop of blood by pricking herself (the marks were apparently still evident).

Not being finished with men, Elizabeth asked Satan to provide her a new one: the Fraunces who gave her her surname. Again, the caveat was that she must give herself to him before their marriage – though this time the nuptials were carried through afterwards and a daughter was born. Before the child was two, Elizabeth found herself inexplicably 'stirred (as she said) to much unquietness and moved to swearing and cursing' and wished the infant dead. Satan obliged. So too did the cat provide when she wished her husband, Fraunces, to be lamed. Some years afterwards, for reasons of 'weariness', Elizabeth traded the cat for a cake from a 'poor woman', Agnes Waterhouse. These events all took place nine years before Elizabeth's confession.

The sixty-four-year-old Agnes in turn confessed she had received the cat with instructions to feed it drops of blood along with its bread and water. It was to retain its name. Agnes tested Satan's magical abilities by having him kill one of her own hogs in return for her blood and a whole chicken. In what is probably a holdover from the old conception of witchcraft as heresy, Agnes admitted (or was compelled to admit, or the chronicler of the confession interpolated) that she would say her Paternoster in Latin after issuing every demand. If witches had increasingly been linked to anti-Catholic faiths and sects by the Catholics, they were as easily linked to anti-Protestant faiths by the Protestants.

Agnes then turned Satan's power on one Kersey, who had offended her, killing three of his pigs. Emboldened, she then killed one of Widow Gooday's cows and three geese belonging to another neighbour, spoiled still another's butter, destroyed the local brewery (to save herself labour), killed yet another neighbour 'with a bloody slice', and finally turned her attentions on her husband. He had been killed too, all through the intervention of Satan, whom Agnes could apparently transform into a toad.

Finally, Agnes's eighteen-year-old daughter, Joan, made her own confession. She admitted only that she had once seen her mother carrying a toad – but that she was never taught witchcraft. Rather, from observing her mother's interactions with the cat, she had called it herself after being refused bread and cheese by a neighbour's child, Agnes Brown. The cat came, albeit in the guise of a great dog. At this point, her confession took a decidedly devilish turn. The dog asked her what she would give him in return for seeking vengeance on the child, and when a terrified Joan suggested a red cock, the beast answered, 'No! Thou shalt give me thy body and soul!' She acquiesced. The dog grew horns, further scaring her.

Little Agnes Brown was called forth to testify that she had indeed been tormented by 'a thing like a black dog with a face like an ape, a short tail, a chain, and a silver whistle about his neck, and a pair of horns on his head'. This grotesque apparition capered about, scorning her and making a nuisance of himself in the milk-house. This went on for some days, leading the girl to ask advice of her aunt, who sent for a cleric, who told her to use Jesus's name to the monster. This she did, and the creature retorted that she 'spoke evil words in speaking that name', before departing. When he made further attempts to confront her, again Christ's name banished him. At the last, he came with a dagger in his mouth, which he indicated with a nod towards Agnes Waterhouse's house was hers, issuing threats to stab Agnes Brown – until her last invocation of Jesus finally rid her of him for good.

Agnes Waterhouse was incensed by this testimony, pointing out that she owned no dagger. Her daughter, Joan, also cried out that Agnes Brown was lying – pointing to the fact that she herself had only seen a dog without an ape's face. Fairly, the queen's attorney said he would dispatch the witches from prison if they could make the creature appear before the court, but 'by and by, no sayeth the said Agnes Waterhouse, I cannot, for in faith if I had let him go as my daughter did I could make him come by and by, but now I have no more power over him'. Still unconvinced by all of this strangeness, the attorney asked Agnes again if the creature had fed on her blood, and she changed her tune, denying that it had. He bid the gaoler lift the old woman's kerchief up, 'and there was divers spots in her face and one on her nose, then said the queen's attorney, in good faith Agnes when did he suck of thy blood last?' 'Not this fortnight,' admitted the cowed woman. She made her full confession: she had been a witch for twenty-five years. Thus unburdened, 'she bewailed, repented, and asked mercy of God, and all the world forgiveness'.

What to make of this? Certainly, it shows the development of the witch 'conspiracy': the belief on the part of the courts that one witch might induct others into demonism. The Satanic pact is impossible to ignore – these witches were entering into contracts, sealed in blood, with their 'Satan'; and here it is collapsed with the familiar spirit in the form of a pet. But if we (as we obviously must) discount the notion that any of the fantastical elements are true, we are left with rather a sad tale. It all began with the child, Agnes Brown, being in a dispute with Joan Waterhouse. The girl's tale of the ape-faced dog is obviously pure fancy, and in other circumstances her pathetic tale of banishing it with the name of Jesus would be endearing. The problem was the can of worms it opened up. Joan Waterhouse might well have been surprised by a dog (such creatures routinely roamed around poor areas searching for food) and might even have seen her mother with a toad. Agnes Waterhouse's confession (patchy and contradictory as it was) might well have been wishful thinking, at least in that she had privately cursed her neighbours and husband and seen their animals – and themselves, in her husband and one neighbour's case – die. The unpopular and apparently feared Elizabeth Fraunces, whom the trail led back to, seems to have suffered postnatal depression and might have been self-harming in some way. There is a suggestion, too, that in her first sexual encounter – with the man she allegedly bewitched to death – she was taken advantage of.

The real question regards the confessions themselves. There is no indication torture was used, and thus we are left with dejected women, some of them on the lower end of the social order, telling magistrates what they thought they wanted to hear: hazy devilish compacts, archetypal devilish traits, and – and this is key – murder as a result of witchcraft. That would be the key element in witchcraft trials under Elizabeth I. Joan Waterhouse, who had killed no one by her meddling, was acquitted whilst her mother was hanged two days after her trial. Elizabeth Fraunces – clearly a long-unhappy woman – was pilloried, but she was freed, despite her confessions of murderous witchcraft, only to see courtroom twice more, in 1571 and 1579. On confessing to killing a neighbour, Alice Poole, through the use of a spirit in the form of a 'little rugged dog', she was finally hanged. Her fate made it into print in yet another pamphlet: *A Detection of Damnable Driftes, Practized by Three Witches Arrainged at Chelmifforde in Essex, at the Late Assizes There Holden, Which Were Executed in Aprill, 1579*. Chelmsford became something of a hotspot: in 1589, Joan Prentice (who apparently kept a ferret named Satan), Joan Cunny, and Joan Upney all went to the gallows for murderous witchcraft, their fates being recorded in *The Apprehension and Confession of Three Notorious Witches Arraigned and by Justice Condemned and Executed at Chelmsford*.

This kind of thing was common: not just places but people's reputations became tainted, and once someone had gained a bad reputation it could be difficult to shift. Like Elizabeth Fraunces, Mary Belsted of Boreham and Joan Osborne of Hatfield Peverell faced repeat allegations. John Samond – the same beer-brewer who had been acquitted for bewitching a man and woman in 1560, two years before the Witchcraft Act – was so notorious that he faced charges of killing two cows by witchcraft in 1570, and in 1587 he finally went to the gallows for killing a woman by magical means. Alongside him went three women who had bewitched cows and also been found guilty of killing a person. Sometimes, it seems, these unfortunate people were community troublemakers and malcontents, or folk who could be viewed as social outsiders.

Not infrequently, when finally sentenced to the gallows, witches would name others – but this did not lead to widespread panics, at least in England. Still, doubts were voiced: in 1578, whilst suing one Ralph Ode for slandering him by falsely accusing him of witchcraft, William Netlingham had to meet his opponent's claimed scepticism about witchcraft by asserting 'that there were many sorcerers, called witches, within this realm of England, and that the aforesaid art of sorcery, called witchcraft, is a monstrous transgression and offence against the word of God'.⁹ This dubiety was in contrast to affairs on the continent, where ideas about witchcraft were developing rapidly. In France, Jean Bodin published his *On the Demon-Mania of Witches* (1580), which recognised the phenomenon and outlined what was becoming a familiar continental idea: that witchcraft was a *crimen exceptum*, or a crime so unusual and evil that it did not require the standard levels of evidence for prosecution, and which in any case was unusually difficult to prove because its operations were cloaked in the supernatural. The Elizabethan authorities, however, continued to resist any wide-scale witch hunts and stuck to the formula of the law: they wanted proof of harm (and in the most serious felony cases, murder) caused by witchcraft.

What, one wonders, did Queen Elizabeth think of this startling new manner of crime, punished as it was in her name? In the 1570s, following the failed Northern Rising, she was at the height of her reign, and she remained at the top until after the high tide of the 1588 Spanish Armada. This was the time of the spectacular Kenilworth festivities of 1575. Elizabeth was still considered a desirable match and still able to play the part – and it was an act – of the blushing prospective bride to Europe's princes and her courtiers at home. Since Mary Queen of Scots had entered her kingdom – and been imprisoned – the English queen had, however, felt more insecure than ever. Her growing intelligence network, overseen by Sir Francis Walsingham as secretary of state since 1572, was active against potential and active Catholic conspiracies (which escalated with the arrival in earnest of Jesuit campaigns from 1580). Elizabeth could have been seen off by a dagger thrust, poisoned tarts, a bullet (as had been her Scottish ally, the Regent Moray), or sorcery. Even at Kenilworth, where the Earl of Leicester made one last, especially flamboyant attempt to win the queen as his bride, the celebrations were lent a cloud when a possibly stray hunting bolt (or was it a deliberate one?) was shot too near to the royal person.[10]

A conspiracy involving sorcery was uncovered in 1579 and immortalised in the pamphlet *A Rehearsall Both Straung and True, of Hainous and Horrible Actes Committed by Elizabeth Stile, Alias Rockingham, Mother Dutten, Mother Deuell, Mother Margaret, Fower Notorious Witches, Apprehended at Winsore*. The four women were tried at the Berkshire assizes in Abingdon on charges of having killed multiple people by bewitchment. Whilst under investigation by Sir Henry Neville, it was Elizabeth Stile, moved to Abingdon by Reading gaoler Thomas Rowe, who gave the fullest confession – and a dark one it was. The sixty-five-year-old – already having gained something of a reputation for being 'lewd, malicious, and hurtful', and dealing in magic – had, apparently, been selling her ability to cause harm.[11] She had, through magical means – and she kept a rat called Philip as her familiar, feeding it with blood from her wrist and occasionally receiving gifts of milk and cream in return – turned her hand to murder. Again, the lurking danger of conspiracy was apparent. She named as her co-conspirators one Father Rosimond (whom she claimed could shapeshift into any beast – typical stuff doubted by some of the more sceptical high medievalists) and his daughter. She accused Mother Dutton, of Clew011the, of keeping a toad, fed with blood from her side, as a familiar spirit which allowed her to read minds. Mother Devell, who despite her poverty kept a black cat named Gille (again fed on blood-infused milk), was also named. Finally, Mother Margaret, a poor woman who went about on crutches, was said to have kept a kitten to which she gave her blood along with bread. The master of their group was one Mother Seidre, who had apparently died some time before the confession. All of these people, claimed Elizabeth as she unburdened herself, had offered their right sides to the devil.

What was frightening and scandalous about this group was that the witches supposedly met together to conspire: they held secret meetings in the backyard of one Master Dodges, there to plot their villainous acts. It was during such a meeting that they schemed to kill Lanckforde à Fermour and his maid, Master Gallis (a former Windsor mayor), and two local butchers. They achieved their design by having Mother Dutton create four red-wax images of the victims, which they then pierced in the hearts with hawthorn prickles. A man named Saddock also drew Elizabeth's spite. When he refused her a cloak he had promised, she clapped him on the shoulder, whereupon he went home and dropped dead. Numerous others in the community were afflicted with sickness, supposedly by this active little group, and animals, too, were not spared. Their reputation grew so that those in disputes would come to them and purchase wax images of their enemies – although disputes could equally arise amongst the witches, so that one might prick an image and cause illness only for another to cure it.

Elizabeth's story seemed to have gained corroboration when a local ostler, from whom she used to beg alms, remembered an episode when he had had little to hand over, after which he was afflicted with pains in his limbs. Seeking respite, he went to none other than Father Rosimond, whom he knew to be a 'wiseman'. Rosimond's advice was to draw blood from Elizabeth. Presumably overcoming the agony in his limbs, the ostler did so, going to the old woman and scratching her face. Doing so had apparently cured him. A similar story is recounted in the pamphlet of a local boy walking home with his pitcher who, on passing Elizabeth's house, threw stones at it. Elizabeth, in a fury, grappled his pitcher from him and sent him on his way. When forced by his father to return to the house to retrieve it, he screamed in agony. One of his hands had begun twisting, rotating, until 'the palm thereof did stand where the back did'. This manifestation of body horror was only cured by the intervention of either Father Rosimond or Mother Devell.

Naturally, as a result of Elizabeth's confession and the evidence in support of it, she was kept confined and the other witches rounded up. It was noted that whilst Elizabeth herself had been in good health, Mother Devell – a poor woman – had so exhausted herself in the doing of evil that 'her toes did rotte [off] her feete, and she was laied upon a barrow, as a most ugly creature to beholde'. The women were hanged, with Father Rosimond (and presumably his daughter, who had not explicitly taken part in the murders) escaping the noose. Witchcraft was, again, the weapon – and murder the ends. To the *Rehearsall*, the source was not in doubt: 'It is Satan that doeth all that plagueth with sickness . . . the witch beareth the name, but the devil despatcheth the deeds, without him the witch can contrive no mischief.'

At root, this episode tells us a little about local communities of folk magicians: would-be healers and harmers who might well have formed little bands, entertained their own delusions, and developed their own jealousies (especially as commerce came into play, with some selling curses and others cures). Elizabeth's confessions are typical enough and the kind of thing that had been debated for centuries; familiar spirits, *maleficia*, and even the demonic pact, though it had not taken on totemic dimensions across Britain, was present. These were, in the main, poor and unpopular people who appear to have been trying to scratch a living by selling what they might have believed were abilities. The confession itself was simply larded with the developing tropes of witchery.

What gave the case such spice was not just its early indication of what would, in future centuries, be called a coven (the supposed requirement for thirteen members being a modern invention), but the high-level interest it drew. The reason for Sir Henry Neville's involvement (he being a former Groom of the Privy Chamber to Henry VIII) and that of the Dean of Windsor, William Day, was not simply a meeting of the secular and the ecclesiastical. Elizabeth's

Privy Council had specifically tasked them with investigating this case, because, it claimed, 'here hath lately been discovered a practice of that device very likely to be intended to the destruction of her Majesty's person'.

The year prior to Elizabeth Stile's trial, 'a countryman had found, buried in a stable, three wax figures two spans high and proportionately broad. The centre figure had the word "Elizabeth" written on the forehead, and the side figures were dressed like her councillors'. The left sides of each figure had been pierced with pigs' bristles, and 'when it reached the queen's ears, she was disturbed, as it was looked upon as an augury, and great enquiries have been set on foot, although hitherto nothing has been discovered'. The queen feared attacks by magical means, because – not unusually – she believed in the existence of magical forces. She trusted, however, in the secular authorities to deal with such threats and in the talents of men of deep learning who might use magic to uncover the secrets of the universe (not least foretelling her own good fortune within it). Conjuring, in the cases of men like Dr John Dee, was not the demonic witchcraft of rough peasants, but another tool in the educated man's box (an idea which would itself be opened up to comic interrogation in Christopher Marlowe's *Doctor Faustus*, first performed in the early 1590s, in its elision of the lines between a polymath's lofty magical pursuits and the unthinking dabbling of the lower orders).

Obviously, the queen was not found to have been targeted by these particular witches. However, that did not mean she was safe from witchcraft, which might be especially potent if such people could band together. Witches working together was conspiracy of a higher order than even one witch inducting another, and this raised the profile – and the interest of authorities – in the case. With Elizabeth's cold war against the Spanish increasingly moving towards outright conflict, she sought ever greater security. This she attempted by escalating relations with her cousin James in Scotland, despite the fact that his mother still sat – plotting her freedom – in various English country-house prisons. In 1583, she despatched Francis

Walsingham north to lecture the young Scottish sovereign for daring to switch councillors (this after the failure of the Ruthven regime, when the Earl of Arran was riding high) without first seeking her guidance. Outside Perth, Walsingham came face to face with a witch called Kate, who had apparently been hired by James and his new government to openly harass, curse, and taunt the English envoy and his eighty-strong entourage. The king, at this point, clearly – and despite his knowledge of political sorcery and probable knowledge of witchcraft in and around his capital – was still content to use witches to his political advantage. Kate, unlike the women of Leith, for example, who had already been strangled and burnt, was paid £6 Scots and given a new plaid for her troubles. Mercifully for James, Walsingham, who had not wanted to go to Scotland at all, largely thanks to his ongoing physical illnesses and the concomitant need for an uncomfortable coach, did not allow this to derail his mission to ensure young Scottish royal deference to older English wisdom.

It is unlikely James knew much or cared much about the danger to Elizabeth's life from potential political sorcerers, save that he might well have wished that one of them would succeed, provided it gave him her throne. Yet the affair of the Windsor witches recounted in the *Rehearsall* and the earlier *Examination and Confession* tell us much about developing English attitudes and tastes, high and low (given the burgeoning popularity of print and its ability to be mass-produced, read aloud from, and shared). The press sensationalised these crimes and undoubtedly helped revile the witch that they were, simultaneously, helping to construct (out of healers, unpopular local oddballs, widows, or troublemakers) and disseminate. If there were witches at work in Boreham, Abingdon, and Hatfield Peverell, why not in St Osyth and Wapping and Llandyrnog and Stanmore?

St Osyth saw the unusually high figure of fourteen women tried (for murder and beer-spoiling) and several executed in 1582. Wapping discovered Margaret Hackett in 1585: a sixty-year-old hanged for having killed two neighbours by witchcraft, her case providing more pamphlet fodder. In Wales, the thrice-married Gwen ferch Ellis, a weaver and folk healer reputed to be disputatious, went to the gallows for murderous witchery in 1594. In 1599, authorities in Stanmore uncovered Anne Kerke, who could allegedly travel through locked doors. When a barber tried to cut her hair to test an old notion about witches' tresses, he found his scissors battered and spoiled, the hair then causing fire to fly away from it.

More ominously for the country's future relationship with witch-craft, in 1589 an entire family – the Samuels – fell under suspicion when nine-year-old Jane Throckmorton began suffering fits of sneez-ing, convulsions, and trances. Local doctors diagnosed bewitch-ment, and soon Jane's sisters and the Throckmorton servants began showing similar symptoms. The girl pointed to seventy-six-year-old Alice Samuel, a local dependent, as the cause of her affliction. Oddly enough, she and her sisters fell into these fits when the time came for their lessons in Biblical study – a sign, to the doctors, of possession put on them by a witch (and not children avoiding schoolwork). The girls' parents had more sense and did not pursue old Alice. However, things took a dark turn when the family was visited by Lady Cromwell, wife to the extremely wealthy Sir Henry Cromwell (grandfather of Oliver). Lady Cromwell was apparently not sensible. On seeing Alice in the area, she tore the bonnet from her head, cut off a lock of her hair (intending to burn it as a folk-remedy defence) and denounced her as a witch. Alice, for her part, made the mistake of saying, 'Madame, why do you use me thus? I never did you any harm, as yet.'[12] The final clause was her downfall.

Lady Cromwell returned home, reportedly suffered nightmares in which the old woman tore flesh from her body, and fell into a sick-ness which lasted fifteen months, killing her in the summer of 1592. Meanwhile, Alice was forced to live with the Throckmortons, whose daughters continued their conniptions – and their accusations, now enlarging them to encompass the old woman's husband and daugh-ter. A crude test was undertaken, by which the girls scratched the old woman: drawing the alleged witch's blood, it was thought, would provide relief to the bewitched, as it had in the case of Agnes Waterhouse. This produced results. Alice was encouraged to confess by the end of year, though she almost immediately recanted. Pushed again, this time by the Bishop of Lincoln, William Wickham, she again confessed. All three Samuels were forced to cure the children by casting the devil out of them (the conjunction of words appearing to take effect) and were subsequently hanged in 1593, despite the aged Alice attempting to 'plead her belly' (claim she was pregnant) to escape the death sentence: a sad act of desperation which apparently led to laughter and a ritual examination. Worse, her corpse underwent an appalling posthumous examination which uncovered a 'teat' on her private parts: proof, evidently, of a Satanic pact. The whole affair found its way into print in *The most strange and admirable discoverie of the three Witches of Warboys arraigned, convicted, and executed at the last assizes at Huntingdon.*

This had all been done on the word of children – and it became a cause célèbre in the English advancement of witchcraft blamed in cases of apparent possession. Possession itself was taken seriously and its symptoms already the cause of some debate between those who saw demonic activity at work and those who saw madness. In 1573, Alexander Nyndge had supposedly displayed unusual strength and violent behaviour, his chest swelling, his eyes protruding, and curious lumps manifesting about his body. As he shrieked laughter and foamed at the mouth, his brother Edward, an Oxford graduate, claimed he spoke sometimes in the 'horrible roaring' voice of a hellhound and sometimes in a 'hollow-sounding' voice. As he twisted and bashed his head against the walls, his body apparently took the form of a 'devil in a play' (which itself raises questions about life imitating art). Edward's writings on the case would find republication, and elaboration, in 1615, when interest in such matters had grown further. And grow it did. Men like John Darrell enjoyed, throughout the 1590s, pseudo-celebrity status as exorcists of those afflicted by witch-driven possession – much to the disgust of good Protestants, who thought the whole business reeked of popery. Those accused might find themselves treated abominably in the attempted removal of curses, as did 'Mother Rogers', who in 1593 was thought to have bewitched a child; it was recommended she be stabbed in the buttocks to free the young victim.[13]

People died, fell ill, and experienced mental illness and night-mares unexpectedly across the country, and anyone who had access to (or the ability to) read pamphlets might turn suspicious eyes on those who had bad reputations, had been in some form of dispute with the deceased, or were otherwise known to tell tall tales about their magical abilities. Might not the local beggar have uttered some-thing dangerous and deadly on being refused a crust of bread or a cup of milk? Was the loss of the family cow, dead five years, perhaps linked to the old woman who had since been bragging of her power to cure beasts? It was possible.

Yet this did not produce a widespread climate of fear, any more than did the existence of thieves, fraudulent beggars, coney-catching con artists, and killers who murdered by non-magical means. Although witchcraft-related murders were evidently unusual and scandalous enough to warrant pamphlets, they no more caused mass paranoia or panics than do modern-day sensational crime books or news stories. Nevertheless, local, apolitical, deadly witches became a recognised part of life (albeit that recognition was spread unevenly across the nation), although it was yet rare enough to cause a frisson of public interest, just as political sorcery had been a part of life in elite circles since time immemorial.

This English pamphleteering culture, nascent though it was, did not go unnoticed by James in Scotland. Nor did the counter-reac-tion to its witchcraft tales. Indeed, stories about the new brand of criminal activity embodied by people like Elizabeth Fraunces, Agnes Waterhouse, John Samond, and Elizabeth Stile provoked something of a backlash, albeit a rarefied one. The issue of English witchcraft was already raising scholarly eyebrows.

*

As it had during the Catholic medieval period – both before and after the publication of the *Malleus Maleficarum* – the reality of witchcraft continued to provoke debate. In 1563, the year of Elizabeth I's Witchcraft Act, the Protestant physician Johann Weyer published his sceptical *De praestigiis daemonum* (*On the tricks of demons*), which took a cautious view of matters, asserting that the majority of witches were simply delusional. This, he argued, was why so many were old women; their age and sex inclined them to melancholy (then a broad term for disorders of the mind), and their weakened mental health led them to spout all manner of untruths. Further, the horrors of their confessions again led Weyer to suspect their veracity – he could see, as we can see now, that these were embroidered and fanciful laundry-lists of evil acts. Any claims that charms (then a byword for minor magical acts via object or incantation, which were endemic across society) had caused actual harm, he claimed, ought to be rigorously examined. Above all, to at least his Protestant mind, it was unthinkable that God should so derogate His miraculous powers as to let Satan make merry on earth.

In 1584, the English country gentleman Reginald Scot entered the debate, publishing a lofty, exhaustive enquiry into witchcraft, again from the Protestant perspective. This was *The Discoverie of Witchcraft*, which appears to have been a real labour of love, given the author personally investigated cases to expose the frauds and jealousies which underpinned them. The book – a doorstop packed with fascinating detail – rebutted previous authors point-by-point, drawing on Catholic theology, Bodin's writings (including a reprinting of his compendium of named demons, from Astaroth to Flauros to Zagan), Calvinist hermeneutics, and, of course, the Bible. It was, moreover, loaded with the kind of acerbic humour which makes it a still-lively read: the author recounts, one imagines with a twinkle in his eye, the kinds of wonder ascribed to magic: 'We read . . . of a woman that brought foorth a young blacke Moore, by meanes of an old blacke Moore who was in hir house at the time of her conception, whome she beheld in phantasie, as is supposed; howbeit, a gelous husband will not be satisfied with such phansticall imaginations.'[14]

To Scot, common witches were, again, the products of old wives' tales (which bore no real Biblical ancestry), unpopular scolds, simple poisoners, Catholic-infected con-artists, deluded melancholic folk perhaps plagued by confused dreams, or the victims of local jealousies, petty revenges and suspicions. Ordinary people could and did engage in what they considered sensible, self-protective magical acts – but they were better smirked at than indulged. Scot lambasted the charms of 'conjurers, bad physicians, lewd surgians, melancholike witches, and couseners [cozeners]' as mere purveyors of superstition and ignorance: bad-faith creatures who preyed on the gullible.[15] Their powers were imaginary in that 'the power and will of a witch [were only what] may be accomplished by natural meanes . . . for manie a knave and whore doeth more commonlie put in execution those lewd actions'.[16] These were the kind of people who told their clients that headaches could be cured by wearing around their necks nooses which had hanged felons; that scorpion bites might be relieved by whispering in a donkey's ear, 'I am bitten with a scorpion'; that certain magical herbs could open all locks; that thieves' eyes could be put out by sorcery; and that those men magically robbed of their privy members might regain their manhood by eating a haggis or pie, anointing themselves with the gall of a crow, or stooping to 'pisse through a wedding ring' (with what is not stated).[17]

The demonic pact was likewise a figment of the imagination, as were the litany of bacchanalian orgies the continental witches were being accused of (and confessing to) engaging in. Scot held up for scrutiny – and not a little mockery – the idea that old women were pledging themselves to Satan via 'their oth and bargain . . . by protestation of words, or by obligation in writing, sometimes sealed with wax, sometimes signed with blood, sometimes by kissing the divels bare buttocks'. Moreover, these things were impossible; the 'joining of hands with the divell, the kissing of his bare buttocks and his scratching and biting of them, are absurd lies; as everie one having the gift of reason may plainlie perceive'. The fact that Satan was mere spirit, according to Scot, made a nonsense of any such claims – and the fascination with (or terror of) dancing which his fellow Protestants seemed to evince revealed more about their prejudices and obsessions than it did about the people they alleged were witches. Scot criticised English law itself for taking such papistical nonsense-peddlers seriously; after all, was not legislation against witchcraft akin to the 'popish laws' against witches, which were 'foolish and lewd . . . tyrannous [and] cruel'?[18] The machinations of the Catholic Inquisitions were held up as examples of what *not* to do. Certainly, people might be justly investigated and – if guilty – punished according to the law for denying God, blaspheming, devil-worship, committing infanticide, indulging in cannibalism, or killing beasts. But the rest – demonic pacts, conspiring to induct others into such pacts, having sex with spirits and thus producing more witches, and boiling unbaptised infants – was bunkum, attractive only to superstitious fools.

But Scot and others of sceptical bent, whatever their faith, were not arguing in a vacuum. To them, the rise of 'witchcraft' as a problem, whether a real one, an imagined one, or an academic one, was a live issue: they could see what had once been a relatively niche question suddenly costing lives – every year more – whilst giving rise to new thinking and stoking hysterical fears. And it seemed to be catching.

On the continent, Catholic zealots such as the Jesuit-educated Archbishop-Elector of Trier, Johann von Schönenberg, had already launched a campaign of terror against those accused of such crimes in his diocese – and it was one that snowballed into a panic or series of mass trials that lasted over a decade (and in which hundreds were executed, the persecution not sparing children, the nobility, or justices who objected to the horrors). In Lorraine, the jurist Nicholas Rémy was likewise active – he boasted of having witnessed the torture and execution of over 800 people for witchcraft in the 1580s. In response, critics such as the Catholic Cornelius Loos produced his *True and False Magic*, which was quickly suppressed (with the author being forced to recant his apparently heretical opinions). His spiritual successors in the Catholic stand against witchcraft persecution, and the hideous tortures involved to extract confessions, included Alonso de Salazar Frías and the Jesuit Friedrich Spee, early in the next century. On the Protestant side, Reginald Scot's heirs included the Calvinist Anton Praetorius, author of the *Thorough*

Report about Witchcraft and Witches (1598). These men were, however, minority voices arguing against what was the prevailing orthodoxy in both Catholic and Protestant intellectual and theological circles – and these circles were not simply English or Scottish or German or French: they embraced the entire Christian world. Very few, whatever their faith, wished to appear either soft on, or in denial about, what was an easily identifiable popular enemy, synthesised from a whole host of negative characteristics so deep-rooted and ancient that their existence was incontrovertible (even if individuals might or might not really be one of them).

Those who argued against the reality of witchcraft were, it must have seemed at the time, contrarians on the wrong side of history: the eruption of accusations and trials surely proved (in what appears to have been a grand case of self-fulfilling prophecy) that there was a problem and that the doubters were wrong, either wilfully or due to having failed to apply their minds properly to the issue. Furthermore, the sceptics were hamstrung by the simple fact that they were not (whatever the more hysterical of their opponents might have claimed) arguing from a modern, atheistical position; they were not, that is, expressing doubts about the existence of God or Satan. Rather, they were variously arguing that the devil simply couldn't or didn't do certain things; that accused witches were mentally ill or tricksters; or that emerging methods of proving witchcraft – torture, for example – were inadequate or faulty. This kind of fastidious, stickling argument, situated as it was within a Christian framework in which good and evil, or God and the devil, still very much existed, was simply less appealing – less mainstream – than the popular line that a cosmic battle was being fought and the devil was converting weak souls into foot-soldiers. Popular fears, as ever, invited populist approaches to combating them, and nuance was at best the preserve of intellectuals and at worst an indication that the contrarian was a secret convert to devilry.

Thus, as Europe tore itself apart over the question of which was the true religion, conditions were perfect for an 'ancient enemy' to emerge as a theological football to be fought over by competing faiths. The flames would, further, be fanned by the increased pan-European use of that revolutionary new technology, the printing press, which widened and sped up the spread of intellectual debates. So too would the press, to some degree, democratise and popularise discussion. The academic case for witchcraft leapt from cloisters and libraries to bookstalls and debating halls across the continent (and beyond). Ensuing popular interest could then be enflamed by comparatively cheap print runs of sensationalist pamphlets. The imaginary threat of witches was thus made real by paper and ink; it was legitimised by serious men taking it seriously and seeking the most God-fearing and effective solutions, and further confirmed by the apparently real cases reported and gobbled up by growing readerships. Witches, in short, were becoming big news in sophisticated continental elite circles and amongst the hoi polloi.

This remarkable scope of appeal allowed politicians and religious leaders (and in this period the two were inseparable) to lead populist moral crusades. In an age of intensely personal governance, the beliefs, preoccupations and obsessions of rulers – whether of nations, cities or parishes – mattered, and, if the supposed problem of witchcraft was one of their interests (and, if they were keen readers, it was natural that it should be), these men increasingly had the legal instruments, spiritual justification, and popular support to stamp it out. In a phenomenon familiar to many eras of history, the persecution of witches allowed leaders to appear tough on crime whilst encouraging subjects and citizens to do their bit by airing private suspicions, jealousies, and fears. Everyone won, it seemed, except those unfortunates who found themselves accused – and, across Europe, the age-old and seldom-true advice held: only those who had something to hide had anything to fear. Those accused were, undoubtedly, what Reginald Scot suspected – a mix of the disadvantaged, outcasts, deluded people, troublemakers, actual murderers, and the victims of local and personal spite – but they continued to be arrested, tortured, and hanged because, at root, people wanted to believe an enemy within their communities existed and could be identified and disposed of. As a result, any enemy who might once have simply been an irritant – whether one's enmity towards them arose due to their appearance, their behaviour, their unpopularity, their inconvenient social or political position, or their sharp tongue – could be a witch. People were being told, essentially, not only that a problem most of them had always believed in – even if in a muted way, based more on rural superstition and self-protective practices than active fear – was very real, but that it was growing ever more dangerous, and they ought to do something about it. Unsurprisingly, many did.

As a result, Scot's book simply became part of the ongoing elite cultural conversation, or debate, about the reality of witchery and its real-world effects. This world thrived on disagreement and rebuttal, and the debating chamber was as wide as the continent. Soon enough, Scot's text caught the eye of someone with a voice far more powerful and influential than an English country gentleman's. His mockery of those who believed in the weather-commanding power of witches would soon be rebutted – with horrific consequences – by a man who had witnessed that power for himself. *The Discoverie of Witches* was about to become a target of obloquy for the young King of Scots.

6

Denmark's a Prison

In February 1587, the unthinkable happened. At the instigation of an aggressive Parliament and the persuasions of her councillors, Elizabeth I signed the warrant that sent Mary Queen of Scots to a rough, black velvet-draped wooden block in the frosty great hall of Fotheringhay Castle, the remote and semi-ruinous fortress which had become her final prison.

Mary's crime was to have engaged with desperate men who sought to free her from captivity with the aim of setting her on Elizabeth's throne. In this she had been entrapped, not in the sense that she was innocent but in that the English government, having secured a league of amity, the Treaty of Berwick, with Scotland in 1586 (which granted James an annual pension), now felt secure enough to rid itself of the woman Francis Walsingham called the 'bosom serpent'. Mary was thus allowed what she thought was covert communication with her supporters in the outside world: communication which was in fact put in place by the English intelligence network and subsequently monitored for signs of treacherous dealings against Elizabeth. These were not long in coming, as the Catholics John Ballard and Anthony Babington approached Mary with a plan for her conveyance out of her current prison. This would, naturally, have been accompanied by the assassination of the English queen – something that Mary tacitly acknowledged, even if she preferred to think only of her long-awaited freedom. She was thus guilty of plotting against Elizabeth, and her argument that she could not be guilty of treason, in that the Elizabeth was not her sovereign but her peer, availed her nothing.

News of his mother's trial – and its verdict – in late 1586 struck fear and eventually panic into King James. He had formed nothing other than a morbid fascination with Mary, and he certainly did not want her returned to Scotland (the monarch of which she still claimed to be, her demission of queenship having been gained under duress), but he did not want her subjected to what looked on the world stage like English butchery. He wrote panicked letters and sent hapless and rather unwilling delegations south to plead for her life, suggesting that she might be kept in even closer confinement with guarantees for her good behaviour. But it was all for nothing. Elizabeth, after her habitual vacillation, signed the warrant. A dropsical, stooping Mary, who had undergone something of a spiritual awakening – Catholic, naturally – went serenely to the block, diminished in stature but not dignity, and was given a less than serene execution. It took two blows of the axe and, reportedly, some sawing to sever the final gristle. James, when he heard the news, was seized by shock at the scandal of an anointed monarch being executed, as Mary had put it herself, 'like a criminal', and apprehension. This intensified when he saw the reaction from certain of his advisers and people, who called for immediate armed revenge against England. A threat to his hard-won new pension rose, as unwelcome as it was dangerous to his estate.

But, as emotions cooled and it became clear that Elizabeth herself offered a diplomatic way out for them both without either losing face – Mary's execution was to be presented as an accident, caused by a clerical error in the dispatch of the death warrant – he began to see the benefits. He was now Scotland's sole sovereign. And that made him, suddenly, a far greater prize on the international marriage market.

Despite James's basic bisexuality and romantic attachment to men, he was certainly capable of romantic feelings for women, or at least for his fantasy version of submissive, obedient women. His marriage had been the subject of debate since his earliest days, when a Spanish Catholic match had been mentioned (to the horror of his mother's Protestant councillors, magnates, and subjects). By the late

1580s, a Calvinist match with the older Catherine of Bourbon, and a Lutheran one with a young daughter of Denmark, were the front runners. James's canniest but possibly most unpopular (at least amongst the nobility) councillor, John Maitland of Thirlestane, was in favour of the Bourbon match, but riots against Scotland's possible involvement in the French Wars of Religion, and in favour of trade with Denmark, led James to favour a Danish princess. Maitland – brother to the side-switching, Machiavellian William Maitland of Lethington, who had intermittently served Mary Queen of Scots until his death in 1573 (and who had earned the punning nickname Michael Wyllie, or Muckle Wily) – lost the argument, but he had no intention of losing his influence with his king. He resolved, as he always would, to come out on top.

By 1589, once the death of the Danish King Frederick II had put an end to his demands that the Orkney and Shetland islands be returned by the Scots (these having been pawned by a previous Danish monarch and never redeemed), the remaining daughter of Denmark was Anna, a spirited, intelligent but not academic girl of fourteen. The marriage contract was signed and a proxy wedding held in Copenhagen in August 1589.

This was an act of boldness on James's part. For years, he had chafed against the delaying tactics and contradictory noises made by Queen Elizabeth regarding his position as her successor and her attitude to his marriage. In truth, Elizabeth had not wanted him to marry at all, as she had not wanted his mother to marry. From Elizabeth's perspective, the marriage of her potential successors to anyone – and the likelihood of their bearing children – could only rebound to her own discredit and risk her own popularity. If that meant Scotland, and very likely England, would suffer a dearth of Stuart heirs as it suffered a dearth of Tudor ones, that was not her problem but God's, and God would provide. James, however, had no intention of remaining unmarried and childless. When he heard rumours of the 'queen's [Elizabeth's] dislike of the match', he insisted that the English ambassador, Ashby, remain for the wedding to quell them – and, one assumes, to demonstrate that it was a *fait accompli*.[1]

James did his new wife the honour of clearing his bedchamber of the pretty men who had come to be regarded as his 'bedfellows', and announced himself eager to prove that he was not a 'barren stock'.[2] However, when Anna and her retinue set sail for Scotland, in the autumn, their ships were driven onto the coast of Norway (then pertaining to the Danish Crown) by the most ferocious storms anyone could remember seeing. Indeed, a cannon on the new queen's own vessel, the *Gideon*, broke free and almost crushed her. The Admiral of Denmark, Peder Munk, crawled on all fours to tell her that the prayers of the onboard divines were proving useless. In Scotland, James, who had been at Seton awaiting her arrival, was reported as being racked with impatience, because 'he is not like to see his love and joy before the spring'. The prayers and fasting he ordered appeared futile. He had been troubled, too, by news that a ferry carrying women (including his mother's faithful lady, Jane Kennedy) bound for Anna's household had sunk in the River Forth after colliding with another vessel. Around sixty people drowned. This was ominous, but as yet there were no whispers (or at least none were recorded) of any supernatural dealings.

After sending out scouting parties which only confirmed the freak weather conditions, James took another bold step: he elected to go to Scandinavia himself, taking with him a suitable retinue, including Maitland of Thirlestane, and leaving behind that councillor's chief enemy, Patrick Hepburn, 5th Earl of Bothwell, in dual charge alongside the young Ludovic Stuart, 2nd Duke of Lennox (son of Esmé Stuart, the memory of whom remained strong with the king). It was the former choice that was to raise eyebrows. Already, Bothwell had a reputation as inconstant: 'the most turbulent' of men. Between him and the callow Lennox, there was a danger, at least to the observant eye of Elizabeth's chief minister, William Cecil, now Lord Burghley, 'that some stirs and trobles maye be moved in the Kinges absence by the papistes and that faction'.[3] Although Bothwell, when given a little of the power he craved, would largely behave himself, James in time came to be horrified at the devilish pastimes the earl was soon accused of leading.

For the moment, though, the royal romance took precedence. James sailed from Scotland. Despite being beaten back to Pittenweem by storms in late October, his party of ships, decked out gaily with red taffeta on their sails, reached the frigid Norwegian coast at Flekkefjord. James moved inland to Tønsberg and on to Oslo, where he met his bride and, despite her initially refusing a kiss (that not being the custom in her country), they were able to chat amiably in their shared language of French. The following day, they set a date – 23 November – for their marriage proper. This took place at the Old Bishop's Palace, with the pair making a well-suited couple. He was twenty-three, golden-haired, fair-bearded, tall and slim, with deep-set, mournful eyes; she was nearly fifteen, tall, blonde, had striking features, and appeared deceptively docile. With alacrity, the newlyweds accepted an invitation to the Danish court (which Anna had not long left) to spend the winter.

James's time in Scandinavia was to be the happiest period in his life thus far, not least because he was free of the threat of seizure by political enemies and – despite the interminable and unedifying warring over precedence and place amongst his retinue – he was treated with dignity and deference. His time in Norway was spent partly in hunting and outdoor pursuits – which were a mania with him – and partly in hard drinking, at which the Danes excelled. But so too was he able and eager to indulge his other overriding passion: learning.

He was lucky. Copenhagen was a true Renaissance city, in the process of a rapid modernisation, which reached new heights under Anna's brother, Christian IV. It was a place of high culture, thanks in part to the dowager Queen Sophie's patronage of artists and drama-tists, and it boasted an excellent university established by papal bull in 1475 and inaugurated four years later. It was home also to leading European thinkers, such as Tycho Brahe and Niels Hemmingsen, both of whom the Scottish king spent time with (the former at his magnificent Uraniborg and Stjerneborg: an island observatory and laboratory). The latter engaged with James at Roskilde Cathedral, where the subject under debate was predestination. The elderly, white-bearded Hemmingsen was also an authority on witches and witchcraft, having in 1575 penned *Admonitio de superstitionibus magicis vitandis* (*Advice for Avoiding Magical Superstitions*), which defined witchcraft as the belief in the power inherent in symbols (words, signs, figures, or characters), which could only be exercised through demonic means, whether or not an explicit compact with Satan had been made.[4] Though Hemmingsen was sceptical of claims that witches could fly and of their supposed nocturnal mass assemblies, he was nevertheless critical of what he did recognise: traditional rites and practices of 'divination, conjuring, augury, incantation and both *maleficium* and beneficent magic'.[5] In the case of the latter, any physical cures came at the expense of the soul; more generally, most magical acts were implausible and their effects illusory. He did not censure esoteric practices – learned practices – of future-reading, but he didn't have to; the devil's job was to corrupt and pollute, and whether individual witches entered into a pact with him or his minions or not, their work, whether it was effectual or not, was *de facto* demonic. Yet Hemmingsen was no zealot. That the public and some judicial leaders were so interested in witchcraft – particularly in ghastly prosecutions and executions – was a problem, he argued, given the relatively rare nature of the beliefs manifesting as real-world effects.

There is no evidence that James discussed witchcraft with Hemmingsen during their time together. However, the king had shown an interest in the phenomenon: in April 1589, he had asked for one Marion MacIngaroch, accused of using magic to cure a man, to be given a royal audience. Marion, it seems, faced no accusations of devilry as a result and was not prosecuted. Yet if James retained his intellectual interest, the eminent scholar Hemmingsen was not the only man in Denmark whose mind was also attuned to the issue of witchcraft. The trials in Trier under Johann von Schönenberg were ongoing and thus current news (in the form of pamphlets), and debates were then at fever pitch in the academic world about the rights and wrongs of torture and execution (or at least the most valid methods); the precise nature of witches' powers and activities; and the correct role of the upright Protestant state in approaching the phenomenon. Any good intellectual Protestant thinker – and James counted himself one – ought to arrive at some learned opinion on the matter. Further, Denmark itself had had laws against witchcraft (when it resulted in death) since the twelfth century, and, like other European states, interest had been revived in the sixteenth – particularly in the context of storms; in 1543, witches had been accused of using magic against ships due to sail against the Holy Roman Emperor, Charles V (he of the codification Lex Carolina, which had drawn secular and ecclesiastical authorities together in punishing witchcraft), and in 1566 Copenhagen witches were said to have raised storms that sank the Danish fleet's best vessels.[6] In 1571, an enterprising trader named Doritte (or Dorothea) Nippers had also been tortured and executed despite her refusal to confess.[7]

Though James and Anna would leave the country in the spring of 1590, James must, during his time in Denmark – amidst the revelling, lively debates, and infighting of his party – have heard, too, news that had already begun circulating about witches active in and around Copenhagen. In April, when the royal couple were leaving Denmark, a woman named Ana Koldings – known infamously as the 'Mother of the Devil' – had been arrested on charges unrelated to the storms and confessed to her crimes (which made any future tortures permissible).

The seeds had been planted for what would be an enduring interest – and they would not be long in sprouting.

*

The active agent in pushing Copenhagen's witchcraft trials was the Danish admiral, Peder Munk, who was hardly a disinterested party. Even before transporting James and Anna home, he realised that he might be blamed for having poorly provisioned the royal fleet – and thus risking the life of Queen Anna and, by extension, the King of Scots who felt the need to sail out to retrieve her. He initially blamed the Treasurer, Christoffer Valkendorff, for not providing sufficient funds to the navy. Valkendorff balked at this, and the affair ended up, on Munk's return, in the Danish High Court, which found there had been no funding problems. As this particular thread of investigation was being unspooled, its uncertain outcome (and it was not concluded until the late summer, in Valkendorff's favour) left the admiral vulnerable. If simple weather had been to blame, then he might yet have questions to answer about his seamanship – and judgement – in attempting to sail in it. But the weather had not been simple. Obviously, someone had been responsible for the freak gales and tempests. Ironically, it was Valkendorff who provided the solution. He pointed out that witchcraft, already under investigation via the unfortunate Ana Koldings, might have been responsible. Munk had every reason to see what would prove to be ongoing and multiple witchcraft trials through to guilty verdicts.

Ana was once again induced to confess. This time, she admitted that she had been encouraged to use her powers to ensure that 'the lady [Queen Anna] would not reach Scotland on the first attempt': a formulation which recurred so often in the ensuing confessions that it was likely put in her mouth by the interrogators.[8] Moreover, she named others. Karen Vævers (or Weaver) was accused of being the ringleader of the attempts against the royal party. Karen, in turn, corroborated Ana Koldings' claims but named Kirsten Söndags, Margrete Skrivers, and a farmer's wife as the ones aiming at the destruction of the royal ships. Although she confessed to witchcraft, it was Karen's contention that the others had taken her 'Apostle' (or familiar spirit), Langinus, from her and – against her will, as her relatives were part of the fleet – sent it to sea in an empty beer barrel with the job of raising storms. Karen, on retrieving Langinus, had sent him to kill the farmer's wife so as to prevent the group's maleficent designs. Ana Koldings, who had outlived her usefulness in telling the authorities what they wanted to hear – that her witchcraft had been put in the service of causing the freak weather, and that she was only a junior member of a wider conspiracy – was executed by burning.

Before her death, Ana had provided more names. Knocks came on the doors of, amongst others, Maren Mads Bryggers (a brewer's wife), who confessed under interrogation to have met her fellow witches at Karen's house, where little clay vessels were used to represent the ships to be sunk or harassed. After – probably, but not certainly, given it was technically illegal to apply it before conviction – being tortured, Maren named yet more women (some of whom, like Kirsten Söndags, had already been accused). Another Maren, Maren Mogens, who had previously been accused and found not guilty of witchcraft, was then interrogated. She also named Margrete Jakob Skrivers (a scribe's wife with an existing reputation for witchcraft) as another experienced witch. A narrative was now taking clear shape. These women had all met at Karen's home and hatched and enacted their plans to destroy the fleet. Margrete's husband, Jakob Skrivers himself, was accused of being the true leader – the one who had hired the others with the aim of raising the storms. Not coincidentally, Jakob, a well-to-do former mayor, had previously been involved in an altercation with Peder Munk – by now being called an 'inquisitor' in the affair – which had resulted in blows being exchanged. The design had apparently first been put into practice on Michaelmas of 1589, with Jakob enlisting the women's services as revenge on Munk. The by-now familiar story was rehearsed, featuring meetings at Karen Vævers's house and the use of familiars (not just Langinus but Maren Morgen's Pilhesteskou and Ana Koldings's Smuck). Most of the women were executed in the late summer and early autumn, with only the Skrivers kept in confinement.

Given their position in society, Margrete's nephew attempted to intercede for her via the Court of Appeal, which held authority over death sentences in such trials. This failed and, sadly, she was sentenced to death in October and burnt at the stake in early 1591. Jakob (who had allegedly attempted suicide in prison after a failed escape attempt) had his goods forfeited but was allowed to live on, ruined socially and financially. Admiral Peder Munk had won.

What are we to make of this? On the surface, it appears a clear case of a man high in government leading a charge against witchcraft – and executing innocent women – out of pure self-interest. To some degree this is true, but it doesn't follow that Peder Munk, who enjoyed a good career and appears to have been faithful in Danish royal service, was acting entirely cynically. It might be that, given the evident belief in witchcraft then current (as proven by Ana Koldings's confinement on unrelated charges), he found it reasonable to believe that she and a group of cohorts had indeed raised the storms that had so vexed him and the royal party. Arguing against this are the confessions. Obviously, we can discount the idea that any of these women possessed demonic familiars who could travel to sea in barrels and harry the keels of ships. But did they attempt, however, misguidedly, to endanger Queen Anna's and King James's travels, and did they do so at the instigation of Jakob Skrivers?

The answer is almost certainly not. These women might well have fancied themselves to have had some supernatural powers, given some had reputations for just that – although it is worth noting that Maren Mogens had expressly been found not guilty in the past. But beyond that, the way in which their narrative was shaped into a conspiracy leading to Jakob Skrivers smacks of inquisitorial intervention (if not invention). In this way, Admiral Munk took advantage of the situation. The authorities had discovered what was, to them, a real crime. With Munk's guidance as a quasi-inquisitor, the accused women duly produced a relatively coherent story of how their ostensible plot had operated, and they were frightened and tortured into agreeing with all that was put to them (including the involvement of the Skrivers). In all, the Copenhagen witches were guilty of nothing more than having a poor choice of friends. Yet the outcome of the trial affirmed, for those so inclined to believe in the reality of witchcraft, that weather-changing and attacks on royalty were threats that should be taken seriously by good Protestants. It indicated that common witches might well be engaged by politically jealous and spiteful paymasters.

News of the affair was soon in Edinburgh and London, adding yet more to the debate. In July 1590, a woman from Lübeck even attended Queen Anna, begging her to tell James that 'learned magicians' had prophesied that he would undertake noble acts: 'The king and country,' it was reported, 'think her a witch, yet he is purposed to hear her.'[9] Later that same month, Peder Munk was openly being bruited as the driver of the Copenhagen hunt, the affair was being linked to Edinburgh witches accused of roasting wax images of the late laird of Wardhouse, and the Lübeck woman was forced to flee. Witches were not and had never been a Catholic problem and certainly their activities weren't mere papist superstition; they were real, dangerous, and if the Catholics had failed to deal with them adequately during their monopoly of Christianity, it was time for godly Protestants to take charge.

The target of the witches – by accident if not design, given he had felt the need to ride out the storms in pursuit of his bride – would prove to have been listening to all that had gone on in Denmark attentively. King James, long wary of his rebellious and treacherous subjects, noble and common, would turn suspicious eyes on his own kingdom.

PART III

Obsession

'They ought to be put to death according to the law of
God, the civil and imperial law, and the municipal law of
all Christian nations'
— James VI and I, 1597, *Daemonologie*

7

The King's Evil

The Scotland to which King James brought his new queen was not particularly strong on the international stage, given its recent history of political instability. It is often said that it was a poor country, and though it was not as rich as many of the better-populated and centralised nations of early modern Europe, it would be fairer to say that it had a poor Crown. James had been in debt since his minority and, given his country was – and had been for decades – possessed of rebellious nobles and barons, and its Highlands and Islands had a somewhat loose association with central government, he was unable to consistently enrich the royal coffers at his subjects' expense. The majority of those subjects were the rural poor, with only a minority living in the larger towns and cities and thus engaged in commerce and forming part of the emerging middle classes. What money there was in Scotland – and it could be considerable – largely remained in private pockets, with the king only extracting taxes on special occasions (such as the festivities incumbent on the country in welcoming its new queen, which saw a £100,000 Scots levy voted in by the Estates).

Immediately on the royal couple's return, time and money were spent in the pursuit of Queen Anna's reception (which involved a tour of her jointure properties, intended to safeguard her future in Scotland), her triumphal entry through Edinburgh, and her spring-time coronation. At the latter, ongoing tensions between the king and Kirk, or at least between him and the hotter reformist ministers, raised their head, with disputes arising over the godly rectitude of anointing the queen with holy oil. James, who was a believer in what some ministers thought a 'superstitious rite, borrowed from the Jews', insisted on having his way, and Anna received her anointment.[1] This was just the latest in what would be a long-lasting difference of opinion between those churchmen who espoused ecclesiastical governance by presbyteries (elected or nominated assemblies of Kirk elders) and an Erastian monarch who believed in appointed bishops and, ideally, the pre-eminence of the sovereign in spiritual affairs.

The value of that role – and of James's attitude to justice – was about to be tested. In May 1590, just over a week before the new queen's coronation, a woman had been placed under investigation for witchcraft (some of her alleged crimes dating back nearly a year) by her local Kirk Session in Haddington. This was Agnes Sampson, a respectable healer, widow, and midwife whose remedies had, reputedly, not always been particularly successful. As was standard practice, she was imprisoned in squalid conditions in the Haddington Tolbooth and subjected to interrogation. It is probable that, at this point, she was reticent to admit to much more than healing through prayer and natural remedies – and it is clear, too, that she was aware of the dangers into which a healer might fall if those remedies looked like falling under the banner of witchcraft (it being thought that a witch might remove the curse or bewitchment laid on by another witch). She was far from the only person in Scotland currently accused of witchcraft under the 1563 Act, and neither was her case all that unusual. It would, however, take a darker turn.

At some point later in the year, a young servant came home and found herself face-to-face with a suspicious and threatening master. Geillis Duncan was suspected by her employer, David Seton, of witchcraft. This in itself was not shocking news to the wider world. In addition to witchcraft trials having become part of the cultural landscape in Scotland, even if a new and rare one, there had recently been a handful of cases in East Lothian.[2] Yet what arguably should have happened – the girl being investigated, tried, and found either innocent or guilty, before being released or punished accordingly, as would happen in other scattered trials throughout the year – did not.³ Seton's reason for suspecting her was, apparently, that she had been leaving his house at night. This was dangerous; there was always something covert – something unnatural – about nighttime business. He then decided, on his own initiative as a bailie depute (or a local deputy alderman), to strip the girl and search for a mark that would indicate her interaction with Satan. This was not an original belief but one which was still in the process of development: did all witches receive a physical stamp as part of their demonic initiation, or just some? Could such marks be distinguished from normal physical marks? Were these a sign, as in some of the English cases, of a familiar spirit feeding on the witch's blood?

Crucially – and it is here worth noting that much of our knowledge of Geillis's case comes from a source in which James had a hand – the king was a believer and, given his education and academic interests, probably far better placed to have an opinion on the matter than David Seton. Further working on his suspicions, Seton almost certainly began torturing the girl – and probably his desire to do so played a significant part in his real motivations.

The fates of these two women, Agnes and Geillis, are intertwined – and it was very likely at the instigation of the king that they became so, with Agnes being transferred from Haddington to Edinburgh. James, who had heard by late in the year the true extent of the Danish witch trials, with their revelations of an implicit plot against his life, began to take an active interest. This was probably born of paranoia. Throughout his youth, threats and plots had been manifold against him, and here was the latest and most insidious. By late November, it was being reported that he was busy with ongoing prosecutions. For the first time, witchcraft was now under investigation by the king and his Privy Council acting as a court, their courtroom no less than James's magnificent palace of Holyroodhouse.

According to her (rather confused) surviving deposition, Geillis confessed to a meeting in the middle of the Firth of Forth with none other than one of the Copenhagen witches. She had also, so she claimed, attended an assembly at the old kirkyard in North Berwick, the doors of which were kept by one 'Grey Meal': a man named

John Gordon, who was probably also rounded up. This group had, moreover, bewitched the Laird of Balnaird, one William Douglas, and one Alexander Douglas, and had engaged in ritual dances. Geillis named Agnes Sampson as another of the party, alongside a slew of other names: ship's captain Robert Grierson; schoolmaster John Fian (alias Cunningham); Bessie Thomson; Irish Marion; George Mott's wife; Christian Lud; the goodwife of Spilmersford; Kate Graw; and Davie Steele (the latter two of whom had already been executed for unrelated witchcraft convictions). These people had, by Geillis's admission, raised the storm which wrecked the ferry carrying Jane Kennedy in September 1589.

By means of a cord, the witches could apparently raise the devil up and answer in affirmation that they'd become his good servants. Thereafter, Satan appeared several times to Geillis, once 'like a man clad in black'. The end of all this group activity was 'to raise the storm for the stopping of the queen's coming home', with the additional desire (on Geillis's part) that her master, David Seton, should suffer sickness. It is a confused story: a gallimaufry of demonic acts and meetings stretching back years, with the critical elements being those details of the supposed plan which tally closely with what had been confessed to (or rather constructed) in Denmark. Geillis, terrified and abused first by Seton and then by the Privy Council, poured forth a hotchpotch of demonic and maleficent tropes, and almost certainly agreed with what the councillors were really interested in. That was what all early modern governments were paranoid about: a conspiracy (which witchcraft, with its long if uneven association with secret assemblies, lent itself to) to kill the sovereign. As in the Danish case, Michaelmas (when Jakob Skrivers had first launched his storm-raising plans) played a role, with that being a prelude to destroying James himself.

Agnes Sampson, under torture, eventually corroborated the story, such as it was. Although initially she still denied the charges laid against her and confessed only to her use of such folk remedies as whisky, eggs steeped in vinegar, and fleur-de-lis steeped in white wine (this in early December 1590), the older woman was put on the spot by the king himself. James was quick to note inconsistencies in Agnes's tales of healing. She did, for example, admit to knowing when someone was bewitched and how best to remove the curse. She claimed to have learnt from her father how to use prayers to lengthen or shorten others' lives. She mentioned, several times, a black dog she had seen during various of her healing activities. All this smacked very much of witchcraft, and, despite Agnes's denial that she knew Geillis, the king was intent on proving a conspiracy.

Following, probably, another round of torture, Agnes responded to James's desire that she 'straitly confess the truth'. Suddenly, the black dog was the devil, who demanded to be referred to as 'Eloa' (or 'Elva'), and she had sworn to serve him. Following this, Satan had begun appearing sometimes as a man, sometimes a foal, sometimes a stag, and he had given her a mark (a further indication that the importance of the devil's mark, or witch's mark, did not originate with David Seton in Scottish cases but with King James). More witches were named, some of whom had, again, already been executed on unrelated charges; again, the idea of conventicles (assemblies of witches) loomed large, with Agnes admitting she had coerced Grey Meal into joining what was, clearly, a coven (even if the name was still not in use in the context of witchcraft). As Geillis had been forced to admit, Agnes agreed that an assembly took place at North Berwick, wherein there were six men and the rest – numbering above a hundred – were women. There, they had opened up three graves at the devil's command, 'and took the joints of their fingers, toes, and noses, and parted them amongst them . . . to make a powder of them to do evil withal. Then he [the devil, in a black gown and hat] commanded them to keep his commandments, which was to do all the evil they could. Before they departed they kissed all his arse.' On another occasion, the witches had gone to sea in a boat like a chimney, the devil passing before them 'like a rick of hay', to wreck a ship called *The Grace of God*.

With this corroboration ongoing, Geillis was again brought to confess. One of those women she had earlier named, Bessie Thomson, had by this time provided testimony (again, probably under torture), and so Geillis was once more induced to confirm the conspiracy. By now it had grown to include details. She, Agnes, John Fian, and one Meg Din had apparently baptised a cat, Margaret (it being blasphemous to baptise an animal), tied the exhumed and severed body parts to it, passed it three times through the links of a crook and three times under a chimney, and at midnight cast it into the sea. The cat thankfully survived this ordeal and 'came back again', but the work was done: by these means a storm was raised.

By now, the tragic Agnes and Geillis had been thoroughly identified as two of the prime agents (along with John Fian, who managed to escape captivity but was swiftly recaptured) in what the king and his councillors believed was treasonable witchcraft: a shocking collision of age-old political sorcery with all the modern theories about demonic witchcraft and mass assemblies grafted on. Both women, under unimaginable conditions of stress, terror, and physical agony, gave conflicting, contradictory accounts, doubtless in response to their treatment. Agnes, in January 1591, went further again, admitting to associations with one Barbara Napier (a wealthy woman who had probably at some point consulted her as a medic) and Eupheme MacCalzean (the only daughter of Lord Cliftonhall, who had likely done the same). Both were now accused of political sorcery in killing the late 8th Earl of Angus and, predictably, of being part of the plot to kill the king. It might well be that these accusations were seized on due to the two women's political connections (and property), but this must remain conjectural. What is more likely is that Agnes had had some connection with them, and authorities were quick to seize on their involvement in the bigger plot. The hunt was now on to uncover all the arms and legs of that conspiracy. Significantly for the future, amongst the slew of names Agnes Sampson and her unfortunate alleged co-conspirators had given was one Ritchie Graham: a 'notorious and known necromancer' who boasted associations with some of the most influential men in Scotland.[4]

*

At the end of January, crowds lined the streets of Edinburgh, their faces excited and expectant. The city was then composed of one long, wide street – as wide as any continental boulevard – which stretched from the rocky volcanic plug on which looms Edinburgh Castle to the Netherbow Port which led into the neighbouring burgh of the Canongate (and so on to Holyroodhouse). Leading off from this street, now known as the Royal Mile, were dozens of rabbit warren-like alleys, vennels, and side streets. Overlooking it were the projecting upper floors and galleries of merchants, ministers, tailors, and city wives. All would have clamoured for a view of John Fian, by now known as a notorious witch who had sought the king's death, as he was led – probably amidst jeers and showers of spittle – to the forecourt on Castle Hill. The man had been broken by months of accusation, torture, confession, and days spent staring into the implacable face of an enthroned King James and his steely, unforgiving councillors. His feet and ankles had been broken by the use of the 'Spanish boots': instruments of torture which shattered the bones. His fingernails had reportedly been torn out with pincers called 'turkas', and irons pins forced underneath. On Castle Hill, John made his speech. As the English ambassador, Robert Bowes (who wrote to Burghley with news that some accused witches had tried to implicate him, crowing that they had described him inaccurately as 'a little black and fat man with black hair' and so not won the approval of the king), noted, 'at his death [he] denied all he had acknowledged, saying he told those tales by fear of torture and to save his life'.[5] This was the simple truth. Nevertheless, John Fian was throttled to death before his emaciated and shattered body was burned. The next day it was Agnes Sampson's turn, and the crowds again turned out to see her end. Justice, from the royal perspective, was being done. But in Holyroodhouse, matters were not settled. In that low-lying palace, a good distance from the choke of the smoke, the king brooded.

King James was not, by his nature, a vindictive man. Throughout his life, before and after the irruption of witchcraft as an imagined force against him, he showed himself gregarious, bluff, and generally merciful, at least to those he had taken the time to get to know. Yet something had been fired in him. It would be easy to blame pure cynicism: to imagine that, given his rivalry with the Kirk and its Presbyterian ministers, he sought to glorify himself as Satan's enemy – but this would be unfair. Whilst it is clear that he did see the benefits of presenting himself as God's anointed and thus the right man to be both the target of the devil's wrath and consequently his strongest foe, it is certain that he believed this to be true. For the first time in the British Isles, witchcraft was not simply being tried as a crime like any other but cracked down on via the systematic excavation of a wide-ranging conspiracy. This is because the king believed, genuinely, that he had discovered a new and insidious plot against himself, as real as any rebellions staged against his mother or any of the numerous Jesuit conspiracies to assassinate Queen Elizabeth. He had seen the proof of it in the storms, and it was evident that continental thinking – even if not all of it – was on his side or moving towards it.

The gathering of depositions, the recording of 'dittays' (legal indictments), and the trials continued. Geillis and other accused witches, Jane Stratton and Donald Robson, continued to do as they were compelled. Stories were recorded of conventicles at Acheson's Haven at Lammas in 1590; of toads dropped in urine to procure the king's death; of the creation of images of James, delivered to Satan with malevolent intent; and of the potential role of the 5th Earl of Bothwell, who had been left in charge (along with the young 2nd Duke of Lennox) when the king had been in Scandinavia. Bothwell was quickly arrested and warded in Edinburgh Castle, pending a planned trial by his peers (which did not eventuate due to lack of enthusiasm from those magnates). He emulated his famous uncle by staging a daring and successful escape – as legend has it down the sheer cliff-face of the castle mount. Ritchie Graham, who probably did know him, offered to reveal all he knew, particularly regarding Bothwell's desire to calculate the king's date of death, provided he could escape the death penalty and be protected from any revenge on the earl's (or his followers') part.

This was all explosive stuff – more explosive than the litany of charges made against even those prominent women Barbara Napier (who was sentenced to death but found guilty only of consulting with witches, thus escaping the death penalty – much to James's fury) and Eupheme MacCalzean, who was found guilty and went to the rope and the flames days after Bothwell's escape in June 1591 (albeit there were almost immediately strenuous attempts to posthumously clear her name). Geillis, whose master had begun the horror, and who was undoubtedly innocent of even knowing important people and probably of any type of effective (or ineffective) magical healing, was executed on Castle Hill in December 1591, denying at the last that she had ever known Barbara and Eupheme. Although Janet and Donald retracted their confessed knowledge of Bothwell, the mud stuck.

Two things were now foremost in the king's mind. The first was trumpeting what had occurred – or rather what he had narrowly escaped – far and wide. In essence, James believed he had discovered and foiled the equivalent of a modern-day terrorist plot. In June 1591, he stood up in the Tolbooth in Edinburgh and gave a long speech discoursing on the iniquities of Scotland – particularly, he was concerned with the rifeness of criminal activity, and of those activities, particularly witchcraft, 'which is a thing growen very common amongst us . . . and I have bene occupied these three quarters of this yeere for the siftyng out of them that are guilty herein'.[6] Yet the rest of the world – and particularly England, which he expected one day soon to govern – must be told of and appreciate the matter. In this way, he was in tune not just with the growing pamphleteering culture of England and the continent but its potential role in spreading political propaganda. Although he did not write it (the author of at least some of the raw material probably being James Carmichael, minister of Haddington, who had lived in London), the result was 1591's *Newes from Scotland*: the most famous record of the Scottish royal family's escape from a witchcraft-powered murder plot. In its anglicised form – the better for English readers and newsmongers – the pamphlet appeared south of the border, and

James, tellingly, made no diplomatic attempts to have it suppressed (this despite him not being shy about pressing English authorities to hand over any Scottish witches who fled southwards, and at other times attempting to suppress texts which failed to meet his approval). It is obvious why he made no deprecatory comment.

The *Newes* is a masterpiece in drama, rich in climaxes and not shy about presenting the king as the hero of the hour: a man initially sceptical of the trials (which the records indicate he was not) but suddenly reconciled to the true horrors afoot when Agnes Sampson had, in Holyroodhouse, whispered to him the words he'd spoken to his new bride on their wedding night. This fanciful dramatic turning point is probably just that. The *Newes* is equal parts salacious – it recounts, for example, the shaving of Agnes and her silence until the devil's mark is found 'upon her privities' – and packed with memorable details: the sailing of witches to North Berwick in 'riddles or sieves' and the disorderly dancing of reels (an emerging bugbear of upright Calvinists) at the conventicles, with Geillis accompanying the dancers on a 'Jew's trump [harp]' (which James is said to have asked her to perform in the palace as proof). It is the only record, too, to suggest the operation of torture in the course of interrogations (although naturally the surviving depositions do not include what went on between the confessions). The truth of the practice's use was confirmed, however, by the Privy Council's establishment in October 1591 of a royal commission explicitly designed to arrest and interrogate witches (though it did not allow commissioners to try them). This commission, six men-strong, was authorised to use torture in its examinations. Whatever had been going on before, which was evidently *ad hoc*, the king was now intent on centralising the discovery of witchcraft in his kingdom – or at least those parts of the realm in which the royal writ operated smoothly. The right to allow examination and brutalisation of suspects became King James's prerogative and, though this commission was time-limited, he believed it should remain so.

In the *Newes*, elements of what was then modern thinking on demonic gatherings are rehearsed: the kissing of the devil's backside and its coldness, and the copulation with him which none are said to enjoy because of the chill. Remembering the affair years later in his memoirs, Sir James Melville (knighted at Queen Anna's coronation) added further to the picture: 'He caused all the company to come kiss his arse, which they said was cold like ice, his body hard like iron . . . his face was terrible, his nose like the beak of an eagle, great burning eyes, his hands and legs were hoary, with claws upon his hands and feet like the griffin. He spoke with a low voice.'[7]

This story needed the devil. Even if Satan was assumed to be present in all cases of witchcraft, here his centrality was underscored enough to require comment – and that is because a king deserved and was given an enemy prominent enough to make for an adversary. To this was appended the moral of the story. In attempting to destroy King James, the devil and the witches, with Agnes as ringleader of the latter, had learned that he was protected by God: 'His Highness carried a magnanimous and undaunted mind not feared with [scared by] their enchantments but resolute in this: so long as God is with him, he feareth not who is against him.' James had survived this multi-pronged demonic assault because 'God would as well defend him on land as on the sea'. Again, the king himself was neither gullible dupe nor malicious cynic. He was, by training and inclination, a ferocious reader accustomed to familiarising himself with both sides of a debate, weighing them up and reaching what, to his own mind, must be the logical conclusion. He was not, however, an original thinker, original thinking not then being a prerequisite of a Renaissance man. Having considered the arguments for and against witchcraft, he positioned himself in favour of its reality. That meant those arguments in favour of it – produced by previous cases of discrete and political witchcraft, the writings of advocates of witches' powers, and received wisdom about the devil's role and appearance – were valid. Those accused could thus be rightly forced to confess to these things under duress and by leading questions. That this allowed James to preen as Satan's enemy – and thus give a fillip to any censorious Kirk ministers who doubted royal supremacy – was a boon. But it wasn't his motivation.

In the *Newes from Scotland* and in the various confessions (and retractions), we can conclude, ironically enough, the innocence of those accused. The details confessed to are closely aligned with developing thinking on demonology and royal concerns: the icy-cold devil's arse (politely emended to the 'devil's ears' by Victorian historian Agnes Strickland), for example, had been recounted in earlier French cases as well as in Edward Fenton's *Certaine Secrete wonders of Nature* (1569), and the low voice is found in English ones. These modern tropes are unlikely to have been at the forefront of the minds of local healers, serving women, or even a local school-master or wealthy city women. It is inconceivable they either invented them or had the necessary experience of witchcraft studies to parrot them. It is even more difficult to imagine these people had the slightest interest in advancing any new Scottish Protestant theo-logical position on the reality and workings of witchcraft. Yet their admissions appear engineered to have done just that. This means they had to have been put in the mouths of those accused – and if these fantastical elements were forced upon them, there is no reason to believe much of anything else, save the vague possibility that some prominent healers had some prominent clients. The role of King James and his council is thus all-important, not in the sense that they bullied victims into confessing (which they did) but in why – and in terms of who was chosen as part of the conspiracy. The witches executed throughout 1591 as part of the anti-royal plot were, certainly, victims of the king's belief that the Danish witches had not been working alone. Just as in Denmark existing accused women had been forced into the roles of storm-raising political assassins, so too were existing accused women in Scotland, who could then be forced to name their co-agents. The biggest name of all, however, might well have been the product of James's council-lors, and one of them in particular.

Bothwell was in no doubt about who this was. Even prior to the king's voyage to Norway, the rambunctious and self-important earl had been at loggerheads with James's chancellor, John Maitland of Thirlestane. On learning he had been accused of witchcraft – indeed,

that he had conspired with a gaggle of witches to destroy the king
– he named, and would continue to name, Maitland as the architect
of his unfolding downfall. More dangerously, he proved he was not
above taking the law into his own hands, springing a follower who
had been arrested from the Tolbooth whilst James and his council
were in the building.

Bothwell was far from popular, least of all in England. Though he
was occasionally paid by Queen Elizabeth and her government to
cause mischief in Scotland, he was a loose cannon. In September
1589 it had been reported that he had given succour to an English
malcontent, and in 1590, shortly before the accusations landed on
him, Bowes recorded with some glee that 'upon [my] request for
reformation of the disorders of Liddesdale, the king has dealt with
Bothwell far more roughly than he has been accustomed, letting
him know that albeit he had promised largely, yet he had performed
little, having ever found shifts to delay the accomplishment. The
king charged him to be careful, and to fulfil his promises speedily, or
he would withdraw his good countenance from him, and cause his
pleasure to be executed by others, to the earl's disgrace.'[8]

James was thus primed to believe the worst of the vainglorious
earl, who, although he had governed Scotland competently during
the winter of 1589–90, was possessed of that tiresome fault common
to sixteenth-century magnates in every country: he viewed himself
as one of the realm's natural leaders by dint of his birth and position,
and he wasted no opportunity to agitate against any lower-born or
upwardly-mobile interlopers. This had led him to clash already with
Chancellor Maitland, who was viewed with the same green-eyed
asperity as had been, for example, Thomas Cromwell and Lord
Burghley (and later his son, Robert Cecil) in England, and David
Riccio in Scotland.

Following his escape from Edinburgh Castle in June 1591,
Bothwell was declared an outlaw (or 'put to the horn', in Scottish
terminology) for having 'had consultation with necromancers,
witches, and other wicked and ungodly persons'. This was not
James's ideal; Scotland's law against consulting with witches was far

less strictly enforced than the crime of wielding magic directly – but it served the purpose of removing the earl from the political scene. Bothwell thereafter began a guerrilla campaign, which outlasted the executions of his accused co-conspirators by some margin; leading bands of followers, he harried King James and Queen Anna, all the while ingratiating himself with the Kirk by presenting himself as one of its unjustly maligned honest sons (and, when opportunity knocked, accepting cash from English coffers, Elizabeth I banking on him as a reliable means of keeping the Scottish king busy). Although Anna, to James's chagrin, attempted to intercede on the renegade's behalf, Bothwell proved himself a nuisance. After a failed attempt at seeking mediation with the king and Council, he appeared at various locations issuing challenges to Maitland, always fleeing afterwards, so that in December there were rumours – entirely false – that he had disappeared to Caithness in the far north.

He had gone nowhere. In December 1591, he surprised the royal couple at Holyroodhouse. As James's English courtier Roger Aston reported, 'the Earl Bothwell entered the palace, accompanied with the Laird of Spott, Mr. John Colville, and others to the number of sixty, in armour, assailed the house in all parts and took as many as they pleased, and pursued the chancellor's house [apartments] with great rigour'.9 James barricaded himself in the monarchical apartments in the palace's opulent tower block and remained there even as his door was set ablaze, whilst Maitland likewise defended his chambers. Even the queen's rooms were assaulted, with the intruders – some fifty-strong – attacking her door with hammers. When the people of Edinburgh were alerted, as they generally were to any fracas in the nearby palace, they descended, driving off most of Bothwell's men. In the event, at least two members of the royal household were found dead and several of the rebels captured and hanged.

This, along with the recent horrific revelations of the witches' attempts on his life, had done nothing for the king's paranoia. Already, it was being reported that his young friend the Duke of Lennox was a 'favourer' of Bothwell. Queen Anna, too, had shown him some sympathy prior to the assault on Holyroodhouse. James continued to see conspiracy everywhere. In February of the following year, Ritchie Graham, the infamous necromancer, was finally tried, found guilty, strangled, and his body burnt, his offer to reveal all about Bothwell in return for protection having availed him nothing. In June, the Scottish Parliament ratified the earl's forfeiture, underlining his outlaw status – though the same sitting would repeal James's 1583 'Black Acts' via the new 'Golden Acts', removing his favoured episcopalian structure of the Kirk and instituting presbyteries (though James retained nominal spiritual supremacy). Henceforth, Kirk Sessions, which had replaced the old ecclesiastical courts, would be bulked up and granted greater licence to snoop into parishioners' moral lives. The thin line between private and public was further blurred, with individual sins now communal sins. Presbyterians were riding high – but they had little real interest in witchcraft, being far more eager to suppress Catholicism and further the cause of reform.

Yet James was far from toothless. Although an order for joint Kirk-Crown commissions was drafted (which included, as an afterthought, the right to hold criminal courts and thus have jurisdiction over witchcraft), it was probably never implemented.[10] James retained the right to dispense royal commissions of justiciary for the trial and punishment of witches. He need only await the next outbreak.

Probably in response to the confirmation of his forfeiture, Bothwell struck again, this time attacking the king's hunting lodge-turned-palace at Falkland. Again, the invaders were repulsed – and again the king felt conspiracy clutching. It was little surprise that he was found 'lamenting his estate', and soon even his bedchamber seemed unsafe; when he was sleeping with Anna at Dalkeith, one of the queen's ladies helped a Bothwell partisan, John Logie of Wemyss, then imprisoned elsewhere in the palace, escape through the royal bedroom window. If James thought he might find sympathy from his peer, Queen Elizabeth, he had another think coming: in requesting advice on dealing with Bothwell from the English queen, she 'answered by letter that it was [his] own fault, that he spared the offenders in his power, and that those who will attack a king are worthy to stretch on

a halter'[11] (which was hypocritical more than ironic, given her willingness to encourage Bothwell's troublemaking).

As his friend the Catholic 6th Earl of Huntly had, in February
1592, murdered the glamorous 2nd Earl of Moray (known to history
as the 'bonny' earl) in the climax of a blood feud, with James himself
accused of complicity, the king had reason to imagine that his reign
was in danger. Rumours of his growing unpopularity swirled,
enflamed further by Huntly's involvement – alongside other Catholic
magnates such as Erroll and Angus – in the 'Spanish Blanks' affair,
whereby these prominent men were caught sending, effectively,
signed blank cheques to Philip II of Spain, that His Catholic Majesty
might fill them in as he pleased. To the Kirk, this was the king's fault;
he had been, was being, and would be far too soft on Catholics.
James thus found himself and his wife in the unenviable position of
being in competition with (and sometimes under attack from,
particularly when it came to courtly dancing) the Kirk, surrounded
by potential treachery, and unjustly accused of outright murder.

A new low seemed to have been reached when Bothwell launched
a fresh attack on the king, again at Holyroodhouse. This one was
successful, in that the earl managed to gain entry to the royal apartments, where he threw himself at James's feet, proffering his sword
to his sovereign in a show of submission. James, who had attempted
to flee to Anna's rooms but found the door locked, had no choice
but to accept this. But it was pure show. James did not believe
Bothwell had been maligned by Maitland (who had at this point
retired from court partly due to an ongoing property dispute with
the queen); he believed the earl had consulted with witches aiming
at his death. Yet, as long as he had made this apparent peace, he was
forced to allow a show trial which acquitted the rebel of charges of
treasonable witchcraft. This changed nothing. As soon as James felt
he could do so safely, he once again had Bothwell outlawed – this,
interestingly, only weeks after Chancellor Maitland had reconciled
with the queen and returned to court.

Not surprisingly, all this turmoil had given James a knock – and
he was fast gaining a reputation for duplicity. Even the news of

Anna's pregnancy did not restore him to popularity – although the birth of an heir, Prince Henry, in February 1594 did much to raise royal prestige. The king felt secure enough, at any rate, to attempt to repulse Bothwell when the earl, furious at his treatment, assaulted Leith – although James found himself embarrassed by the lack of support the royal presence drummed up. He was pressured, too, to make a stand against the Catholic earls, via the reduction of the fortresses of Huntly and Erroll. In the end, it wasn't the king who ended the terror of the supposed witch-leader earl but Bothwell himself. In his desperation to be avenged on Maitland, whom he still considered the main actor in his downfall, he joined with the Catholics. This lost him the Kirk's goodwill and in February 1595 he was excommunicated. In April, his money (whether his own or that taken from the English) ran out and he was forced into exile. Bothwell remained on the king's mind – and recurs in state papers as a potential threat – but he would not darken James's doorway, or attempt to burn it down, again.

Throughout these messy affairs, with their heady mix of murder, accusations of witchcraft and conspiracy, religious disputes, and ecclesiastical development, the Earl of Bothwell, the supposed paymaster of the witches, remained resolute in his claims that Maitland of Thirlestane had been his chief accuser. Historians have generally written this off, reasonably, as the earl defaulting to the rhetoric of the 'evil counsellor' (which was emulated, for example, by Elizabeth I's famous 2nd Earl of Essex during his own coup against her chief minister Robert Cecil). Yet there is some evidence that he might have been telling the truth – or at least he might have been more right than he knew.

Corroborating evidence of a kind can be found in the attitude of Queen Anna, who was no mean political player in her own right. She had conceived such a dislike and distrust of Maitland over what she believed to be his appropriation of lands pertaining to her jointure properties that in January 1592 it was reported that '[the] chancellor is drawn hereby, and by other occasions, into the evil conceit of the queen'.[12] This was exacerbated, apparently, by 'some speech uttered in the queen's presence and hearing by the chancellor's wife, touching the favourites of Bothwell's late attempt, and which the queen conceives much otherwise than the lady meant'.[13] Particularly during Bothwell's early guerrilla campaign, rumours had risen about the queen's (utterly false) close relationship with the earl. Anna did not doubt that the source was the Maitlands, whom she found to be political schemers. Later, when they did manage to reconcile (mainly because they had found a common adversary in the Earl of Mar, to whom James had granted custody of Prince Henry despite Anna's opposition), it was reported that queen and chancellor were hatching a plot. In response, 'the king . . . sent to the chancellor to know if he were participant of this purpose. He denies that ever he was made acquainted with any such matter.'[14] This was a lie. Maitland encouraged Anna's opposition to Mar from the sidelines, advancing her cause – in what became a protracted custody battle – for his own ends.

Maitland, in his fifties by the time of Bothwell's fall, was a political veteran born of a deeply political family (with not just his famous brother having served Mary Queen of Scots but his poet father having been a senator of the College of Justice). He was, without doubt, one of James's ablest ministers – and he was a consummate survivor. Part of this stemmed from his intimate knowledge of the king's mind. Maitland was fully aware, at every step, of his master's growing obsession with witchcraft and the supposed plot against his life. It is entirely possible – even likely – that it was he who took advantage of the forced confessions (and possibly uncovered the real link between Ritchie Graham and Bothwell) to have his great and long-standing enemy accused. As the saying goes, just because the earl gave every appearance of being paranoid, that does not mean they weren't out to get him. The evidence of Maitland's duplicity, cunning, and willingness to secure political capital as events presented themselves is suggestive. If there is no smoking gun proving that Bothwell was right in claiming that the chancellor was the man who forced the accused witches to falsely incriminate him, then it is worth noting that Maitland, his fellow councillors, and the king sent people to the gallows on far slimmer evidence. Whatever the truth, Maitland lived only to see Bothwell's departure. The chancellor died in October 1595, whilst the exiled earl lived on, in increasingly straitened circumstances, until November 1612.

For the moment, Scotland's king could count himself thankful that he had eliminated a devilish plot. However, the results of it – the accommodation with the Kirk on prosecuting witchcraft – would have many sequels. The problem of witches was no longer just a matter of scattered incidents (although these would continue under the new central oversight). The king had demonstrated the lurking danger of Satan, the potential anti-witchcraft militancy of the Scottish state, and the political threat of large assemblies of witches working in tandem with great men.

The North Berwick witch trials lit a flame which flared brilliantly, if horrifically. It died down but was not extinguished for well over a century. James had, in short, fuelled and overseen the first Scottish witchcraft panic. It would not be the last. For the moment, his mission – in addition to bringing his perennially unruly realm to heel – would be to justify all he had done. It was time to declare to Scotland and the wider world that his nation's leader had reached his conclusions on the reality and danger of the witches.

8

These Detestable Slaves of the Devil

Although not published until 1597, it is likely that King James began writing his *Daemonologie* in the wake of the North Berwick witch trials. The book was a crystallisation of his thoughts based on what he had seen, learned, read, and experienced in the course of the events of 1590–91. It was, moreover, a deliberate rebuttal of those who had doubted the phenomenon of witchcraft and a vindication of those, like Jean Bodin, who had spoken out against it as a real danger.

James's book is short (at least in comparison to some of the weightier tomes on the subject) and makes a virtue of its brevity. From its preface, the king's motivations are clear. He essentially views his job as a patriarchal one, and that involves educating his ignorant children – those of his subjects who harbour doubts – about the realities of demonic magic. In this he is joining the theological conversation not only as an interested party but as a scholar; it is his duty to rebut the 'damnable opinions' of such men as Reginald Scot and Johann Weyer, the latter of whom, chillingly, is noted as betraying himself 'to have been one of that profession' – an early example of a sceptic of the phenomenon opening himself up to allegations of witchcraft: something that would have horrifying reverberations in the next century. James makes no attempt to go into any great depth, as previous writers had, about the actual practices of sorcery; to provide details would be 'both unnecessary and perilous', given that more ignorant readers might try their hands at the devilish arts. The bulk of the text is thereafter composed of a classical dialogue between the fictional Philomathes (the lover of knowledge) and Epistemon (the knowledgeable), as the former exhorts the latter to eliminate his doubts about the reality of demoniacal powers, which Epistemon does, in such didactic terms it is obvious that he stands in for the moralising king.

Above all, *Daemonologie* is a Protestant text and the king's own attempt to stake out an official Scottish Protestant position on witchcraft. Biblical interpretation is present throughout, with the general theme being the role of the devil (who is held to be unable to predict the future, as witches delude themselves into believing, but only to guess at it). God is held to be the supreme power, who treats Satan as his 'hangman'; the devil is allowed some licence on earth to, for example, tempt humans and thereby test their faith. The Calvinist doctrine of predestination (which was far from universally accepted amongst Protestants – Elizabeth I, for example, resisted attempts by some of her bishops to introduce it in England via the Lambeth Articles in 1595) emphasised the notion that humanity had been pre-divided by God into the Elect and the Non-Elect (or the Reprobate) after the Fall (at which point man, despite having been made in God's image, had lost His grace). The Elect – those granted favour in the postlapsarian world – would, ideally, feel their spiritual awakening and thus appreciate their salvation by God's grace – but even they might be tested by the devil. The Non-Elect, by contrast, bear Satan's image and are inclined to evil. The devil is not content with these people, however; he is thought to tilt at more converts. Witches, in *Daemonologie*, are the most wretched humans of all: they willingly and with full knowledge of their actions turn away from God's service and make direct homage to their master in exchange for earthly powers. The book is clear: Satan personally harnesses and directs malice rather than personal malice motivating sorcery and witchcraft.

That people – of any rank – might turn to the devil was probably never in doubt to James or his contemporaries; Satan was, after all, as real as any other figure. The vast majority of people had, for example, never seen the pope or the King of Spain, yet they naturally accepted their existence. God and Satan were equally unseen, but, to the majority at least, they were mighty potentates, with God ruling from his divine domain above earthly sovereigns and Satan in hell (though perhaps, to increasing numbers of believers, apt to walk the earth). The devil was thus an enemy within: the arch antagonist of the godly, who might corrupt the souls of neighbours, friends, or kinfolk and sway them to his diabolical cause. He was every rebel, traitor, and foreign enemy rolled into one – and his terror lay in his ability to create disciples whose inner corruption could be masked by benign outward behaviour. What was needed was reliable means of discovering who'd been won over.

In the book, James finds those who turn to necromancy and magic, and those who turn to witchcraft and sorcery (the two branches of demonic practices he recognises as deriving from Satan) to have done so out of earthly ambition (here he might well have been thinking of Bothwell), or due to greed or simple poverty. To the ambitious, necromancy and magic appeal; whilst to the poor and greedy, sorcery and witchcraft offer opportunities. Essentially, these are the types entranced by magic in Marlowe's *Doctor Faustus*, in which the high-flying German doctor seeks ever more esoteric knowledge, and his servants make merry with his magic book, at one point seeking no more than a shoulder of mutton. The devil, who has been watching humanity and learning its foibles since the Creation, knows exactly who to target and how; the learned 'masters' and the foolishly ambitious he embroils with necromancy and magic, whilst the unlearned witches and sorcerers, whether rich or poor, are merely his slaves. Once again, the lessons of North Berwick are apparent. Satan, effectively, makes generals of men like Bothwell, who in turn might command armies of slavish witches and sorcerers, whose earliest tools are 'word, herb, and stone . . . unnatural charms without natural causes'. These differ from the non-criminal tricks and generally non-criminalised charms long-beloved of 'daft wives' (though both are in, in their way, in defiance of natural reason). The lower sort of witches might then graduate, on Satan's guidance, to the ubiquitous wax or clay images, poisons, and powders, none of which have material effect in themselves but all of which act as symbols of the devil's work. All witches, however, high or low, are subject to the demonic pact – it is by such means that an astronomer might fall into devilish astrology, thereby hoping to learn the future, and that hapless women might cross from harmless folk healing to fuelling their superstitious charms with demonic power. If the Witchcraft Act had effectively outlawed all manner of magic users, then James intended that it should not be toothless or reactionary but an active law.

The means of raising the devil by magicians and necromancers is of apparent interest to Philomathes, and Epistemon states that by the drawing of circular and geometric designs, conjuration, the presence of Holy Water (anathema to Protestants), and the offering of a live gift, the master could be summoned. Crucially, this is more effective the greater the number of practitioners: again, the fear of conspiracy is latent. The devil might then appear in animal form (whether a dog, a cat, or an ape) or, in the case of skilled necromancers, in the form of a corpse or a servant, and press those he has tempted into summoning him to seal their pact. His appearance is, and accordingly continued in confessions to be, fluid: a beast, a man (usually black in clothing, hair colour, skin, or countenance, although the original sources are rarely explicit), or even an unfamiliar infant.

In return for their homage, the summoners are promised the power to cure diseases, to manage affairs in their lives according to their desires – or, if they are of the higher order of magicians, they might be given secret knowledge of the affairs of nations and battles. All is, naturally, false. Satan is a deceiver who delights in granting mere fancies and playing upon the silly desires of humankind, and this he is well placed to do, having long experience of the world's ways and skill in illusions that are never to be equated with God's miracles. Crucially, *Daemonologie* places emphasis on the physical manifestation of the pact: '[It] is either written in the magician's own blood . . . or else [the devil] touches him in some part, though peradventure no mark remain, as it doth with all witches.' When it comes to baser witches, Satan requires less of a welcome; to these people, who might be driven by a desire for revenge, discontent, or poverty, he will manifest as a man and approach them when they are alone, making equally false promises and, on securing their souls by having them renounce God and their baptisms, leaving them with a mark which will thereafter be impervious to any pain not caused by failure to serve their new master. At this renunciation and re-baptism, the witch places him- or herself outside of God's protection and beyond the grace of any Christian prince.

Given the wickedness of witches, James is unequivocal. Those of the higher type – magicians and necromancers – deserve the same punishment as the more common witches and sorcerers: death. These people are not mad or melancholic (an argument which sceptics had put forward) except in those wilder cases in which men claim to be rabid werewolves. Indeed, some of those lately executed had been 'rich and worldly-wise, some of them fat or corpulent in their bodies, and most part of them altogether given over to the pleasures of the flesh, continual haunting of company, and all kinds of merriness'. Such merriness hardly indicates a desire for melancholic solitude. To these conventicles, James allows the possibility of magical flight through the air or spiritual attendance whilst the physical body remains inert at home. This is the Calvinist in the king speaking, but it is also the politician, frightened as ever of the prospect of conspiratorial dealings amongst a mob of rebels (and rebels against the monarch were, to James, rebels against God and His order). Fear, too, is apparent in his recognition of what all servants of the devil aim at: enlarging Satan's tyranny over the world by worshipping him in numbers and causing harm to others (that is, those not, as James fancied himself to be, protected by God).

It is the Calvinist – perhaps even a shadow of the misogynist tutor George Buchanan – too who explains the reason why more women than men fall into witchcraft: 'The reason is easy, for as that sex is frailer then [then] man is, so is it easier to be entrapped in these gross snares of the devil, as was over-well proved to be true by the serpent's deceiving of Eve at the beginning.' This was conventional thinking. It is worth considering what James does not say, but what he does explicitly reveal, in acknowledging why women were so much likelier to be accused (and punished) for witchcraft than men. It was a Christian (and thus both Catholic and Protestant) commonplace that women were the weaker vessel and had been for centuries. Women were thus historically viewed as second-class citizens, and as such made far easier targets than men. Additionally, being barred from the institutions of education, women were also generally relegated, if they were so-minded, to folk education: to traditional remedies for illnesses and solutions to problems. Any law prohibiting all forms of magic was bound to find a wider pool of female victims, and those victims, when pressed for the names of co-conspirators, would be bound by the same society's misogynistic bent. They would often name other women.

Lawful proceedings against these people – whether male or female – is judged crucial by the king; the more 'slothful' the magistrate, the more likely God will be to allow Satan to operate against him. Once caught, the witch must be subject to strict confinement. Then, God should step in and offer gaolers protection against any demonic reprisals. If the entrapped witch continues to deny his or her craft, the devil might visit them privately (perhaps in the body of a corpse), entertaining them with false hopes of relief or inducing them to commit suicide. Only by confession – which would be the real goal of King James in his attitude to witchcraft suspects – could the witch be freed from Satan's grip. Execution – whether by fire or any other means under the law – is then necessary, in all cases except those of children, who might be spared due to their ignorance. According to *Daemonologie*, this is held to be equally necessary for those who consult with and thereby enable witches – a feature of the 1563 Act which, to the king's displeasure, was more honoured in the breach than the observance.

James-as-author is not, however, so blinded by bloodlust that he would take in the innocent with the guilty; on the contrary, he argues that due form and process must be carried out, and that the word of just one infamous accuser should not be taken seriously. Nevertheless, given the gravity of the crime – a treason against God – even the word of a witch might suffice as evidence against another witch. This is, indeed, necessary. Given the conspiratorial nature of witchcraft, only witches might know who were truly other witches. It is axiomatic, too, that those who have seen visions of witches must be telling the truth – for God would not allow the devil to mimic the forms of innocents. With this logic, King James gave, and King James took away, the chance for many to escape guilty verdicts. Besides, the finding of the devil's mark should provide physical evidence, as would a new innovation James had read about but not yet seen instituted in his realm: the floating or swimming of the suspect.

That Satan should appear on earth is not in doubt. To James, those who deny this denied also God. His Protestant credentials in espousing this belief are not forgotten; the Catholics had, in their centuries of errors, neglected the reality of the devil to the extent that they had failed to see him walking amongst them. The upright Protestant should not make this mistake. The key theme of *Daemonologie* is, in fact, the setting out of a clear, Calvinist view on witchcraft and what must be done about it. The text's consistent focus is on the devil at work within the bounds prescribed by God, albeit Satan encourages his enslaved followers to imagine his and their powers to be much greater than they are. In codifying this, James is keen to point out the accepted – or, as he would have it, the real – forms of demonic spirit that torment humans: spirits who haunt lonely places and houses; those who harass people; those who possess people; and mischievous fairies. The first might be conjured by magic or witchcraft, or else they might operate according to their own malign behaviour – although they are barred from having to do with good Christian society by God. Chillingly, they might, again, inhabit dead bodies and creep through doors and windows to harass the living. Wraiths – or the spectres of people newly dead or about to die – are also the devil's work, as he fools the living into believing they are being visited by good angels in the form of friends or relatives. Corpses, to King James, are all the devil's playthings, being bereft of souls. Prayer and Christian living are, unsurprisingly, the solution to being thus terrorised.

Those who find themselves harassed by spirits (for example, being continually offered demonic service or warned constantly about lurking dangers) or possessed are, likewise, thought to have fallen from the Christian path and thus allowed by God to be tormented or seduced by Satan's imps.

Possession, which might be attained by means of *incubi* (wherein the devil would steal the cold sperm of a corpse and deposit it within a sleeping female victim) or *succubi* (Satan using the body of a woman to seduce a sleeping man), is inevitably a fruitless affair, with female victims especially deluding themselves into believing they will produce or have produced monstrous, semi-demonic offspring as a result. This grotesque thinking was not new, being at least as old as the anonymously authored fifteenth-century *Recollectio*, which responded to the Arras witch trials. The *Malleus Maleficarum*, too, had had much to say on the dual-subjects of obsession (control and torment of a person from without) and possession, both of which it recognised as forms of bewitchment, whether by *incubus* or *succubus*; by the devil-sent infection of great passion or hatred; by the devil's presence in the body in the form of sickness; or by spells. The answer was, naturally, Catholic exorcism. In Scotland (and in England), bewitchment likewise came to be understood, in time, as the product of witchcraft and a possible explanation for unusual or aberrant behaviours. To James, however, the victim of possession (control of a person by an invading spirit working from within) can be distinguished from a mad person not, as the Catholics would have it, by terror at Holy Water or crosses, but due to their inordinate strength, swellings, unnatural contortions, and the speaking of foreign languages unknown to the subject. James is, typically, unequivocal in arguing that the Catholics have no innate powers of exorcism; in those few cases in which they are successful, the reason is due to fasting and prayer – tools available to any Christian, having been prescribed by Christ.

No less terrifying are vain fancies about fairies: to James, pagan holdovers and products of perpetual ignorance. Those who believe in such things as the riding out of the goddess Diana or the courts of fairy kings and queens are, in their fantasies, entertained by the devil, who delights in encouraging them to believe they have been transported to magical lands and given prophecies. As ever, *Daemonologie* holds that the magical is not magical. It is demonic.

In totality, James's book represents a watershed not only in the king's thinking on witchcraft but, in the setting out of that thinking and given his position, of Scottish theological thinking on the phenomenon. The word 'Scottish' is key. It is natural to wonder whether James thought the problem of witchcraft was a British or even a European one. Did it affect all nations equally?

The answer is no, as his own preface to the book makes clear: 'The fearful abounding,' he writes, 'at this time and in this country of these detestable slaves of the devil, the witches or enchanters, has moved me (beloved reader) to dispatch in post this following treatise of mine.'[1] He was speaking no more than the truth. James believed, truly, that his nation had fallen into errors and disorder in part, at least, 'for the great wickedness of the people'. He had and would continue to have a jaundiced view of Scotland, due not only to his religious stance but to his youthful experiences and his country's recent history of deposition, assassinations, kidnap and kidnap attempts, and a general lack of deference towards his coveted position of spiritual and secular master. In short, Scotland and its people made, to a deeply religious autocrat at the cutting edge of developments in witchcraft studies, rich pickings for the devil. His attitude – although his book was not published for some years – was clear to all in the wake of the North Berwick witch trials. Scotland was infested.

It was now time to begin the purge.

*

Towards the end of *Daemonologie*, James's Philomathes raises the issue of so-called monstrous births – the results of copulation with demons – in such far-flung places as Lapland, Finland, and Scotland's own Orkney and Shetland. It was in Orkney that, in 1595, a local magnate attempted – and failed – to launch his own witch hunt.

Patrick Stewart, 2nd Earl of Orkney, was a son of one of James V's several illegitimate children (by one of his many mistresses, Euphame Elphinstone). Stewart was no stranger to the king, being one of his favoured courtiers in the 1580s and '90s and being brother-in-law to the diplomat Patrick Vans of Barnbarroch, who had accompanied James on his Scandinavian tour. Indeed, the nobleman served at Prince Henry's opulent baptism at Stirling Castle in the late summer of 1594. Yet Stewart, who since the 1593 death of his father enjoyed semi-regal authority over Orkney and Shetland in the manner of a feudal prince, was an intriguer, a tyrant, and every bit as paranoid as his sovereign could be.

Stewart's paranoia ran particularly high when it came to his family. In December 1594, he accused a servant of his younger brother, the Earl of Carrick, of trying to poison him. The unfortunate servant was arrested on Stewart's command and tortured for over a week. In the course of this, he accused an Orkney healer, Alison Balfour, of witchcraft with murderous intent (an accusation he later retracted). Alison, he claimed, had been hired by Carrick the previous year – and soon she found herself under arrest and transported to Kirkwall for interrogation. Damningly, there was found in her purse a piece of wax. A hideous programme of torture followed, with Alison and her family suffering indescribable agonies: 'She answered that at the time of her first deposition she was tortured divers [many] and sundry times in the Caschielaws [iron boots heated by fire] and sundry times taken out of them for dead, and out of all remembrance of good and evil; as likewise her goodman [husband] (he was eighty years old) being in the stocks, her son tortured in the Boots, and her daughter (a child of seven) put in the pilliwinks [thumbscrews].'[2]

Alison confessed. She went to her execution recanting, however, insisting that she would die innocent of witchcraft and having confessed only due to the horror she had endured; she, so she claimed – undoubtedly honestly – only ever carried a piece of wax intending to make a plaster at the request of the 'Lady of Stenhous'.

This was of a piece with many isolated cases of witchcraft tried locally and without a commission issued by the king and Privy

Council. It is probably for that reason that Alison's confession never erupted into a plethora of cases. To James, if he heard about it, it would have been anathema: Stewart had acted illegally, both wielding the law outside central authority and showing himself uninterested in due process. The earl had, essentially, dealt in feudal power and had, moreover, invoked what was increasingly looking like antiquated political sorcery: the invocation of witchcraft against political enemies and without any reference to the devil (the neglect of whose role would continue for decades, despite James's beliefs). The king was no stranger to hypocrisy and, throughout his life, showed himself sceptical of nakedly political accusations of witchcraft unless the ends of the accused witches were directed against his own person.

Stewart had blundered, probably never having even considered his sovereign's views in the matter. It would not be the last time. In 1596, he wed one of Queen Anna's ladies (Margaret Livingston, widow of Lord Justice Clerk Lewis Bellenden), though he only involved her in his mountain of debts. In the following century, his tyranny caught up with him and the Privy Council took an active interest in his behaviour in the Islands. On being imprisoned in Edinburgh and Dumbarton, he commanded his son to raise a rebellion in Orkney, which failed – and both father and son were executed in 1615. The man who had ordered the merciless torture of an innocent family was thus the cause of his own family's fall from grace. Patrick Stewart had had the machinery of local justice at his disposal, and used it – but he lacked what any large-scale hunt needed: a powerful leader driving matters from the top (and issuing a commission of justiciary) and a populace willing to engage more fruitfully in accusations and counter-accusations. The people of Orkney appear to have been as unsure of what was expected of them as Stewart was unisinterested in what his sovereign expected. This was, in total, evidence of a demonic pact (rather than old-fashioned political *maleficia*), open confessions – with names named – of conventicles, and a centrally authorised commission to oversee the affair legally.

It was becoming increasingly clear in the mid 1590s that Scotland was changing. Its sovereign was increasingly autocratic both in his political and spiritual goals, and he was intent on dragging Scotland out of its – to his mind – backwards-looking view on the problem of evil and into the light of modern theological thinking. After the 1590–91 North Berwick trials – and the ongoing problem of Bothwell – had retreated, James was left with bad harvests and ensuing dearth, local tensions, and a militant and muscular Presbyterian Kirk. He was, however, growing in confidence, buoyed by his potency as a dynastic patriarch (and he would show himself no heir-and-a-spare man but a prodigious procreator) and his towering intellect. In the latter, he would find reason to continue his witch hunts, not leaving them to the vagaries of self-interested noblemen but ensuring the machinery of justice remained under his guiding hand. Soon he would put that hand, and that machinery, to use.

9

Here Be Monsters Again

In the late summer of 1596, King James and Queen Anna had cause for celebration. They had produced their second child: a fair-haired daughter, Elizabeth, who could one day be expected to make a prestigious match. The child was named after the king's cousin, Elizabeth I of England, in a rather shameless piece of ingratiation. In truth, both parents were more desirous of the English queen's throne (to which James had the strongest hereditary claim) than her goodwill.

Yet this procreative success (and Elizabeth was followed by Margaret in 1598, Charles in 1600, Robert in 1602, Mary in 1605, and Sophia in 1606 – though only Princes Henry and Charles and Princess Elizabeth would survive infancy) did not win universal accolades, at least not in Scotland.

The problem, as ever for James, was the Kirk. By 1596, both king and queen were under fire for their perceived Catholic sympathies – and in both cases, these had been particularly overt. Although it is often claimed Anna converted to Catholicism (with various priests seeking credit for having done the deed), the truth is more elusive. What seems equally likely is that the royal couple were engaged in careful – and often friendly – handling of powerful Catholics, whom often they both liked personally, in order to broaden their appeal as the future King and Queen of England. To James, England was an unknown quantity. Though the country was certainly Protestant under Queen Elizabeth, the strength of numbers of Catholics – and the strength of individual Catholic magnates – was harder to calculate. The king wanted no opposition in England or on the continent to what he hoped would – ideally very soon – be a smooth succession to the elderly English queen's crown. This type of politico-religious machination was, however, unconscionable to Scotland's more fiery Kirk ministers, who demanded outright rejection of all Catholics, high or low, and for the King of Scots to accept his spiritual place as a member, and not the head of, the established Church. A particularly heated exchange took place at Falkland in 1596, when the preacher Andrew Melville – long a thorn in James's side – plucked the king's sleeve and called him 'God's sillie vassal [merely God's instrument]' and informed him that, whether he wore a crown or not, he was subject to 'Christ Jesus, the king of the Church . . . of whose kingdom he [James] is not a king, not a lord, not a head, but a member'. Even more insultingly, David Black of St Andrews denounced all monarchs as 'devil's bairns' and claimed that 'Satan was in the Court, in the guiders of the Court, and in the head of the Court': a view which was the direct opposite of James's own view of kingship as a sacred position ordained by God.[1]

The devil was apparently active in the country, however. In October, Alison Jollie was tried and acquitted for hiring a witch to kill Isobel Hepburn of Fala in a dispute over land. Less lucky was Christian Stewart, who was arrested in November and confessed to having used 'ane blak clout [cloth] with a thing made of iron in it. She left the clout near a gate' where one Patrick Ruthven often walked. Thereafter, 'she gave the black clout to the devil'.[2] In this way, she allegedly cast a sickness upon Ruthven, which she then attempted to undo when it became likely that her crime would come to light. Her interrogation demonstrated the law – the centralised law – operating at its most anodyne level, with the occasional witch turned up by reactive rather than active authorities; but according to due process and his own interest, James himself was able to take an active role in Christian's case, being present for her interrogation at Linlithgow, where he had her brought. She went to her death, and it is to be wondered how much the demoniacal aspects of her confession were tailored to the king and his Council. Yet cases such as Christian's proved something. The legal machinery was only as effective as those who operated it. If the authorities under the king were not conscientious or otherwise interested in pursuing suspects with vigour and to the letter of the law, witch hunts would not be particularly productive.

Yet nothing, thus far, had constituted a national persecution with regions up and down the country producing mass trials (although the North Berwick panic had certainly produced accused witches from as far afield as Aberdeenshire). This was probably because religious leaders (or at least the more outspoken ones) and king remained disunited. This was not to James's taste, and even the more moderate ministers sought some kind of working agreement between Kirk and Crown. This was, however, impossible as long as the extremes – the king on one hand and passionate Presbyterian reformers on the other – fundamentally disagreed. Neither was an extended stalemate, such as had existed since the 1592 Golden Acts (which had torpedoed episcopacy and established presbyteries), likely to last. The storm broke in December 1596, following the return of the Catholic Francis Hay, 9th Earl of Erroll, to Scotland. Erroll had long been one of several *personas non grata* to the Kirk, having been involved in just about every Catholic plot, from Huntly's rebellion to the Spanish Blanks affair. Huntly, too, had returned to the country despite his stronghold having been razed, and it looked to all as if James, historically known for being far too lenient towards Catholic peers, was again going to embrace these men back into the fold.

The result was an attempted coup against the king, in which Kirk leaders and militant laymen took advantage of a rising of the Edinburgh mob, which had been moved to fear not by witchcraft but by the imagined threat of Spanish Catholic invasion. James, at the time of the sudden rising, found himself trapped in the city's Tolbooth, where he had been presiding over a meeting of the Privy Council. He was able, with consummate skill, to talk his way out and thereafter he made preparations at Holyroodhouse and, the following day, decamped to Linlithgow on the pretext of going hunting at Dalkeith. On the road, he suborned the 7th Earl of Argyll, whom once he'd charged with reducing Erroll and Huntly and who was being groomed by the rebellious Kirk ministers as the leader of their new movement, and won him to the royal cause. Shorn of a leader not just in Argyll but in Lord Hamilton (whom the king also won over), the rebels scrambled to save face – but it was in vain. James consolidated his position from Linlithgow, drawing loyalists to his side, and, in a gesture born more of necessity than magnanimity, blamed the entire affair on Edinburgh's civic authorities (who had, in fact, done their best to subdue the mob). More than this he had no need to do; the hotter sort of reformist ministers had already delegitimised the cause of Presbyterianism through their failure to win the day.

As the dust settled, both James and the Kirk leaders continued to seek to shore up their positions. In one way they could meet. Just as Protestants and Catholics (or at least significant numbers of both) were increasingly agreeing that witches were a problem that required a solution, so too could King James and Presbyterian Kirk ministers; both were intent on creating a godly society, after all.

The creation of such a society needed a systematic approach to ridding itself of Satan's slaves. The shoots of a witch panic appeared first in Slains, Aberdeenshire, when Erroll received a royal commission of justiciary that empowered him to try and execute named witches, the better to ensure speedy justice at minimal expense to the community. In nearby Dyce and Fintray, and at roughly the same time, Kirk Sessions began to seriously investigate local women of notorious reputations. These included a local wise woman, Isobel Strachan (alias Scudder), who claimed to have learned magic from her mother, who had allegedly been mistress to an elf. Isobel's crime was thus demonic in origin, though her activities involved charming a man to stop him beating ('dinging' is the ameliorative word used in the dittay) his wife by means of sewing papers together with coloured threads and hiding them amongst his corn. This supposedly prevented him from meting out domestic violence. Isobel was executed in March (although her daughter, also besmirched by public accusation, was acquitted), alongside one Katherine Fergus, a midwife accused of transferring sickness from a woman in labour to the woman's husband and son. The city of Aberdeen received its own commission of justiciary with the aim of prosecuting a burgess's wife, Janet Wishart, who had a litany of charges against her (from causing a stillbirth to spoiling ale to casting spells to using the parts of a hanged man to attempting to poison a child). In all these cases, several things were apparent. Public interest in witchcraft was awakening in Aberdeenshire; interrogations were deemed unnecessary given the weight of accusation (which probably derived from personal jealousies, suspicions, and fears); and the importance of the demonic pact was not yet universally accepted.

This was, however, already changing. Only days after Janet's execution in February 1597, her son Thomas Leys was arrested and interrogated, and he confessed to both making a pact with Satan (who appeared to him as a 'little cuttie [short] fellow with a staff') and attending conventicles. Moreover, he named several women as having danced with him at the Fish Cross on Halloween 1596. These women were also arrested, and they confessed, some of them naming more witches. This was, from James's perspective, the ideal course of affairs. The civic authorities appear to have realised it and they sought a new commission – this one not aimed at any individuals but wide enough to try any who might be named in the course of the investigation. On 4 March a five-year general commission (so-named because it allowed for the trial of anyone charged) was duly granted. On the strength of it, Aberdeen's authorities began a campaign of terror and torture, beginning with those Thomas had named and working through those that ensuing captives accused. Throughout March and April, sometimes in the teeth of unwilling or bemused local Kirk Sessions and landowners, more witches were rounded up. This persecution went on, in Aberdeenshire at least, until the end of May, digging into localities and the histories of their locals. Dozens had been accused, twenty-seven executed (whilst two died in prison, one of suicide), five acquitted, and eight convicted of offences which did not justify the death penalty.[3]

This type of narrative set the new pattern for large-scale witchcraft hunts: first, anxiety might arise regarding local named suspects. There would follow an application to Edinburgh for a commission of justiciary to try them. If the local authorities were conscientious enough – or ruthless enough – to discover further names, a general commission would be sought, empowering them to try any offenders they might root out. This, naturally, opened the door for any number of personal – or religious – motives to drive local hunters. Thankfully, these panics never became the norm. Outside of them, the default position was the occasional turning up of a witch or small group without any ensuing mass-trials or avalanche of names.

1597, however, was already becoming one of those years which was not normal. South of Aberdeen, in Fife, witchcraft was also under investigation. The Kirk Session there heard five cases. James's councillor, Colonel William Stewart (who had played a key role as a go-between when the king was separated by storms from his new bride, who became godmother to Stewart's son), was active as a local investigator. Stewart had, during the troubles of Bothwell, shown himself an enemy of the late Chancellor Maitland and thus lost influence (and had even been arrested). He had since been rehabilitated and was evidently keen on showing himself an upholder of royal policy. This now meant working with the Kirk – in Stewart's case the Presbytery of St Andrews. According to Robert Bowes, the English ambassador, 'the number of witches exceed': the devil's mark, he claimed, was being sought out in their flesh.[4] Tellingly, Bowes, writing to Burghley in England, expected fuller details of the increasing number of trials to be published – probably because the king had attended St Andrews in order to pay close attention to events.

Fife, like Aberdeenshire (and Atholl, and Perth), was in the grip of a panic. This was the purging of witchcraft as the king imagined it operating: direct rule from the top, officious lawmen in the middle, the common people doing their duty in denouncing the ungodly in their ranks, and the witches themselves revealing the truth about their colleagues. But out of the climate of fear and paranoia came opportunity – and that in the form of one extraordinary accused witch named Margaret Aitken.

*

Margaret Aitken was a canny woman. She also had something of a reputation in her hometown of Balwearie, in Kirkcaldy. As panic spread across Scotland's lowlands, she was thus apt to be caught up in it. This she was, and, on being arrested and interrogated, she not only confessed to being a witch but offered names. On seeing the reaction this got from her interrogators, she took her chance. She offered to cooperate fully: in other words, to name more names provided she be allowed to live to 'purge the country of them' and thereafter be spared her life.

Margaret knew what her interrogators wanted and she delivered: it was in her gift, so she claimed, to spot in the eyes of other witches a secret mark which betrayed them. Beginning in April 1597, she was therefore transported from town to town, plying her gruesome new trade. Her success inspired other local authorities to do the same – to loan out accused witches to neighbouring localities to help produce more suspects. In Glasgow, the minister John Cowper evidently took her gift of instantly identifying other witches very seriously. Margaret apparently fingered several local, wholly innocent women who were interrogated. This involved, for the first time (and possibly the last) the use of 'floating' or 'swimming' in Scotland. James certainly endorsed this grim trial by ordeal, whereby the accused would be bound at the toes and thumbs and thrown into water to see if she floated (in which case she was a witch) or sank – after all, it had been described as theologically justifiable – and valid – in Wilhelm Adolph Schreiber's 1583 pamphlet *Epistle on the Trying and Examination of Witches by Cold Water*.

Margaret's trickery was only revealed when she accidentally pointed out one unfortunate victim as guilty and then, when the same person was shown to her the following day, forgot what she'd said previously and pronounced the victim innocent of witchcraft. She was promptly shipped back to Fife where she was denounced and tried, confessing that she had been a fraud, and was sent to her death. Despite what she had done – which had likely resulted in the deaths of several innocent people – it is hard not to sympathise with her. She took advantage of her captors' gullibility and attempted to use it to save her own life.

This was, however, a major embarrassment – not least for James, who had not only granted a commission to the Glasgow authorities for the trial of witches but had probably also authorised Margaret's transport about Scotland because he genuinely believed in the ability of one witch to identify others. Those over-credulous (or over-eager) authorities themselves would, within a year, be subject to railing libels which spread the story of their foolishness – and the miscarriages of justice it caused – throughout the country. A weak attempt at a moratorium was placed on the ongoing trials whilst the dust settled in August – probably at the instigation of the king's councillors rather than James himself – with the focus being on preventing executions born of personal vendettas or jealousies. In reality this revoked only some commissions and, as Julian Goodare has argued, probably saved few lives.[5] It was, at best, an attempt to restore some more rigorous form of central control over affairs which must have seemed, at least to some on the Privy Council, to be running away from it. It was at this time that a Parliament was summoned, at which it was expected that the way proceedings should be undertaken would be revisited.

James, for his part, was by nature disinclined to embarrassment – or at least to letting it get in the way of his decisions and actions. This particular woman had been a fraud, but she had been rightfully exposed and executed. Individual counterfeits – and this is key in understanding both the king's later attitudes and the recurrent nature of trials and occasional purges – did not invalidate his demonological theory or belief system. He intended that the purge of witches should continue and, as if responding to his personal fears about the threat, one Malcolm Anderson was soon found who had sought his destruction and that of Prince Henry (ensconced at Stirling Castle under the care of the Earl of Mar). One suspects this was what the king had been looking to find all along.

At this point in what had become Scotland's biggest witch hunt, James was in his element and it is not surprising that he chose this year to revise and publish his *Daemonologie* (with its indication that, whatever had happened with Margaret Aitken, witches could identify other witches), the better to educate his ignorant people out of their retrograde beliefs and into the progressive view of the elite Protestant demonologist. There was, further, no better time to do so. Given the fiasco of Margaret's case, not only certain councillors but certain Kirk ministers were expressing doubts about the ferocity of the witch trials. Outbreaks of plague only heightened the sense of God's judgement on the land. Into this climate of hesitancy James could step as the true enemy of Satan and his minions. If the king ever did act cynically – and there is no reason to believe he did not truly believe what he'd written in his book – then it was when the witch trials looked like being reined in in late 1597. Yet it is important not to judge him too harshly. James was simply responding to advances in demonological thinking and marching with the vanguard of elite scholars. The real problem was, as with contemporary advances in, for example, early modern medicine, elite views could too easily be errors built on misunderstandings founded on mouldering fantasies and misconceptions. James might have been aggressively academic, but given that what was being taught in academic circles was at best wrong and at worst dangerous, it is uncharitable to blame the accomplished graduate student.

In reigniting the flames, he had partial success. Local panics continued around Stirling in the autumn, and James ordered at least one accused 'prickat witch', again, to be brought to him at Linlithgow for examination. By now, the 'pricking' of suspects was becoming a feature of interrogations and trials, as Bowes had noted. This cruel method involved discovering what was a devil's mark (as opposed to a natural mark) by the jabbing of sharp objects (such as needles) into any unusual marks found on the accused witch's body. As James had written, those blemishes left by the devil were insensitive to pain. Thus, whilst any thrust into a natural mark might produce a cry of anguish, any touching the demonic mark would result in silence. As the devil was thought to leave his stamp on 'secret parts' of the body, it can be imagined how sickeningly invasive, perverse, and prurient the process would have been. The torture performed on the unnamed witch brought before James in the environs of his magnificent

Renaissance palace naturally had results: she (and by this time male witches were often, if not consistently, being referred to as 'warlocks' or 'warlows') implicated Captain Patrick Heron and his wife (who fled). Both of these more notable figures were enemies of Sir William Menteith of Kerse, who pursued them through the justiciary court in the capital – and thus the whole thing was probably a personal dispute which exploded in unexpected directions. James might not have approved of the former, but the results – the catching of witches under his supervision – might well have excused matters. The rising (or re-rising) of prosecutions this time encompassed Edinburgh, which heard a case again four witches in November.

The Parliament, which had been called in late summer, met in December 1597 (following yet more trials in Aberdeenshire and under Lord Ochiltree in the Borders) and it did, indeed, pass an Act Anent the Forme of Proces Against Witches. Unfortunately, the text is lost; however, it is apparent from later references that it touched the value of evidence to be considered admissible in witchcraft trials as a result of the Margaret Aitken affair. This implies that the Act itself was designed to ensure that the king and Privy Council were to consult with physicians, ministers, and lawyers in deciding whether or not any witches could be transported about the country naming others. This it probably did by the setting up of a commission. It was likely a result of Kirk ministers getting cold feet about the low quality of evidence (as proven by Margaret's fraud and the trial by 'floating') and James being required to give ground. The unity which had kept Kirk and king working together against a common enemy had broken down – although it was James who emerged from the great panic, which had petered out in its intensity by the end of the year, in the stronger position. Although he might have failed to keep the mass trials going, with Scotland slipping back into its 'normal' state of more or less occasional witch trials, he had published his book, proclaimed himself the leading Scottish authority on all matters demonic, and positioned himself as a more muscular crusader for a godly society than the more cautious Kirk ministers. From a modern perspective, he might appear the villain of the piece. To the godly, he was the victor.

Yet what the king lacked was any great national – or international – recognition of his role as God's champion. This he continued to crave, as he had craved it when having his escape from the North Berwick witches trumpeted. He was, however, about to find himself at the mercy of a direct plot. It was one of the strangest and most debated episodes in Scottish history – and at its heart would be a 'conjurer of devils'.

10

Let the Blood Run Free

In 1599, the Swiss traveller Thomas Platter visited England and was afforded the honour of passing by the royal guard, in their red-and-gold liveries, and entering the perfumed presence chamber of the elderly Queen Elizabeth. There, under a canopy, on a low chair piled with red damask cushions embroidered in gold, sat the famous sovereign. Platter left to history the following description:

> She was most lavishly attired in a gown of pure white satin, gold-embroidered, with a whole bird of paradise for panache, set forward on her head studded with costly jewels, wore a string of huge round pearls about her neck and elegant gloves over which were drawn costly rings. In short she was most gorgeously apparelled, and although she was already seventy four [sic], was very youthful still in appearance, seeming no more than twenty years of age. She had a dignified and regal bearing, and, as noted above, rules her kingdom with great wisdom in peace and prosperity and the fear of God, has up till now successfully confronted her opponents with God's help and support, as can be testified by all the histories, and although her life has often been threatened by poison and many ill designs, God has preserved her wonderfully at all times.[1]

In Scotland, James was nothing if not disappointed at that interminable preservation. The Queen of England, now approaching sixty-six, certainly did not paint herself in inch-thick Venetian ceruse (as modern screen depictions insist), but to Platter her sprightly carriage, vibrant wigs, and gamine frame suggested eternal youth. Elizabeth seemed determined to appear immortal, and she had, to her Scottish cousin's simmering fury, pronounced no word either in his favour or against it in terms of his succession to her throne. He might have been more interested in Platter's observations, had he known of them, when they noted the occult dangers lurking in England and the relatively lenient treatment of them: 'Numerous witches are found in England, for report goes that they do not punish them with death there, because the queen was once on the water, and a number of witches had planned her destruction in a storm, but another witch prayed for her and held off the tempest, as she herself confessed, and so although the belief is that they bring on many hailstorms, they are not punished with loss of life.' Platter was technically correct in that English witches were still executed only if they caused death, but it is hard to credit the rumour he had picked up of this being a result of one witch saving Elizabeth's life against several who had treasonably sought to end it.

For all her apparent vigour, Elizabeth was, in her demonological position, falling behind the times. Her England remained intent on executing those who wielded witchcraft as a murderous weapon; generally, the courts were reticent, and the constables unwilling, to hunt down harmless healers or old-style cunning folk (unless they were caught up in political sorcery or prophesying). Elizabeth and her government, in short, had failed to declare a godly war against domestic magic users and consulters. She was far too busy haemorrhaging money in her interminable war with Spain (begun in the mid 1580s and threatening several invasion attempts, including the famous 1588 Great Armada).

The English queen was a good Protestant, but she was a moderate one who saw no reason to advance the reformist cause domestically. Moderation, however, like tolerance, was an increasingly dirty word, to Presbyterians and Puritans as well as to extremist Catholics. In the same year as Platter's visit, the Dutch Jesuit Martin Antoine Delrio, no stranger to the Spanish Netherlands, which was a key battleground in the Anglo-Spanish war, began publishing his *Disquisitiones*

Magicae (*Magical Inventions*): a six-book, three-volume disquisition into witchcraft and magic from the Catholic perspective. Drawing on ideas found in the *Malleus Maleficarum* and 1595's *Daemonolatreiae libri tres* (*Three Books of Demonolatry*) by Nicholas Rémy, the French jurist who claimed to have executed over 800 witches. Delrio's book reiterated the need for Catholic trials and punishments, recognising (as Protestants like James had done) the link between witchcraft and devilry and going further in recognising the problem as a universal one, with witches present across Europe and in the New World. In a world of competing faiths, the true one was that which was seen to be doing most good – or rather rooting out most imagined evil – in the world. The Catholics wanted that reputation. So did the Protestants – and in Scotland, arguably, they were in competition with the king. The rivalry as to which faith was better qualified to deal with the perceived threat of witches was well underway – and it was a lackadaisical or incompetent leader who would let the other side emerge as the prime exponent of opposition to Satan's forces.

In Scotland, James was anything but lazy. He couldn't afford to be. In addition to getting his own house in order, he was determined to wrest from Elizabeth an acknowledgement of his succession rights. This looked unlikely when, early in 1598, the English queen heard that he had, in his recent Parliament, complained of the unjust execution of his mother; repeated a rumour that Elizabeth planned to engage in her own bit of unorthodox necromancy by disinterring Mary from her Peterborough resting place in order to burn her corpse; criticised the withholding of his English pension; and complained that the English sovereign still refused to recognise his succession rights. In response, Elizabeth 'wondered what evil spirits had possessed him to set forth such infamous devices void of any show of truth'.[2] In a display of gender inversion, she reminded him that he 'dealt with such a king [herself] as will hear no wrongs nor endure infamy, and without large amendments she may not, and will not, slupper up any such indignities'.[3] For a brief moment the threat of war arose. In March 1598, she backed down, asking the English diplomat George Nicholson to restore James's pension and requesting that he 'have that part left out which mentions the burning of the body of the king's mother'.[4]

The whole ugly episode – one of many diplomatic troughs – was to be forgotten. The underlying bad feeling wasn't. As ever, James and Elizabeth were yoked together by politics, religion, and geography – and, as ever, the harness occasionally galled them both beyond endurance. The real point of suspicion between the rulers was, at this time, Irish affairs, and James's knowledge of how he might use them to his advantage: Elizabeth's war of domination in Ireland was costing her, if anything, more than her war with Spain, and she was perennially suspicious as to James's dealings with what she considered her rebellious Irish subjects. It did not help that such troublemakers as Valentine Thomas, a thief and 'debauched villain' arrested in England, declared that he had been hired by James to kill his English cousin – a claim which Elizabeth disregarded but which James fretted over for at least a year. Post packets between the two British royal courts continued to blow hot and cold – and among them were all manner of underhand dealings by which James sought English support outside of the queen.

By the end of the year, it was being reported that 'the king is in a miserable condition, and the nobility contemn and disdain him'.[5] This was an exaggeration, but it is fair to say that James remained paranoid about those around him, unsatisfied with his realm and people, and still at loggerheads with the Kirk. Following the Christmas Revels which he kept at Holyroodhouse, this despite the official position of the Kirk long having been against keeping Christmas, he was sharply rebuked. In January 1599, he warned his critics, 'If ye speak against me, my crown or my estate, hanging shall be the pain of the first fault.'[6] This put something of a damper on the birth of Princess Margaret, who, sadly, lived no longer than March. Discontent with the Kirk continued, until it was being reported that 'the king will not endure the Church discipline', he having expressed 'bitter prosecution of them in his last book': *The True Law of Free Monarchies*, which set out the royal stall on the sacred absolutism belonging to kings.[7] On the subject of books, those not to the king's taste were, in December, prohibited from publication without royal licence – notably 'libels, defamations, invectives, chronicles, annuals, or histories'. A similar desire to be at the head of affairs – seen already in the witchcraft trials – arose in his opposition to a proposed Anglo-Spanish peace in April 1600, or rather in his unhappiness at not being fully briefed on affairs. James was, in modern parlance, as keen as other rulers of his age to control the narrative. This desire stood him in good stead in the late summer of 1600, even if his conflict with the Kirk threatened to undermine him.

It was in August that news broke of an attempt on James's life, which he only narrowly escaped. James's story was that he had been hunting in Perthshire when the out-of-favour courtier Alexander Ruthven, the Master of Gowrie, had approached him with news of the discovery of a pot of gold. James had mulled this over before agreeing to accompany Ruthven to Gowrie House, where Ruthven's brother, the Earl of Gowrie (who had not apparently been apprised of events), threw together a hasty supper. James's entourage, whom he had not invited, followed and managed to overtake him; thus, they were present too. The king was then invited by Ruthven up into a turret room to inspect the treasure. Ignoring the fact that Ruthven locked all the doors behind him, James went. In the room, a mystery man was waiting. Ruthven then turned on his sovereign, swearing revenge for the death of his father (the 1st Earl of Gowrie, who had lost his head back in 1584 for kidnapping the young James and overseeing a government in his name). James had made it to a window, crying, 'Treason!' A few members of his entourage who were in the gardens below, eating cherries, saw their master in distress. Some flew up the main way, seeking hammers against the locked doors. Another, young John Ramsay, found a secret way in. Immediately, he drew his blade and slew Ruthven whilst the mystery man fled. As the rest of James's men, still in the dining chamber being assured by Gowrie that the king had left the property, smelled a rat, they insisted on being shown up to the turret. Gowrie led them, and there the various players converged in a melee. Ramsay killed Gowrie on the spot. In the end, only two men lay dead in what James announced was an assassination attempt: Ruthven and his brother, the Earl of Gowrie, the two would-be assassins.

There are many murky elements to this tale – and this was James's account – not least of which is the baffling geography of the house (which is long gone) and the paranoid king's seeming trust in going alone into a turret with anyone. A number of theories have been put forward, from James organising a 'hit' on the pair (to whom he owed money) to him soliciting sex from Ruthven and being rebuffed (which is equally as unlikely, given he was never a sexual predator). The likeliest scenario is that the pot of gold story was an outright fabrication on James's part, probably invented to cover what Ruthven had really asked him to discuss: some official involvement in the endemic cross-border negotiations with English notables about the succession. Gowrie, certainly, had lately been on the continent and had visited Queen Elizabeth in England – he would have been well placed to engage, and thereby gain favour for his younger brother. Whether Ruthven became annoyed and threatened the king on being refused, or whether James simply took fright at the sight of a mystery man (later officially recognised as one Andrew Henderson) and the reality of having potentially walked into a trap and cried for help is impossible to know. James certainly appears to have believed he was in danger; that doesn't mean that he was.

Of more immediate interest in the study of witchcraft, though, is what happened next. James was keen, as he had been in the wake of the North Berwick witch trials, that his escape from imminent danger be publicised as widely as possible. Certain members of the Kirk, however, were reluctant to humour him; like Queen Anna, who had liked the Ruthvens, they found elements of his story fantastical. It certainly did all look suspicious. Hitherto, James had expressed no real fear of the Ruthven family, and the Ruthven brothers, in turn, appear to have harboured no great resentment over the execution of their father (their brother James, the 2nd Earl, had died in 1588) – although Gowrie was suspected of disliking the witch-hunting Colonel William Stewart. Now, in the aftermath of the

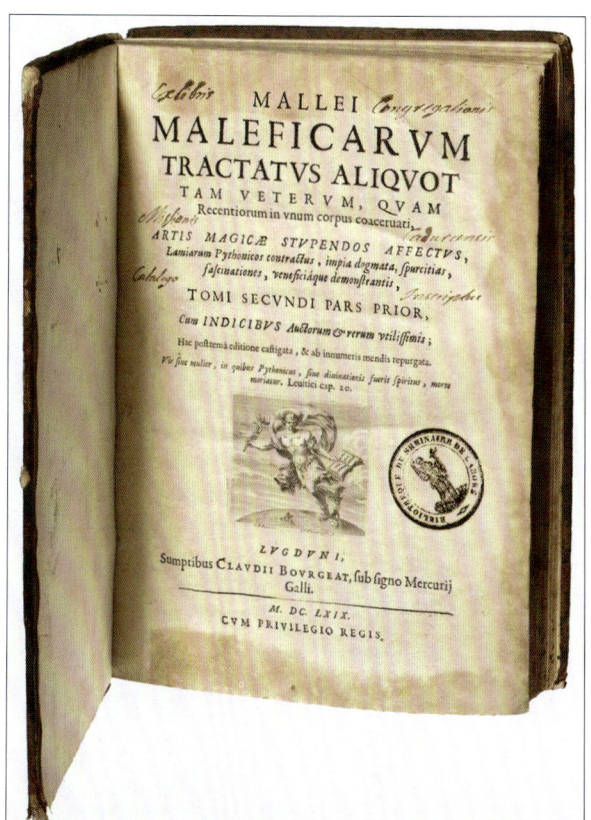

The *Malleus Maleficarum*, by Heinrich Kramer and Jacob Sprenger, was intended to unleash a general purge of witches. It would prove a slow-burn hit rather than an immediate phenomenon. (INTERFOTO/Alamy Stock Photo)

Henry VIII of England considered annulling his marriage to Anne Boleyn on the grounds that it had been brought about by witchcraft. He abandoned this course for more violent methods – but he later oversaw a 1542 Act against sorcery. His kingdom was, however, more plagued by prophecies than charms and spells. (iStock.com/Gwengoat)

Elizabeth I introduced a more successful Act against witchcraft than her father. This was due to pressure from her reformist counsellors, who wished she were a more hardline Protestant. The queen was interested only when rumours of witchcraft touched her safety. (iStock.com/Gwengoat)

The Catholic Mary Queen of Scots oversaw Scotland's 1563 Act against witchcraft in Scotland – albeit this was at the behest of her Protestant counsellors (and, in fact, might have been an attempt on their part to tarnish Catholicism). No great purges resulted – but the queen was slandered as a witch and said to have been bewitched by her second and third husbands. (iStock.com/GeorgiosArt)

The most wonderfull

and true storie, of a certaine Witch
named *Alse Gooderige of Stapen hill,*
who was arraigned and conuicted at Darbie
at the Assises there.

Is also a true report of the strange torments of Thomas
Darling, a boy of thirteene yeres of age, that was possessed by the Deuill, with his horrible fittes and terrible Apparitions by him vttered at Burton vpon
Trent in the Countie of Stafford, and of his maruel-
lous deliuerance.

Printed at London for I.O   1597.

A burgeoning English pamphleteering culture saw an efflorescence of news about witches and witch-
induced possessions and torments, often of (and reported by) children. This increased public knowledge
of witchcraft tales, with possession in particular a popular subject in England. Self-proclaimed exorcists
and debates about children's evidence accordingly blossomed. (Pictorial Press/Alamy Stock Photo)

Right. James VI and I, son of Mary Queen of Scots. He became deeply interested in witchcraft in 1590 and determined to make himself a leading light in academic literature and an enemy of Satan. (ICP/Alamy Stock Photo)

Below. A woodcut from the *Newes from Scotland*. This pamphlet, endorsed by James and intended for international consumption, portrayed the king as God's champion: a hero-king saved from a witchcraft-powered murder plot. (Charles Walker Collection/ Alamy Stock Photo)

Left. Castle Hill in Edinburgh: on the forecourt, convicted witches suffered the horrific 'double death' of strangulation and burning. (iStock.com/serts)

Below. King James personally questioned accused witches at his beautiful palace of Linlithgow (sadly now a roofless ruin, though it retains its fairytale charm). (iStock.com/Heartland-Arts)

Right. In the wake of the 1590–1 witch hunt – Scotland's first successful purge, driven by the king – James wrote his *Daemonologie*: an academic study that would be the last word, he supposed, on the reality and danger of witchcraft. (courtesy of the author, with thanks to Claire McDade and the Royal College of Physicians & Surgeons, Glasgow)

Below. James endorsed ordeal by cold water (variously known as swimming or floating the witch), a 'test' that had found academic backing in Europe's debating chambers. It would see its use – possibly its only use in Scotland – in the king's second great hunt (in 1597). (Chronicle/Alamy Stock Photo)

94

DAEMONOLOGIE, IN FORME OF A DIALOGVE.

FIRST BOOKE.

ARGVMENT.

The exord of the whole. The deſcription of Magie in ſpeciall.

CHAP. I. ARGVMENT.

Proued by the Scripture, that theſe vnlawfull arts in genere, haue bene and may be put in practiſe.

PHILOMATHES and EPISTEMON reaſon the matter.

PHILOMATHES.

I Am ſurely very glad to haue met with you this day: for I am of opinion, that ye can better reſolue me of ſome thing, whereof I ſtand in great doubt, nor any other whom-with I could haue met.

EPI. In what I can, that ye like to ſpeir at me, I will willingly and freely tell my opinion, and if I proue it not ſufficiently, I am heartily content that a better reaſon carry it away then.

PHI. What thinke ye of theſe ſtrange newes, which now onely furniſhes purpoſe to all men at their meeting: I meane of theſe Witches?

EPI. Surely they are wonderfull: And I thinke ſo cleare and plaine confeſſions in that purpoſe, haue neuer fallen out in any aage or countrey.

PHI. No queſtion if they be true, but thereof the Doctours doubts.

EPI. What part of it doubt ye of?

PHI.

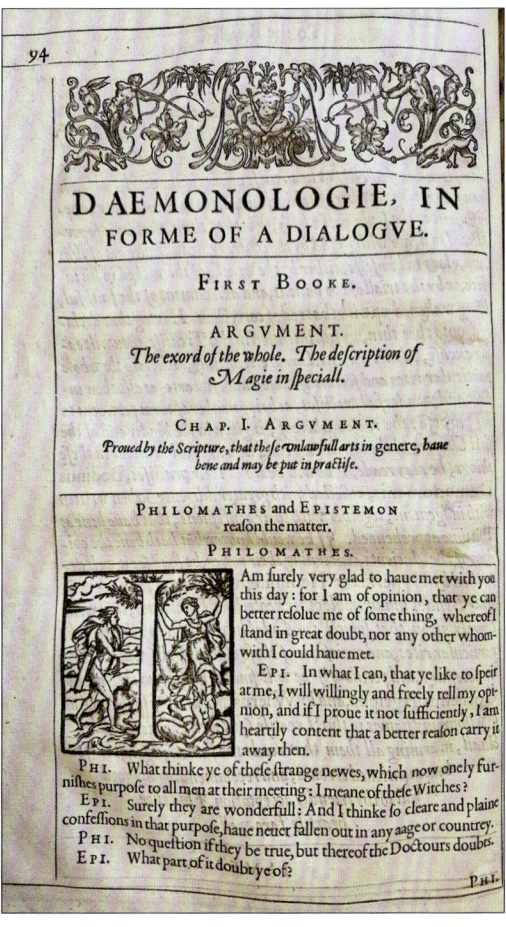

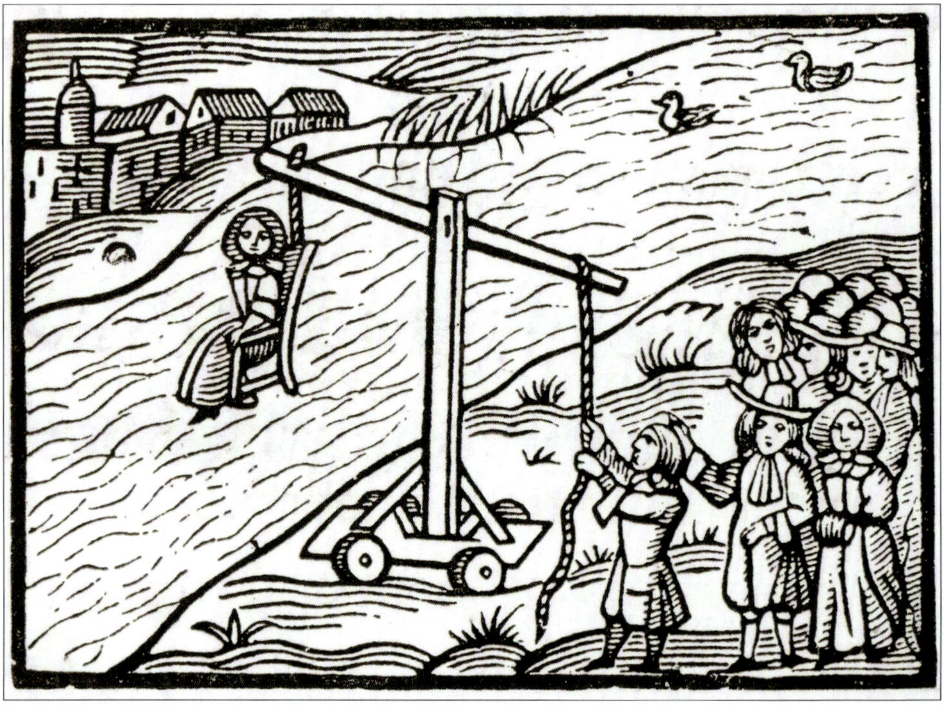

Above. King James acknowledged lowly slave-like witches and more educated generals in Satan's army (as given dramatic life in *Doctor Faustus*). Both, however, were touted as being utterly servile to their demonic master, whose backside they might kiss and who would leave a mark on them (insensible to pain and apt to be tested). (iStock.com/duncan1890)

Left. An avowed Anglophile, James did not think England was prey to Satan in the way he imagined Scotland was. Certain English regions did, however, see local panics, as they had during Elizabeth's reign. (Charles Walker Collection/ Alamy Stock Photo)

IT happened one time that a great number of Lancaſhire Witches were rev-
ling in a gentleman's houſe, in his ab-
ſence, and making merry with what the

The older King James found living in England very much to his tastes. It is often said that he grew sceptical there, but in truth he maintained that his standards of evidence in witchcraft cases had been clearly laid out in *Daemonologie* and that investigators must refer to it. (iStock.com/Thomas Faull)

James I. of England.

On his death in 1625, James left behind a legacy of witch hunts, popular belief in the dangers of witchcraft and the machinery to pursue accused witches to death. But he was not alone. In the post-Reformation world, Protestant and Catholic leaders were apt to compete in terms of who was toughest on the crime of witchcraft. (iStock.com/ZU_09)

James's last and greatest lover, the Duke of Buckingham (the king being bisexual), faced accusations of dealing with witches and wizards; alongside witch panics affecting the lower orders, politicians continued to face politically motivated accusations of witchcraft and wizardry. (iStock.com/Luisa Vallon Fumi)

With an eye for the main chance, Matthew Hopkins presented himself as an expert (having read James's book) in hunting witches. He made a successful business of it in the midst of the civil wars, but his mendacious methods were eventually exposed and he lived just long enough to see himself turn from hero to villain. (Charles Walker Collection/Alamy Stock Photo)

The popularity of the pointed hat came later (in retrospective studies and images of witchcraft), but in confessions across Europe and beyond, people were educated into claiming to have seen 'black men' (which might have denoted clothing or hair as often as it meant skin colour) and shaggy dogs. The devil was implied even when not named. (iStock.com/duncan1890)

Clay or wax figures were often involved in witchcraft accusations and confessions (these being intended to cause harm). Animal familiars (from cats and toads to polecats and ferrets) also loomed large and were amplified in early media (pamphlets being popular). (iStock.com/duncan1890)

As one of the goals of witch purges was to create a godly society, the religious colonisers at Salem imported beliefs about possession and spectral evidence. By the time of Salem, however, James's standards of evidence had become a bone of contention between those who feared atheism and those who maintained empiricism and religion could coexist. (iStock.com/Christine_Kohler)

A memorial to Sarah Good – a victim of the Salem panic who, like the others, died not for being a witch but for denying being a witch. (iStock.com/Kirkikis)

A memorial in Perthshire to Maggie Wall, who supposedly died in one of Scotland's hunts in 1657. Whether she is an apocryphal figure or not, she represents the thousands judicially killed for impossible crimes. (courtesy of the author, with thanks to John Clark)

deaths at Gowrie House, James abolished the family name. More ominously, part of the official account noted the magical – and therefore demonic – items found when the king, immediately following the deaths, had Gowrie's pockets searched and found there 'but a little parchment bag, full of magical words of enchantment, wherein it seemed he had put his confidence, thinking himself never safe without them, and therefore ever carried them about with him. It was also observed, that while they were upon him, his wound, whereof he died, bled not, but incontinent, after they were taken away, the blood gushed out in great abundance, to the great admiration [amazement] of all the beholders.'[8]

For the moment, James made some effort to discover whether Gowrie had in fact been involved with conjurers, sorcerers, or witches. This seemed plausible, given the reputation of Gowrie's grandfather, Patrick, 3rd Lord Ruthven, for dabbling in the black arts and the rumours that his son, the 1st Earl of Gowrie, had consulted with sorcerers. Certain families and kinship networks could be tainted generationally by accusations of witchcraft. Just so, certain towns, regions, and even nations (Scotland being one) could acquire dark reputations as demonic hotspots; they would become bywords for places where witches were expected to be active. This is why panics affected some territories more than others over decades and centuries. Once the first flames had been kindled by enthusiastic leaders, whatever their motives, and erupted into spectacle, a fearful public would huddle around the light. People high and low, in authority and out of it, were frequently eager to blow fresh life into the embers – and occasionally they were very successful at doing so – at moments of social tension. Unsurprisingly, investigating authorities would then seek, and invariably find, supporting evidence.

James Wemyss of Bogie was questioned on 9 August, four days after the deaths, in the course of which he was asked whether he had discussed 'things curious [unusual or magical]' with the late Gowrie. He admitted to having killed an adder in the Highlands with the dead man, upon which Gowrie had supposedly said he could have enchanted the serpent by means of a Hebrew word. Gowrie had apparently also consulted with a man he thought to be a necromancer during his time in Italy; but the fellow had proved only to be a scholar. The earl's tutor was subsequently tortured via the 'boots', and yet he revealed nothing more; yet, rather foolishly, he did admit to Patrick Galloway, a royalist – or episcopal-minded, at least – minister, that Gowrie had indeed owned papers, marked with Latin characters, which he kept on his person. King James and sundry men around him were expert Latinists, of course, which means that either the tutor was wrong or the 'magical words of enchantment' were a deliberate obfuscation in the official narrative.

James found in Galloway a willing vessel by which to communicate his message. On 10 August, when investigations were still ongoing, the minister (who was a Kirk elder in the Perth Presbytery), delivered a sermon which was in effect a holding action, begging the people of Perth (who had apparently respected Gowrie) to form no opinions yet. At the Mercat Cross in Edinburgh he was less equivocal, thundering, 'He [Gowrie] was an atheist, an incarnate devil, in the coat of an angel, a studier of magic, a conjurer with devils, some of whom he had under his command.'⁹ These accusations found more lasting – and widespread – voice in the publication the following year of *Ruvenorum Conjuratio* (*The Ruthven Conspiracy*). More sceptical ministers were hesitant to support the king's story, however. At a meeting in the East Kirk, they decided to go only as far as admitting that James had survived a potential threat. Though they were not the majority, this meant that the official version was not as widespread as the king might have liked. Though he would declare 5 August a day of national thanksgiving (five now being one of his blessed numbers), and though the *Ruvernorum Conjuratio* would do its best to ensure the survival of James's salvation and Gowrie's demonism, the truth was that Kirk and king were disunited enough to make any attempt at lowering the late earl to necromancer status untenable.

Two issues arise from this sorry affair. The first is whether or not James believed Gowrie had been a master of the dark arts or whether this was pure politicking in an effort to bolster his narrative. The answer is probably that he did indeed believe it – his interest in demonology had not waned. He certainly did not set Gowrie up to die because he believed him a sorcerer or witch, but on finding spurious evidence, he was certainly capable of believing that a man and a family evil enough to threaten his person must also have been capable of the rankest devilry. This poses the second question: was Gowrie a necromancer? Here, the answer is probably not. It might be possible, however, that the late earl, in the course of his extensive travels and education, had an interest, however mild and shallow, in the kinds of esoterica practised in various parts of Europe (including England). Under the draconian Scottish law against all magical practices, this would have rendered him suspect.

What we are thus left with is interesting less what for happened (which is fascinating and bizarre enough) than for what did not. James was, at this time, a firm believer in Scottish witchcraft – he would, indeed, warn his son Henry that it was amongst the crimes a ruler was 'bound in conscience never to forgive'.[10] If he had hoped that the Ruthven family would be investigated, universally condemned, and denounced as treacherous slaves of the devil, however, he was to be disappointed. Queen Anna, for one thing, showed herself a staunch defender of the Ruthven women, and occasionally even those who supported the official version of events voiced regret about the earl's demise. James's victory over this particular branch of demonic treason was thorough in that the Ruthvens were extinguished as a political force, and he certainly won his day of thanksgiving, but Scotland had no appetite for a great witch hunt against the family and their followers. No one interrogated, even under torture, confessed that they or Gowrie had been necromancers, nor did they produce a list of demonic associates. James had to settle for the affair being largely understood as a treasonous plot against himself, and even that raised more than a few sceptical eyebrows.

If this disappointed him – and there is no real evidence to suggest it did – then he was about to be let down again. In early 1601,

Elizabeth's last great favourite, the vainglorious Robert Devereux, 2nd Earl of Essex, launched an abortive coup against his queen, or rather against her chief minister, Sir Robert Cecil. This was a disaster for the King and Queen of Scots; both had entered into secret correspondence with Essex and his sister Penelope. In doing so, they had backed a dead horse – in a rather literal sense, given Essex went to the block in February. Thankfully for the Scottish royals, he had burnt his correspondence from James, thereby allowing the king to affect ignorance of the Essex faction's increasingly paranoid and ludicrous machinations. Thereafter, Cecil (whom James eventually elevated to the Earldom of Salisbury), along with the obsequious Lord Henry Howard (later the Earl of Northampton) became his contacts at the English court, with Edward Bruce (later Lord Kinloss) and the Earl of Mar as the Scottish receivers. This chicanery continued beneath the official posts passed between Elizabeth and James, with the idea being that the path to the Stuart succession would be smoothed over by the politicians. If Elizabeth knew what was going on – and probably she did – she held her peace.

All James had to do was wait. He was rewarded in late March 1603, when a muck- and blood-spattered messenger arrived at the gates of Holyroodhouse. Sir Robert Carey, an English courtier, had not let a kick from his horse slow his passage; his news was too great. Elizabeth of England, at sixty-nine years old, had died – 'mildly,' so it was soon being said, 'like a lamb, easily like a ripe apple from the tree'.[11] Carey hailed his new master: James, by the Grace of God, King of Scots, King of England, Ireland, and France (the chimeric English claim to France persisting). This was the news the king had been waiting a lifetime for: he was now no longer expected to ride what he called a 'wild, unruly colt' but a 'towardly riding horse'.[12] That phrasing sums up his view of Scotland – and it explains why his attitude to witchcraft in England would differ so sharply from what he had so recently been expressing, and had expressed from 1590, in Scotland. Although he would be leaving behind the machinery of witchcraft trials – the 1562 Act and a history of mass persecutions driven by a powerful leader, supported by assiduous officers, and fed by frightened subjects – there were no more great panics in Scotland until after his death. If he had failed to purge Scotland of witchcraft and thereby create a truly godly society, that no longer mattered. Others might take up the cause.

In the meantime, it remained to be seen exactly what he would make of England's rather *laissez-faire* handling of an evil that was exercising Protestant and Catholic theologians and demonologists across Europe like never before.

11

Pins and Needles

King James has been criticised – in his own day and since – for being a lazy and neglectful monarch, more likely to be found sporting in the royal parks than attending to state affairs. Yet one suspects the bulk of contemporary criticism stemmed not from his avoiding business but from the extra work his frequent rustication imposed on his underpaid and overworked servants and officials. The king expected to be fully briefed on all great matters, which required a constant stream of paperwork flowing backwards and forwards between London and the countryside, all of it carried by harried servants and worried over by politicians in the city. His predilection for taking off for the field and avoiding his English capital was apparent within months of his gaining the throne. Yet, when matters either interested him or required his presence, he rose to the occasion.

This was the certainly the case when, in the frosty January of 1604, James I of England sat enthroned in the splendid palace of Hampton Court, where only a few years before the Swiss visitor Thomas Platter had had his view of the late Queen Elizabeth. The occasion was his Hampton Court Conference, called as a result of his having learned of some disaffection on the part of Puritans (a catch-all pejorative term for reformers dissatisfied with the late queen's religious settlement). His intention was to nip this in the bud.

James had been a great fan of the late Richard Hooker, a Church of England cleric who had opposed calls for greater reform. In his new Church, the king found the state of religion – doctrine and most elements of worship – to his taste, even if Puritans found it riddled with unnecessary Catholic ornamentation, including, to some, unwanted royally appointed bishops. Though James, in his triumphant ride south in the spring of 1603, had accepted the Millenary Petition (so-called because it affected to have a thousand signatories) calling for reform, in October he had issued a proclamation restraining such requests and discouraging anyone from meddling with the settled state of religion. He boasted, as the conference opened, that he was far happier than his Tudor predecessors, who had, since Henry VIII, repeatedly changed the face of public worship – for he 'saw yet no cause so much to alter and change anything as to confirm that which he found well-settled already'.[1] Moreover, he thanked God for 'bringing him into the promised land, where religion was purely professed'.[2] The English Church was, and would increasingly appear to James to be, close to the original Christian Church before it had become infected with Romish errors.

This, then, was the king's view of England, and it is not difficult to understand why. Despite a devastating outbreak of plague in the south, tens of thousands had flocked to see him. With their roars of acclamation in his ears – a far cry from the scathing recriminations hissed at him from Scottish pulpits – he was enamoured of his new realm and its seeming riches. Even lords and gentlemen lived in palaces every bit as fine as the best of his own royal properties in Scotland. It was the sense of his newfound power, though, that really turned his head. He would, after a politic display of strength for French observers' benefit, turn to ending the Anglo-Spanish war. He had the luxury of considering the grandest European matches for his surviving children (Henry and Elizabeth having followed him south to their own extravagant cheers, and the sickly Charles coming later). He was able to craft a new monarchical image as Great Britain's peacekeeping emperor, determined to unite the continent's Protestant sects as a prelude to a universal accord with the Catholics.

He chaired the Hampton Court Conference with gusto, relishing the role he had long sought in Scotland. Here he was, in his pomp, as the undisputed head of his English Church. He faced a team of hand-picked Puritans and enjoyed himself thoroughly in the minutiae of theological debate (in which he counted himself, fairly, an expert). The results included a slight expansion of the catechism, a ban on lay baptism, royal demands for uniformity under the Book of Common Prayer, and, of course, the institution of a commission, split into teams of experts, charged with producing a definitive, authorised version of the Bible in English (with the king as editor-in-chief).

Confident in his glittering new role, James had no reason to persecute English witches via the kind of purge he had instituted in Scotland. A cynical reading might be that, now that he had unquestioned charge of a Church (despite the Scottish Kirk still taking a cockeyed view of royal supremacy), he had no reason to position himself as Satan's chief enemy. Yet this is not entirely fair. James's goal in Scotland had been to dominate the religious balance, tipping the scales in the monarchy's favour. His goal in England was to maintain the religious balance as he found it – and that was already in his favour. Doing so, and making a success of it, would, he hoped, make union between the kingdoms, with deferential England dominating troublesome Scotland, easier – and he had already made his intentions in that direction known via another proclamation in May 1603. Perhaps more importantly, where he had had a dim view of Scotland and its late disorders, he had a (rather myopic if not blinkered) correspondingly sunny view of England. His home nation had been ripe for devilry, whereas England, to the king, was not. His new kingdom simply did not have an infestation. James was acutely aware that he was now navigating a different culture, political context, and kingdom, and he found England more congenial – and more willing to elevate the role of sovereign to sacred heights – in almost every area than benighted Scotland.

Nevertheless, at his first Parliament, the 1563 Witchcraft Act was updated as an Act against Conjuration, Witchcraft and dealing with evil and wicked Spirits. James's beliefs, expressed in *Daemonologie*, were paramount:

if any person or persons, after the said Feast of St. Michael the Archangell next coming, shall use, practise, or exercise any invo-cation or conjuration of any evil and wicked spirit: or shall consult, covenant with, entertaine, imploy, feed, or reward any evil and wicked spirit, to or for any intent or purpose; or take up any dead man, woman, or child, out of his, her, or their grave, or any other place where the dead body resteth; or the skin, bone, or any other part of any dead person, to be imployed, or used in any manner of Witchcraft, Sorcery, Charme, or Inchantment, or shall use, practise, or exercise, any Witchcraft, Incantment, Charme or Sorcery, whereby any person shall be Killed, Destroyed, Wasted, Consumed, Pined, or Lamed, in His or Her body, or any part therof; that then every such Offender, or Offenders, their Ayders, Abettors, and Counsellors, being of the said offences duly and lawfully Convicted and Attainted, shall suffer paines of death as a Felon or Felons, and shall lose the priviledge and benefit of Clergy and Sanctuary.[3]

This covered necromancy and conjuration. James still had no time for men like John Dee, whose reputation by this time had fallen from the heights his genuine studies of geography, navigation, and astronomy had warranted to the depths of occultism; Dee would fall into poverty, his memories of serving the late queen alone unable to keep him fed and clothed.

Witchcraft, however, was treated somewhat more leniently. The old English anxieties about people using 'Witchcraft, Inchantment, Charme, or Sorcery' to find treasure or lost goods resurfaced, as did worries about them being used with the intent of provoking love, damaging property, or attempting to cause physical harm to others. For these acts, one year's imprisonment was the penalty on first conviction, with quarterly outings to the local stocks for a public pillorying (to last six humiliating and back-breaking hours). If, after this treatment, a witch repeated his or her crime, death was prescribed. Nobles, naturally, were to reserve their right to trial by their peers. The real difference from the 1563 Act was that those who merely wielded witchcraft with bad intent, but who failed to cause harm, would be sentenced to death on their second convictions (when once they had been given life imprisonment); similarly, those convicted of causing physical injury (as opposed to just those committing murder) could now face the death penalty in the first instance.

The 1604 Witchcraft Act, then, was not James's handiwork alone, though it did address his primary demonological concerns about necromancy and conjuration. The English Parliament was no more a cat's paw to the king than had been the Scottish Parliament – as time would show, it could be quite the opposite, having already begun to flex its muscles under Elizabeth. But James's interest in witchcraft was well known; *Daemonologie* was reprinted twice in London in 1603 and, it would seem, it was its discussion of demonic possession which really caught the public imagination.

The new law was duly produced by Lord Chief Justice Edmund Anderson (a man strict on maintaining Church discipline against both Catholics and Puritans), the brilliant jurist (and social climber) Sir Edward Coke, twelve bishops, and six earls. Anderson had been active in the 1580s, when scattered witchcraft trials were common, and then he had remarked that 'the land is full of witches. They abound in all places . . . their malice is great, their practices devilish.'[4] Coke, too, would record in his famous *Institutes* that England had a history of witchcraft: a man had been arrested in Southwark in the 1360s who bore 'the head and face of a dead man, and a book of sorcery'.[5] These were thus not disinterested men. What most likely happened is that those who drafted the new law did so knowing of James's interests and thus found reason – English precedent – for catering to some of them whilst retaining a historically English form of process. Neither they nor the king seem to have sought to either revive Henry VIII's failed 1542 Act or to ape Scotland's all-out war on magic and magic users. The suggestion has thus often been made that James, on coming to England, either lost interest in witchcraft, saw the error of his ways and moderated his views, or even that he was embarrassed by his attempted purge of witches in Scotland. None of these is likely. Rather, he simply did not see witchcraft as a pressing problem in England, his promised land. English common law, he claimed, was a perfect form of law and one he would have happily seen spread north of the border. His partiality for his new kingdom only grew with the passage of time and his apparent elevation, as sovereign of a multiple monarchy, to a seat at the top table of European affairs.

Yet if the new king did not see witchcraft as a blight on orderly England, the English people might. That certainly seemed to be the case in Little Moreton, Berkshire, in the autumn of 1604, when a troubled woman, the twenty-year-old Anne Gunter, became fed up with her ongoing sickness and decided to do something about it. In the summer, she had found herself doubled over in pain and falling into episodic fits. Occasionally, she would recoil in horror at the sight of her own vomit and urine; passing both sometimes involved the disgorging of pins. Although pins were ubiquitous in early modern England, being used for everything from attaching sleeves and skirts to fixing feathers and jewels to hats to pricking warts (and occasionally suspected witches), they were not generally vomited. Pins already had something of a reputation for their use in folk heal-ing. This was evidently an unnatural sickness.

In October, Anne took herself to the authorities, confident about the cause of her illness. It was witchcraft, and she was determined to free herself from it. Anne was a reasonably well-connected young woman of gentle stock. Her father, Brian Gunter, was a lay rector and she was sister-in-law to Thomas Holland (who had married her sister Susan), an Oxford theologian who was on one of the teams setting to work on the new Bible. Three witches were accused of being behind her malady: Agnes Pepwell, her illegitimate daughter Mary, and Elizabeth Gregory. The Gregorys were no strangers to the Gunters. In May 1598, a football game had been played in Little Moreton, which soon descended – as the game often did in the period – into extreme violence. When players John Field and Richard Gregory came to blows and a fistfight erupted, Anne's father, Brian, intervened in defence of his son (Anne's brother), dagger in hand. He dealt blows which led to the deaths, some time later, of two

Gregorys, William and Richard. The Gregorys were incensed, but the whole matter was dropped when a grand jury refused to indict the wealthy Brian Gunter. Thus, a local feud was born, with the Gregorys and the Gunters each looking for opportunities to harass one other.

On hearing rumours of her arrest, Agnes fled, leaving her daughter, Mary, and Elizabeth Gregory to face the investigation. The women had not been accused of killing anyone, but under the new law they faced the prospect of a death penalty (rather than a year's imprisonment for causing harm) nonetheless. Word got around of what was going on, eventually reaching the ears of a Wiltshire gentleman, a relative of the Gunters named Thomas Hinton: a graduate of Queen's College, Oxford. Visiting Anne and making a serious investigation into her affliction, Hinton found himself uneasy about her plight. He began, in fact, to think that she was not all that she appeared. In this scepticism, he was supported by one Dr John Harding, who noticed that Anne, despite her fantastical claims of having gained the ability, could not read in the dark. Brian Gunter, however, was convinced, and he enlisted the help of one Alice Kirfoote, who suddenly began believing herself bewitched and sought to prove it by pricking herself with pins, to help plead his case. At the trial on 1 March 1605, presided over by Sir Christopher Yelverton and Sir David Williams (two men who had played a role in drafting the new Witchcraft Act), a parade of neighbours was brought forward to testify to Mary and Elizabeth's bad reputations (Elizabeth's husband being notoriously unpopular in the enclosed world of Little Moreton). They affirmed Anne's fluctuating weight and height, contortions, fits, and the malign influence of Mary Pepwell, who appeared able to cause these episodes. Brian Gunter, too, stepped forward and demanded that the judges reuse the procedure – the forcing of the accused to 'cure' the afflicted by casting out the devil, thereby proving their demonism – which had sent old Alice Samuel and her family to the gallows in the 1593 Warboys case. The judges, wisely, refused.

In March 1605, following interrogation and investigation, Mary and Elizabeth walked free from court, acquitted of all charges but stained further in their reputations. A subsequent examination of Anne by members of the Royal College of Physicians confirmed Thomas Hinton's suspicions; she had been faking it – a conclusion also reached by her next physician, Dr Haddock. If Brian Gunter, who had relinquished the care of his daughter, who continued manifesting symptoms of possession, wanted the matter taken seriously, he would have to take it to a higher authority.

Happily, King James was still in the honeymoon period of his new reign, which – partly out of his academic interests, partly to save money, and partly to show himself and his attractive family to his new subjects – involved a trip to Oxford. Indeed, so carefree was he that he could, in March 1605, write to his minister Salisbury (whom he nicknamed his 'beagle') a note containing some off-colour humour: 'My little beagle although I have been out of privy intelligence with you since my last parting, for having been ever kept so busy with hunting of witches, prophets, puritans, dead cats, and hares, yet will I not suffer this bearer your fellow secretary to go unaccompanied with this present; who should have carried the witches with him as you desired, had it not been that he rides post and witches ride never post but to the devil.'[6]

He arrived at St John's College on 27 August, to be met by a strange sight. Three 'sybils' – later immortalised as *Macbeth*'s three witches – hailed him at the gates, greeting him in Latin as a descendant of the mythical Banquo. He lodged at Christ Church with Queen Anna, whilst Prince Henry took up residence in Magdalen College, the idea being that he could enjoy the university's academic air. On the day of his arrival, the royal party had a visit as interesting as anything the lecture halls could provide. Anne and Brian Gunter managed to secure an audience and plead their case.

James's ears must have perked up. His interest in witchcraft had certainly not dimmed; he had, after all, written the book on the subject and he decided immediately to revisit the case. Prince Henry, too, was probably more interested in this unusual turn of events than the Latin orations he was expected to sit through, given he lacked his father's scholarly bent. The Archbishop of Canterbury,

Richard Bancroft, was charged with overseeing the affair. Bancroft was – and this was to James's taste – an Elizabethan in his attitudes to the religious settlement, and he was a natural sceptic. His faith was ever in institutions, and the machinery of the English legal system had already exposed Anne Gunter as a fraud. His harsh treatment of her – he reputedly used threats and warnings – availed him nothing. The woman persisted in her claims and her symptoms. Bancroft thus referred her to Samuel Harsnett, another divine who was very much a 'company man' in religious matters and one who had written *A Declaration of Egregious Popish Impostures* (1603) in response to the exorcist John Darrell (who had claimed to show that Puritans could as well exorcise demons as Catholics). Harsnett brought in more doctors, who again confirmed fakery. Although the king believed in exorcisms by non-Catholics, he had, in *Daemonologie*, issued strict guidance on what constituted possession. The possibility of real possession was thus to his taste. Puritans were not.

James's interest, though, had not faded. He had Harsnett set Anne up to be courted by a man named Appleby (or Ashely). The possibility of a romance, mysteriously, seemed to cure her histrionics. In the autumn, the king had three more personal interviews with her. After the last of these (on 10 October), during which Anne admitted the influence of her father and his ally Alice Kirfoote on her (including Brian's administering of emetic oil-and-wine potions), James wrote to Queen Elizabeth's former – and his own current – chief minister, Salisbury (the former Sir Robert Cecil):

> For your better satisfaction touching Anne Gunter we let you wit [know] that whereas not long ago she was a creature in outward show most weak and impotent, yet she did yesterday in our view dance with that strength and comeliness and leap with such agility and dexterity of body that we, marvelling thereat to see the great change, spent some time this day in the examination of her concerning the same. And we find by her confession that she finds herself perfectly cured from her former weakness by a potion given her by a physician, and a tablet hanged about her neck; that

she was never possessed with any devil nor bewitched; that the practice of the pins grew at the first from a pin that she put into her mouth, affirmed by her father to be cast therein by the devil, and afterwards that and some other such pin-pranks which she used together with the swelling of her belly, occasioned by the disease called the mother [hysteria thought to be caused by a wandering womb].[7]

Anne had, then, never been bewitched, the devil had not been abroad in England, and, in fact, the king went on to note her newfound desire only to be wed to Appleby. In a letter to Prince Henry, probably written about this time, James referred to Anne as 'yon little counterfeit wench'.[8]

Probably due to November's foiled Gunpowder Plot (which James certainly didn't attribute to demonic acts, being as ever unwilling to disturb England's religious balance by accusing Catholics of being in league with Satan), the Star Chamber prosecution of the Gunters for their imposture did not take place until early 1606. Brian Gunter was certainly imprisoned, but his actual punishment is unknown (although the Star Chamber was unable to dole out anything more serious than mutilation or, more usually, heavy fines). He lived on until 1628, in any case, having given the local witch-hunter a bad name as a vengeful creature acting out of self-interest and spite. Anne's fate is entirely lost to history – though, given no one had died as a result of her machinations, which were in any case apparently encouraged by her father, one hopes she married her Appleby with royal approval.

Had King James, then, turned sceptic on the whole subject of witchcraft? The Anne Gunter case tells us nothing about him we don't already know and thus cannot be used as evidence that he did. In fact, his letters indicate that he was alive to the possibility of the accused women having really bewitched Anne, but he was – provided cases did not touch him personally and smell of treason – naturally inclined to a reasoned approach to discovering the truth (however fallacious his reasoning might seem to modern readers). He knew the symptoms of 'real' possession: the unnatural contortions and the afflicted speaking in unfamiliar languages. Anne Gunter manifested neither of these. What she did manifest, he could see as well as anyone, was the stuff of parlour tricks: the spitting of pins owed more to hoary and false beliefs about possession than what James considered real proof.

Such obvious frauds discredited legitimate cases, as the king well knew; in the 1597 panic, he had had his fingers burnt by Margaret Aitken's imposture, and in that same year, as the panic was petering out in October, a St Andrews woman had been punished by the Kirk Sessions for falsely accusing her neighbour.[9] In their witchcraft cases and understanding of demonology, the English people were lagging behind Europe (around this time Maximilian I, Duke of Bavaria, was beginning a Catholic purge in his territories) and Scotland. This was possibly even a source of frustration. Despite his *Daemonologie* and such texts as Cambridge theologian William Perkins' *A Discourse on the Damned Art of Witchcraft* (1608), which noted the true effects of witches' powers (notably storm-raising, corn-blasting, murder, and the stirring of passions and torments), certain of the English people were showing themselves ignorant of real witchcraft and real possession. Nevertheless, James might have given a sigh of relief, more than anything, to have been confirmed in his opinion that the devil was not as active in England as Scotland. That meant the attitudes of those religious men he approved of – the middle-ground, Elizabethan-minded Bancroft and Harsnett – were right. There was no reason to rock the boat in religious affairs by declaring war on a devilish enemy who was not truly threatening the country. Scotland had been the problem when it came to witchcraft – not England. James would, accordingly, show himself active in trying to anglicise Scots – in 1610, for example, he encouraged Oxford and Cambridge Universities to repeal hostile statutes against 'Scottishmen'; his goal was to bring Scotland and its people closer to God and make them more prone to English obedience (or, preferably, obsequiousness).

For the moment, the king could rest easy. He was secure in his kingdom (despite financial issues already making themselves known); popular; still vigorous despite his luxurious lifestyle beginning to coarsen his features; eager to promote his much-vaunted but ill-fated union of the kingdoms; and almost as keen to promote his laudable but equally ill-fated universal Christian peace. Having already issued what he considered the last word on witchcraft, James's steel-trap mind had latched onto new subjects. England, as far as the monarch was concerned, was largely free of the devil's grip, because Satan would find poor pickings in such a well-ordered kingdom. Unfortunately, in the north, the English people did not seem to realise that.

12

Out of the Mouths of Babes

In 1612, a sick, cancer-ridden man, prematurely aged beyond his forty-eight years, made a visit to the healing waters at Bath. He left – his already tiny, hunch-backed frame further bent by illness – but got only as far as Marlborough. This was Robert Cecil, 1st Earl of Salisbury, who had been overworked by his king, so much so that he came to regret the death of Elizabeth I, during whose reign he 'had ease at my food and rest in my bed. I am pushed from the shore of comfort, and know not where the winds and waves of a court will bear me.'[1] He went to his grave in May.

According to wits, however, he was heading straight to hell. Contemporary verse libels (pithy little epigrams, often rich in personal invective), which were blossoming in popularity (despite the government's best efforts) were quick to emphasise the role of the devil in the unpopular (if not, apparently, with the ladies) minister's worldly success and wealth:

The divell now hath fetcht the Ape
Of crooked manners, crooked shape.
Great were his infirmities,
But greater his enormities
Oppression, lechery, blood, & pride
He liv'd in; & like Herod died.[2]

Another, equally devilish, ran:

King countrye & commons doe mourne & lamente
For he is gone to hell to raise the devills Rente.[3]

So venomous were the attacks on the dead man that an anti-libel rose, defending him against the mock-demonic charges:

Passer by know heere is interrd
The little great one that so was feard
who in his life none durst think evill
but being dead is said a divell[4]

Salisbury had not been a devil. To his marrow, he had been a king's man, albeit one who to an even greater degree than James was keen on continuity and averse to making any great changes in the antiquated workings of government and religion. Yet his death, and the flavour of the outpouring of vitriol that followed it, was significant for the future. Politically, his loss meant multiple empty positions at the Council table. Despite James having, when in Scotland, distrusted the brilliant politician (due to Salisbury having met his old foe Bothwell in Rouen), he had, in the succession negotiations, come to realise the little man's value. Salisbury had been Lord High Treasurer (a thankless job under the impecunious James) and secretary of state. The king referred the former position to committee and left the latter one unfilled, with the work falling to Robert Carr, Viscount Rochester: a weak-willed and -minded but handsome young man with whom James had fallen in love in 1607. In terms of witches and witchcraft, the libels betrayed a problem that not only remained in England but which was about to get worse: the tendency to fall back on accusations of devilry and witchcraft in the sphere of high politics. For the moment, though, Satan had been busy elsewhere in the country.

The trouble began in the East Midlands, where ten people were accused of murderous witchcraft, causing convulsions via the 'evil eye' (a harm-causing glare), and *maleficia* in July, and at least five (one man and four women) were given the swimming test and searched for the devil's mark (which was found on at least one, Agnes Brown) before being executed. Their apparent evil made its way into print via the scurrilous *The Witches of Northamptonshire* (1612).

More infamous events, however, took place further north: a region
seldom visited by the Tudor monarchs and generally left to government by a special council – and they seem to have begun with a
death.

Alizon Device, a spinster of the rundown Malkin Tower, was
walking the path by the old royal forest of Trawden in Pendle,
Lancashire, when she spotted a figure stumping towards her. She
knew him. His humped back was unmistakeable. John Law, a travelling pedlar with the ubiquitous pack, was approaching – and, on
seeing her, he drew up short. The Devices were known locally as
what might now be called an antisocial or nuisance family, apt to be
found begging and rather feared for their reputed supernatural
powers (a reputation which some of them seemed to enjoy for the
little power it gave them). Alizon requested some pins from John,
though it seems she hadn't enough money to pay for them. John
thus declined the sale and went on his way, but, as he trundled
onwards, he fell to the ground. Recovering enough to stand, he
stumbled to an inn in nearby Colne, where Alizon had then looked
in to gawp at him. Although he was not overly concerned at first, in
consultation with his family, he began to suspect the sudden onset
of illness – probably, in reality, a stroke – had been caused by
bewitchment. When the Laws sought out Alizon, to their surprise,
she readily confessed: she was indeed a witch, she had cursed John
Law, and she begged forgiveness. On both sides, sheer bad luck – the
timing of John's stroke – seems to have convinced both him and her
that a simple curse, born of irritation, had had magical effect.

Alizon was duly reported to the local Justice of the Peace, Roger
Nowell, of Read Hall, in March 1612. Nowell had her, her brother
James, and her mother, Elizabeth, brought before him for questioning. This was evidently because the family had a reputation in the
county for witchcraft, or at least as folk healers for hire. Suddenly,
there emerged fantastical tales of historic witchcraft, with Alizon
confessing that her grandmother, Elizabeth Southerns (known colloquially as Old Demdike), had, two years previously, inducted her
into a demonic pact by inviting the devil to appear on one of their

walks and suck blood from her (leaving a mark which had since faded). Further, Old Demdike, who was in her eighties and blind, had been consulted by a local man, John Nutter, in curing a sick cow; however, she had instead bewitched the beast to death. Not content with this, she had then bewitched the daughter of another man, Richard Baldwin (with whom she was feuding), to death. As her confessions grew wider (probably at the prompting of Nowell, who had suspicions about several people in the area), Alizon then accused another woman, Elizabeth Whittle, who had once stolen from the Devices, of being not only a witch but one who had murdered multiple people (including Alizon's father). This led to various arrests in the Whittle clan: Elizabeth, her sister Anne Redferne, and their mother, Anne, generally known as 'Chattox'.

Elizabeth Device, Old Demdike's daughter, too, made her confession before Nowell. She admitted that her mother had, for forty years, borne a strange mark on her body. Her son James confessed to Nowell that he had seen a brown dog leaving his grandmother's house – a strange occurrence which was followed, nightly, by the ghostly howls of invisible children and the shrieking of cats. By now, it seems, the mysterious dog, familiar from pamphlets covering earlier cases, had become a potent signifier of demonic activity. James was, soon after, tormented by a black apparition, about the size of a hare, which crept in upon him at midnight, sat heavily upon him, and fled through his chamber window. This might well have been a form of sleep paralysis, but to James Device it was real, terrifying, and related to Old Demdike. And it wasn't just his grandmother he accused: he affirmed that his sister Alizon had bewitched a local child, although she had removed the curse at the request of the child's father. This was enough to warrant continued questioning of the apparent doyennes of Lancashire witchery.

The unfortunate Old Demdike, who probably had been a long-time folk healer (and probably encouraged her children and grandchildren to believe in her powers and learn from her) was interrogated despite her age and blindness. Indeed, her appearance had probably enhanced her reputation. The courtier and wit Sir John

Harington had certainly recounted a 1607 conversation with the king during which the pair discussed the prevalence of witchcraft amongst elderly women, with Harington offering a 'scurvy jest': 'The devil did work more with ancient women than others . . . we were taught hereof in Scripture, where it is told that the Devil walketh in dry places.'[5]

For her part, Old Demdike admitted that, twenty years previously, she had met the devil 'in the shape of a boy, the one half of his coate blacke, and the other browne'.[6] He had promised her her heart's desire if she would relinquish her soul, which she did. He had kept his promise in part, appearing intermittently over the next five or six years and asking her what she wished for; but she had continually refused to request anything. It was only when he appeared in the form of a brown dog that she allowed him to draw blood under her left arm, this as she tried to protect her child. She had, too, been taken by her granddaughter Alizon to Richard Baldwin's house with the aim of providing curative services, but Baldwin had apparently called the women 'whores and witches' and demanded they leave or he would burn one and hang the other. On being ejected, the evil spirit – by now named 'Tibb' – appeared and invited Old Demdike to take revenge. She availed herself of this offer. In what sounds suspiciously like the old woman confirming what her captors demanded to hear, she then admitted that the surest way to take a man's life was to stab a thorn or pin into a clay image of the victim and then burn it. Indeed, she had once caught Chattox, her daughter, and her son-in-law doing just that.

The elderly Chattox, taken up on the accusation of Alizon, did as her rival in reputation, Old Demdike, had done and confessed. Her admission was that she had sold her soul to the devil fourteen years past – and through the persuasions of Old Demdike. Satan had accordingly made his mark on her right side, near her ribs, promising worldly wealth in return and producing both a feast (which produced no feeling of satisfaction, no matter how much was eaten) and two accessory spirits, Tibb and the appropriately named Fancie. This was standard stuff – Nicolas Rémy's *Demonolatry*, which we can be certain none of the accused had read, had noted that witches confessed to 'banquets [that] in no way satisfied their hunger or thirst'.[7] Chattox was, therefore, either agreeing with matter put to her or giving voice to ancient fairy stories which had, by this time, become conflated with witchcraft in the popular – and the educated – imagination.

According to Chattox, Old Demdike had bewitched a number of local people to death (and in doing so either, one assumes, trawled her memory for local deaths or was fed names). A parade of local people was brought forward to air their own suspicions and recollections of the misfortunes that had struck them after crossing swords with Old Demdike, Chattox, and their broods. These included, in one unsavoury case, a claim by one Margaret Crook that her brother, Robert Nutter the younger, had in 1595 attempted to seduce Chattox's daughter Anne Redferne, been rebuffed, and thereafter died, along with their father. Chattox confessed to this only on the proviso that young Robert's bewitchment had been brought about at the instruction of his grandmother, Elizabeth Nutter, who was attempting a property swindle. Two other local witches – since dead – had apparently helped the curse along.

This was all, naturally, alarming to Roger Nowell, who appeared to have a case of mass witchcraft in his jurisdiction (albeit, in reality, no more than delusional attitudes to the efficacy of curses, family feuds and rivalries, unfortunate coincidences, and a hodgepodge of folk beliefs spiced up with what were then modern, fashionable interpolations, possibly introduced by interrogators or simply supplied by people who were by now familiar with expectations about demonic pacts). For the moment, he sat on it, unsure how to proceed. Alizon, Old Demdike, Chattox, and Anne Redferne were all locked up in the dungeons of Lancaster Castle.

Yet this apparently did not stop the witches. Within a week, ongoing evidence of a conspiracy had been uncovered at the Devices' Malkin Tower, a meeting supposedly having taken place there on Good Friday. On that day – which would certainly have been of interest to Roger Nowell, whose motivations as Justice of the Peace were as religious as legal – the slow-witted James Device had stolen a sheep to feed a host of Device family members, probably with a view to soliciting help for the imprisoned members of the clan. News ot this reached Nowell, who ordered a raid on the house. This turned up, allegedly, human teeth from a Newchurch Grave and the ever-popular clay pictures. Nowell brought in a fellow Justice, Nicholas Banister. This was now taking on the complexion of the deadliest witchcraft form, at least to authorities: the conventicle, or illegal and deadly assembly.

In this round of interrogatories, not only Elizabeth Device and her son James were questioned, but also Elizabeth's youngest child, Alizon's sister, the nine-year-old Jennet. Elizabeth now confessed to far more than she had previously. Now, she admitted to keeping a familiar called 'Ball' (who took on the by-now familiar shape of the brown dog) and killing by means of clay images. She accused one Alice Nutter – a wealthy local woman – of being her co-conspirator in bewitching to death another local man, Henry Mytton, for refusing money to Old Demdike. James confessed to the meeting at Malkin Tower, which he claimed was intended to call forth the imprisoned Alizon's familiar. He had also, apparently, used clay pictures, as he'd seen his grandmother do: these to kill, in turn, a woman from whom he'd stolen turf and a man who had refused him a shirt. Supporting him in this was a familiar spirit named Dandy. At this point, the fingerprints of the authorities become obvious, as James was induced to admit, too, that Jennet Preston, lately acquitted of murderous witchcraft at York, had been present at the assembly (and soon, she was once more arrested, this time without hope of escape). None of this was true. But James admitted also to the family having discussed blowing up Lancaster Castle with the aim of freeing the captives. This hare-brained scheme probably was true – or rather such a ridiculous notion is probably all that had been discussed over stolen meat and a quantity of ale.

The accusations were not at an end. The youngest Device, Jennet, made a slew of her own. Her age itself was a cause for public interest

– although it is worth noting that there was some precedent in the Warboys case of 1593. Further, contemporary ideas about childhood, although nowhere near as sentimental as in later periods, did acknowledge youth as being bound up with innocence (and it was thus probably inconceivable that a child would lie purely for attention or malice in a cause so grave). Despite her age, Jennet was apparently self-assured; she announced that her mother, Elizabeth, was a witch, as were neighbours John Bulcock and Jane, his mother, as well as Katherine Hewitt and Alice Grey. Though the former pair denied having attended the Malkin House gathering (probably honestly), they confessed to having schemed with Jennet Preston and to have used witchcraft to drive a woman to madness. The latter two, Katherine and Alice, of Colne, confessed to having killed one child in the past and planning another murder with Jennet Preston. Once again, Alice Nutter, the 'rich woman' of Roughlee, Pendle, found herself accused. She joined the rest – and by now everyone involved save Jennet Device had been arrested – in Lancaster Castle. Torture, it should be noted, was forbidden in England without express permission from the Privy Council – but that did not apply to subtler forms of torment: terror, threats, near-starvation, and unsanitary conditions. Under such maltreatment, it is not surprising that suspects would tell their interrogators what they thought they wanted to hear, nor that they would agree with whatever might be put to them.

By now, attention was being drawn to the extraordinary events unfolding – and being confessed to – in Pendle. Roger Nowell and Nicholas Banister were joined by other notables, including the mayor of Lancaster, and interrogations continued. At this point, Old Demdike died, either due to her advanced age or her ill treatment (or a combination of both). Yet the population of the dungeon would not miss her. Joining the foul conditions were Margaret Pearson of Padiham (about eight miles from Colne) and Isobel Robey of Windle (nearly fifty miles distant). Both had historically been reputed as witches, though their alleged crimes were unconnected to those linked, originally, to the Devices. In what appears to have been a further sweeping out of problematic people across the north, Roger Nowell's colleague, Robert Holden, provided his own clutch of accused witches (the majority women, but with two men included) from his jurisdiction in and around Samlesbury. Three of these had been accused by a fourteen-year-old, Grace Sowerbutts: Grace's grandmother, Jennet Bierley, her aunt, Ellen Bierley, and Jane Southworth. In total, nineteen people were on trial for witchcraft at the late-summer Lancaster assizes under the judicial gaze of Sir Edward Bromley and Sir James Altham.

The star witness against those under Nowell's jurisdiction was Jennet Device, who recounted her accusations with clarity. This raised her mother, Elizabeth, to a storm of invective. Jennet's brother, James, had been laid low by whatever treatment he had endured during his interrogations and confinement, and he had to be supported in the courtroom. Jennet informed against him, too, confirming his ludicrous story about a spirit called Dandy. Chattox attempted to deny everything, but her own confession, recorded as voluntary, was used against her. Heartbreakingly, among her last acts was to beg for her daughter, Anne Redferne, to be spared, as Chattox attempted to, at the end, admit that all had been her doing. All three were found guilty – and again it is worth noting that murder as a result of witchcraft formed the bulk of the charges – and sentenced to hang. Anne Redferne, despite her mother's attempts to save her life and despite being acquitted on the charge of killing Robert Nutter, was also found guilty of killing Christopher Nutter (Robert's father) and given the same sentence.

The wealthy Alice Nutter remained obstinate in her denials, and it was the Devices' word against her own. To his credit, Judge Bromley began to suspect at least the young Jennet of lying. Jennet did not take kindly to these aspersions and, after being briefly removed from the courtroom, she was allowed to return, whereupon she gave a clear statement on Alice's presence in Malkin Tower. Alice was found guilty, as was the next accused, Katherine Hewitt (although, curiously, her co-accused, Alice Grey, was acquitted). In both cases, the woman's crime had been murder by witchcraft.

It might have been because they had not confessed to murder (but only to causing madness in one Jennet Deane, who only later died) that there was some dubiety about the next pair, John and Jane Bulcock; however, they too were found guilty. Jennet Preston, as a Yorkshire native, was given her punishment at a separate assize, but it was no less tragic. Margaret Pearson of Padiham was, by contrast, found guilty but sentenced only to a term of imprisonment (this her third time in the dock for magical offences). She and Alice Grey received an ominous warning, however: 'There are amongst you that are as deepe in this action as any that are condemned to die for their offences: the time is now for you to forsake the devill.'[8] This came with a command to attend the next assizes. Isobel Robey of Windle, despite not having been charged with killing anyone, had such a litany of magical crimes laid to her charge that she was found guilty and sentenced to hang.

Thankfully, the trials of the seven witches brought up from Samlesbury had less grisly outcomes. On the witness stand, Grace Sowerbutts gave a confused, unconvincing performance (in contrast to the younger Jennet Device); she had accused her grandmother of transforming herself into a talking black dog which encouraged her to drown herself, before carrying her off to a barn and crushing her. Grace claimed also that her grandmother and aunt, in concert, had stolen a child, killed it, boiled it, and eaten it, reserving the bones to brew up magical ointment. Grandmother Jennet had, allegedly, done her best to induct Grace herself into witchcraft, but the girl had refused even after being flown across water and forced to dance and mate with black apparitions. Jane, the 'Widow Southworth', another woman she accused, had also supposedly carried her off to barns and there laid her low. Neighbours were brought in to corroborate these fantasies. However, it was Grace's testimony that caused the case to collapse, or rather her reaction to being counter-accused of having been coached by a Jesuit priest. Soon, something approaching the truth emerged. Those accused had been recusants who had, eventually, turned to the English Church. Grace had been recruited to ruin them. The thought of discovering a Jesuit and his acolytes – those

Southworths who had supported Grace's story – was, if anything, more attractive to authorities than discovering and ridding the area of witches. This, indeed, might have been the intention of Robert Holden all along. All seven from Samlesbury were acquitted.

Alizon Device, with whom matters – regarding Pendle at least – had started, was less lucky. The testimony of John Law was particularly damning; now, he could recall lying ill in the tavern at Colne after his meeting with her. It now seemed to him a 'greate black-dogge . . . with very fearefull fierie eyes, great teeth, and a terrible countenace' had glowered in his face before Alizon had arrived. She, who had probably mistakenly believed she had been gifted powers which frightened even her, was found guilty and sentenced to hang, the accusations of her brother and young sister ringing in her ears (as they would continue to ring in Jennet Device's in the decades to come, when Lancashire was once again visited by cries of devilry).

Matters had proceeded largely from the unpopularity of one troublesome family and had exploded in unexpected directions, revealing a network of local disputes, fears, and hatreds. In all, the 1612 Lancaster assizes saw ten people sentenced to hang (with the eleventh, Jennet Preston, going to the gallows at York), most of them stemming from Alizon's brush with John Law on the road by Trawden Forest. The whole affair had been a local panic driven by a local witch-hunter prompted into action by misleading confessions and false beliefs, rather than a national one driven by the realm's fount of justice – although in at least some of the cases, the new law against magical harm (rather than simply murder) was in evidence. The law was operating as it should, discovering the devil at work and removing undesirable elements who had apparently turned to demonism in the pursuit of their ungodly quarrels. Legal clerk Thomas Potts, using notes approved by the presiding authorities, produced the definitive account (from which the preceding narrative is drawn): *The Wonderfull Discoverie of Witches in the Countie of Lancaster* (1613). However, King James paid little heed to events in the north; these were local witches not aiming their supposed maleficence at him. In London, he had enough to deal with, Salisbury having died, to be followed – shockingly – by the sudden sickness and premature death of the wildly popular Prince Henry, probably of typhoid, in November. Unlike in Scotland, the king was not greatly exercised by English witches because he did not believe – as he had demonstrated in his handling of the Anne Gunter case – that they constituted a personal threat.

However, witchcraft accusations were about to strike very close to the pampered, cosseted world in which King James, for the most part, now chose to ensconce himself.

13

The Cunning Countess

King James in love was King James at his most magnanimous. In the wake of Prince Henry's death, he found solace in the arms of Robert Carr, Viscount Rochester. His belief in witchcraft had not changed, but his priorities had. Foremost in the royal mind in 1612 was not English witchcraft – which he did not see as a problem in comparison to Scottish witchcraft – but dwindling finances, universal Christian peace, and ensuring that Rochester had everything his heart desired.

What Rochester wanted was a wife. James, in principle, had no issue with this. He was well aware that his male lovers must marry, and ideally marry well, to produce the obligatory heirs. He was thus happy to help Rochester to the altar. The only problem was that Rochester's chosen inamorata, Frances Howard, Countess of Essex, already had a husband: Robert Devereux, 3rd Earl of Essex, son to Elizabeth's ill-fated final favourite. James, indeed, had helped engineer this match back in 1604, when the bride and groom had been teenagers and the union a political match between the Catholic Howards and the Protestant Devereuxs. This was, however, a relatively slight problem. Divorces and annulments were not unheard of, provided the Church of England could be convinced to grant them. Further, the marriage had been notoriously unhappy, with the sullen Essex having been sent on a tour of Europe between 1607 and 1609 and having returned to find no greater liking for his bride.

Few could understand this. Frances was, by common report, a remarkable beauty. Rochester saw this, and there is every reason to believe he genuinely fell for her, and she him. She was also, having been born a Howard, well connected: her father, Thomas, was the 1st Earl of Suffolk and her paternal great-uncle Henry Howard, 1st Earl of Northampton (this being the same man who had worked with the late Salisbury in clearing James's way to the English throne and who was now Lord Chamberlain). Rochester, whose monopoly over the king's affections, which showed no signs of diminishing, was making him unpopular (not least with Queen Anna, whom he made the mistake of scorning), saw the value in allying with the Howard faction. Even before he had fallen in love with Frances, Rochester and Northampton had made promises to support one another in gaining political offices in the wake of Salisbury's death (with Northampton coveting the Treasury, and Rochester Mastery of the Horse).[1] What the handsome young royal favourite was too foolish or callow to realise was that the Howard clan, which had its own body of powerful enemies, did not allow shared loyalties. If Rochester was to be won over to – and eventually marry into – the clannish brood, he would first have to be detached from his existing friends and supporters and made as dependent on Howard good-will as possible, so that their clique alone might bask in the royal favour. This meant Northampton and his ilk were keen to separate Rochester from his best friend, mentor, and possibly former lover, Thomas Overbury, on whose wisdom the young man relied in conducting the state business which had begun falling across his desk since Salisbury's death. At first, this proved difficult: Rochester seemed resolute in his loyalty to Overbury, who provided the brains in his navigation of the snake-pit of the court. But as Frances's charms became ever more irresistible, the chance to sow division would arise.

For the moment, the main thing was keeping the flame which had been lit between the young couple burning. Frances and Rochester probably began a sexual liaison in 1612, with the latter being drawn ever more into something more lasting. Frances, however, was in no doubt about what she sought, and in order to ensure she had time with Rochester – away from her husband and her servants' eyes – she employed the services of a mysterious friend: an attractive blonde widow named Anne Turner. This lady, far from respectable, had been carrying on an affair of her own, with a servant in Prince Henry's household called Sir Arthur Mainwaring, during the lifetime of her late husband, a Catholic physician called Dr Turner. Since Turner's death, Anne had turned businesswoman, selling the yellow starches which had become necessary for the fashion-conscious at court who required *de rigueur* new golden ruffs. In seeking her fortune, and the hand of Mainwaring (who seems to have been content with a sexual affair), Anne had consulted the late Simon Forman, the self-proclaimed, self-educated physician and magus who made a note of having seen *Macbeth* in 1610.

Though Forman had died in September 1611, London remembered the intense, sensuous, rather spooky man who had, despite the law, presented himself as a finder of lost things, an astrologer, a necromancer (on which subject he wrote a treatise), and a prophesier (prophesying, in fact, his own death shortly before it happened). With these mountebanks, the law appears to have been generally toothless or disinterested – unlike local healers and witches, they girded themselves with displays of esoteric learning, and this in turn brought powerful, protective patrons. Magic, whether for healing, harm, or love, was too valuable a commodity for practitioners to stop selling or customers to stop buying. Forman, in fact, had had more trouble historically for running afoul of the College of Physicians (whose business he was busily intruding on) than the Witchcraft Act. At any rate, through Anne Turner, Frances was briefly brought into Forman's orbit, the goal of the women being to procure magical 'jellies' capable of ensuring Rochester's lust blossomed into love. Evidently these worked. Throughout 1612, Anne, with the help of a corrupt old servant named Richard Weston, helped the two lovers meet privately in London for trysts. This was all kept secret but, despite Forman's death, his association with Anne and Frances would have dark repercussions.

For the moment, though, the question became: how best to have Frances's marriage to Essex respectably annulled and her subsequent match with Rochester solemnified? The answer was found in the state of the Essex match, which, it was clear even to Suffolk (who had been slow to see the benefits of his daughter's annulment and remarriage to Rochester), remained unconsummated at the beginning of 1613. Early in the year, Suffolk, probably at Northampton's prompting, went to the king requesting a commission to look into the Essex marriage. It took the countess's father some time, however, to come round to Northampton's codicil: any annulment was not for its own sake but to be followed by Frances's remarriage to Rochester. Northampton wanted this. Rochester wanted this (albeit after Frances had convinced him that in marriage rather than just an affair lay their future). The king, if it pleased Rochester, would soon want this. So too would Suffolk, with some careful persuasion. And Frances herself certainly wanted it.

It was, indeed, Frances's desire to rid herself of one man and replace him with another that prompted her to make contact with one Mary Woods: a self-promoting 'cunning woman' who boasted of her magical abilities and had been publicly whipped for her pains the previous year. Since that setback, she had set herself up in London and continued to fan the flames of her dubious reputation (which saw her sought out by women who wished to be rid of their husbands, people who had lost property, and those who needed curing of bewitchments). Mary was called to attend Frances, who gave her a diamond ring as a down-payment on magical services aimed at, one assumes, getting rid of Essex. This Mary took – and promptly she fled. When Frances's servant tracked her down to Norwich (where she had previously been whipped), the enterprising charlatan admitted that she had already sold the ring and that, if she were arrested, she would tell the world that Frances had hired her to murder Essex. Despite the threat, the authorities were called in, and both Frances's servant and Mary were interrogated. The former produced a cock-and-bull story about his mistress having given the ring to Mary for safekeeping, whilst Mary, as she'd threatened, claimed Frances, Countess of Essex, had sought her out as a poisoner. When later called to London, Mary changed her story, instead insisting that Frances had asked only for powders by which she might conceive. The woman, notorious already and lucky to be thought only a charlatan rather than a witch, was not believed. She was thus spared the horrors endured by Mother Sutton and her daughter in 1613: in Bedfordshire, this unfortunate pair were accused by neighbours of having been witches for decades (and recently having used their familiars, Dick and Jude, to torment a neighbour), and both were forced to endure the swimming test before conviction and execution. Nevertheless, the scandal of the affair raised eyebrows and, for the moment, looked like threatening the ongoing nullity suit.

This the king was not prepared to allow. Much of 1613, the year in which James's daughter, Elizabeth, had made her own Protestant match (to Frederick Casimir, Elector Palatine) as part of the royal policy of maintaining a European religious balance, was taken up by his desire to bring to fruition another marriage. It was not, however, smooth sailing. For one thing, the granting of a nullity suit required approval by an ecclesiastical commission headed by the self-righteous George Abbot, Archbishop of Canterbury, who was hostile to the overweening pretensions of the Catholic-tainted Howards and increasingly disgusted by the behaviour of Frances. For another, Queen Anna – who loathed Carr – found the matter distasteful. Rochester's protégé, Thomas Overbury, was likewise appalled by the affair when it became clear it amounted to more than just illicit sex: he referred to Frances as 'that base woman' and professed himself an enemy to the Howard faction. In this, Overbury bungled. He found Frances to be a scandalous baggage, unfit for Rochester and likely to cause him to lose James's fawning affections. All of this opposition would have to be swept away if the nullity case was to find in Frances's favour – and James was determined it should. Already he had given Rochester much – titles, cash handouts, custody of the signet (traditionally the secretary of state's responsibility). He would not stint at a bride.

The bride herself was even more determined. Secretly, she attempted to press Sir David Wood, who had quarrelled with

Overbury, to murder him and was disappointed only to be promised that the would-be killer was willing only to deliver a thrashing. More realistically and pacifically, James attempted to have the troublesome man posted abroad, with Russia being deemed suitably far away. Overbury, whose deft handling of state affairs too complex for Rochester was undermined by his arrogance and rudeness, demurred, and when the suggestion became a royal command, he doubled down. The king had him clapped in the Tower in April 1613 – an imperious move which shocked even Overbury's many enemies. There he would rest, if not quietly.

The commission into the nullity suit remained a potential problem, albeit one ameliorated by the fact that Essex was willing for the marriage to be dissolved providing he might save face via the admission that he was impotent only with Frances, whom he alleged had some physical defect which prevented penetration. This was not ideal, however, as it would make any subsequent marriage of hers difficult to justify. Further, not all on the commission were willing to roll over: canon law was strict on annulment. The Howards needed a loophole. In the *Reformatio Legum*, codified in 1551, they found grounds for dissolution of a marriage if impotence had been caused by witchcraft.[2] Frances, who had so recently been involved with people versed in magical artistry, now had another card to play.

The stumbling block to the annulment had been – and remained – Archbishop Abbot, who, if anything, found Frances and her family more objectionable with each passing day. Unfortunately, he presided over the commission and made no secret of his opposition to the suit, despite other members of the quorum being in favour. His view was simple: there was nothing wrong with Essex and nothing wrong with the marriage, which both parties had legally entered into with God's blessing. It was, he stated, ridiculous to believe that any man could be impotent only with his wife – and as proof he drew in scurrilous gossip about Essex flaunting his erection to members of his household on being teased about his alleged inability. Frances was no less vulnerable to prurient treatment; she – or a veiled substitute pretending to be her – was subjected to a physical examination by six ladies, which found her both a virgin and capable of sexual intercourse. Still, Abbot demurred, refusing the precedent of Henry VIII, who had annulled his marriage to Anna of Cleves by claiming that he was uniquely incapable with her, on the grounds that Henry had been 'a strange prince in that kind'. All of this having dragged out events, Frances played her card, asserting that witchcraft was behind her husband's impotence.

This drew Abbot's scepticism and James's interest. The king held a private consultation with his archbishop, admitting during it that he had initiated the nullity suit and would see it through. Abbot was unmoved. In frustration, James insisted that the case either be found in Frances's favour or adjourned – presumably so that he might find a way through the deadlock. In response, Abbot laid out in writing his belief that there existed no Biblical precedent for witchcraft causing selective impotence – and even if witchcraft had been attempted, he had found no evidence of the couple engaging in prayers, fasting, or even medical remedies to overcome its effects.

King James was off to the races. He had not only proven, in his own mind and to the world via his writings, that witchcraft could affect people as Frances claimed, but it was the considered opinion of the European intelligentsia that the devil saw in the private parts his 'principle operation'. Abbot, he fulminated, was behaving like a narrow-minded and backwards Puritan (James's own foregrounding of Biblical provenances in *Daemonologie* going unmentioned). Though he doubtless thought his arguments self-explanatory, he was moved also to more practical measures. When the commission reconvened in September, he packed it with new members antagonistic to Abbot. Before the deadline the king ordered for the 25th, the archbishop was given an audience at which Northampton and Suffolk were present. He remained steadfast in his desire to do what he believed was right. The following day, it availed him nothing. James commanded that the commissioners confine themselves to announcing – without explaining their reasoning – their votes, and the nullity was granted. Frances was now free to marry

Rochester, and the pair lost no time organising the nuptials. James paid for a lavish wedding, winning over even Queen Anna (or at least convincing her not to be too vocal about her dislike of the matter) by supporting her in a property dispute. In the midst of all of this, it was scarcely noticed that the unpopular Overbury had mysteriously expired on 15 September in the Tower. He would not, however, rest easy.

*

Rochester, in celebration of his victory over Essex and his winning of Frances, was elevated to the height of his power as the 1st Earl of Somerset, with the idea being that his wife, in losing her title as Countess of Essex, would not be diminished in status. All might have been well, if not for Somerset making a foolish mistake. The young man found himself genuinely in love with his wife. This was not what James had wanted or expected – but it was what the late Overbury had warned Rochester about. Now that the favourite had a wife he genuinely wished to spend his nights with, he was no longer attendant upon his royal lover.

This left the door open for Rochester's enemies to pounce. This they did, with the Earl of Montgomery, his brother the Earl of Pembroke, and the Earls of Hertford and Bedford engaging in their own bit of *maleficia*: the men gathered together and threw dirt at a portrait of Somerset. More pragmatically, they began plotting, eventually bringing Archbishop Abbot and Queen Anna into their plan. The scheme itself was simple enough. James was finding Somerset increasingly petulant, far too much in love with his pretty wife, and drawing away from the royal bedchamber. All that was needed was a new man in the king's life. Their choice was a good one: the sweet-natured, compliant, and remarkably attractive and athletic George Villiers, of good gentle stock and, thanks to his ambitious mother, Mary, reasonably well mannered. With some polish, they eventually induced James to take notice of their man, and the king, with Anna's coaxing, knighted Villiers and made him a Gentleman of the Bedchamber.

Somerset knew he was being replaced and panicked, growing only more truculent towards the enemies he perceived plotting his downfall. For a time, he remained at court, doing his best to retain his position and stand firm against the king's new inamorato. His efforts, however, were in vain. Two of the hostile men Somerset didn't see coming for him were the fanatically anti-Catholic Sir Ralph Winwood, who disliked the whole Howard clan and disliked especially Frances and her husband, and Sir Thomas Lake. These were the new joint Secretaries of State, Salisbury finally having been replaced – but they had found, to their chagrin, that Somerset was usurping their offices. Winwood was thus delighted when a dubious report reached him from the continent. It was supposedly the confession of an apothecary's apprentice, William Reeve, who claimed to have witnessed the poisoning of Thomas Overbury in the Tower. The Somersets were, allegedly, the poisoners.

When rumours began growing louder – and when they began touching on the king's involvement – an investigation was launched. In the course of it, Reeve was, strangely, forgotten. Winwood netted instead the Somersets, Anne Turner, and Richard Weston (who had been levered into the position of Overbury's gaoler by Frances and Northampton, who had himself died in 1614). Under arrest, too, was the hapless keeper of the Tower, Gervase Helwys, who appears to have done no more than try to stop a host of poisoners, employed by Frances, from getting their wares to Overbury. Sir Thomas Monson, Master of the Armoury at the Tower, was also arrested – though he was eventually released. There was no stopping such a large plot and so many plotters from going to trial – and very public trials they were, presided over by the ambitious Sir Edward Coke, Chief Justice of the King's Bench and one of the men behind the 1604 Witchcraft Act.

Revelations abounded about Frances's role – and allegedly Somerset's – in seeking the death of Overbury by foul means. Anne, at her trial, found herself denounced by the eloquent Coke as 'a whore, a bawd, a sorcerer, a witch, a papist, a felon, and a murderer'.[3] Overt female sexuality, witchcraft, and murder were grouped in the early modern mind under the same heading: unnatural. This seemed all the more plausible when her connection with the late Simon Forman, notorious for his lubriciousness and magic, was revealed and Forman's home searched – in it was found the stuff of witchcraft: papers with the names of devils inscribed, these intended to be used to conjure up spirits to provoke Anne's lover, Mainwaring, and Somerset to lust, and to torment them if their passions ever cooled. In Anne's home was found a lead figure of a couple locked in a carnal embrace. It was clear that Anne Turner was a witch or had consulted witches – not just Forman but, following his death, apparently one Dr Slavery. The crime for which she was executed in November 1615, however, was her role in the murder plot. Richard Weston and Gervase Helwys went with her.

Frances fared somewhat better, though her reputation did not. Libels, which had once mocked her as a 'a maid, a wife, a countess, and a whore' were rewritten; now she was 'a wife, a witch, a murderer, and a whore'.[4] She too was found guilty of murder and given the death sentence, as was her husband – and probably Frances really had been behind Overbury's death without Somerset's foreknowledge. In the event, James, always merciful to those he had once loved, commuted the death sentences, thankful that neither of the big fish in the affair had made any damning revelations about his relationship with Somerset. The noble pair – and Frances was by this time pregnant with a daughter – were imprisoned in the Tower before being released to live under house arrest. They never regained public positions, she dying in 1632 and he in 1645.

The allegations of witchery made by Coke are, however, interesting for what they reveal about the ongoing association between allegations of witchcraft and high politics in the era. These were, obviously, nothing new – politicians had made either vague or specific allegations of sorcery against their enemies for centuries. But the claims that Anne and Frances were either witches or had consulted with witches did not explode into anything particularly memorable, nor were they the key features of what was, in essence, a high-society murder trial. The reason is probably that although Coke might have included them to please the king, if he did so he was mistaken. To James, these allegations were as frivolous as the low verse libels and, in any case, he was keen to disassociate himself from this embarrassing scandal. He was unable, though, to stem the English predilection for accusing enemies, for purely political reasons, of witchcraft.

Nor could he stop public interest in so high profile a case. The English were, probably thanks to the relatively new forms of mass media such as pamphlets and railing rhymes, as interested in scandal as witchcraft. The Jacobean court was, seemingly, demonstrating every resemblance to the louche courts of Europe depicted (to public delight and horror) in the London playhouses. So too were playwrights interested in all aspects of devilry. It was probably in 1616, following the Somersets' downfall, that Thomas Middleton penned *The Witch*, a drama safely set in distant Italy, which features Hecate (shown as a sexually incontinent witch), who uses animal parts and dead children in her cauldron-stirring activities, which include flying via the use of magical ointment and causing impotence. Tellingly, Hecate and her fellow witches are visited by powerful patrons unhappy about marriages, who use purchased charms to engage in various sexual and murderous escapades. The group of witches are what had by then become typical: fearsome creatures who fly through the air and meet in numbers to work their evil – an image given a fresh coat of paint by the second edition, in 1613, of Pierre de Lancre's *Tableau de l'inconstance des mauvais anges* (*On the inconstancy of witches*). In *The Witch*, a direct line is drawn between the demonic activity of these creatures and the pride, vanity, jealousy, and iniquity of courtiers. With an adulterous killer duchess in its colourful cast, it is not hard to see how the play's Italian setting might have been viewed as engaging with events closer to home by the upmarket Blackfriars audiences before whom it was first performed. James and Queen Anna understood growing public attitudes to apparent corruption and factionalism at court; Anna's protégé and long-time artistic collaborator, Ben

Jonson, wrote and produced his *The Golden Age Restored*: a masque on the theme of reform achieved via the renewed authority of the king (with Astraea, the Goddess of Justice once associated with Elizabeth I, returning). James made the politic move of requesting the masque be performed again two days later, on Twelfth Night, the better to distance himself from the corrupt creatures whose banishment it celebrated.

The stage was not done with witchcraft, however, and neither was James. In the summer of 1616, the thirteen-year-old John Smith, of Husbands Bosworth in Leicester, fell down in a fit. This became a seizure of some kind, during which John beat himself repeatedly, despite two strong men trying to hold him down. This became an episodic problem, and John went on to accuse fifteen women of bewitching him, six of whom apparently used familiar spirits (a horse, a toad, a cat, a dog, a fish, and a polecat) to do so. These women were arrested, despite the fact that back in 1607, when he was probably still in skirts, John had made similar accusations which had been found baseless. When the accused were brought before him, he made animalistic sounds according to which familiar was tormenting him (whinnying, for example, when the horse spirit attacked). The Leicester authorities did what the judges in the Anne Gunter case had refused to do; they drew on the old Warboys procedure from 1593, exhorting the women to say certain words (for example, 'I such a one charge thee, horse, if I be a witch, that thou come forth of the child'). As John responded by ceasing his violent behaviour, this was held to prove that they were witches. The six were tried, found guilty, and hanged, along with three others.

The remaining five women (one had died in prison after confessing, probably due to cruel treatment) were luckier. James, on his annual summer progress (now with Villiers rather than Somerset), visited Leicester and, his interest in witchcraft still lively, heard about the case. Young John was brought before him and the king 'discovered a fallacy' in his testimony. What this was is unclear, but as John was feigning signs of possession, it is reasonable to conclude that, like Anne Gunter, he had failed to meet the requirements set out in *Daemonologie*. Worse, the boy had apparently been willing to turn his 'possession' on and off at the instigation of anyone who asked. James, always disgusted at any attempts to counterfeit witchcraft to the detriment of genuine devilry, allowed the October trial to go ahead, at which the five were released by red-faced magistrates. What provoked such a young man to masquerade as one possessed (perhaps the attention it gained him) and accuse innocent women is unknowable – but it does reveal that even at a young age, people in the period were being exposed to notions of witchcraft and possession, even if their conception of the latter was, to educated men like James, hopelessly backwards.

The affair of the 'Leicester Boy', once again, found expression in the stage, via Ben Jonson's *The Devil Is an Ass*: a play which does not mock witchcraft but scorns and warns against cheap counterfeits and authorities too ignorant to know false cases from real ones. Prosecution using children – already a subject of debate – had been dealt a blow. Understanding true witchcraft required an academic approach: as John Cotta argued in his 1616 *The triall of witch-craft*, the real witch had to be proven to have freely entered into a contract with Satan. This was very much the king's view.

It can thus be fairly said that James, in England and fuelled by a desire to be seen as the wisest man in the kingdom, saved lives that might otherwise have been lost, whether by direct intervention or due to his rigid view that the devil was not at work in the realm and that cases of witchcraft, consequently, had to meet the idiosyncratic standards of proof he had set out whilst still in Scotland. As proof of his indirect positive influence, the so-called 'Bilson Boy', William Perry, was exposed as a fraud by more analytical authorities who had probably heard of John Smith or Anne Gunter's frauds: Perry was exposed by Bishop Morton of Lichfield and Coventry as a counterfeit who had been instructed by a Catholic priest to feign vomiting crooked pins and straw; accuse an old woman, Jane Clark, of witchcraft; pass black urine (ink, in reality); and fall into fits at the reading of St John's Gospel in English.

James's high standards of proof for true demonic possession had borne fruit. In Scotland, of course, the king had believed Satan to be very active – and there he had undoubtedly cost scores of lives. In 1616, his mind turned back to his native land. It remained to be seen whether his misanthropic attitude to his countrymen – and the devils in their midst – had changed.

14

The King Is Dead

James's single return visit to Scotland, which took the form of an extended summer progress in 1617, demonstrated that his attitude to his countrymen had not changed. For all he waxed nostalgic about his return, his motives were religious. If anything, his preference for England had deepened – now, he found himself not only enamoured of what he had once called 'the promised land' of religion but of the English style of worship. What might now be called 'High Church' practices had become his favoured style: music, gilded statuary, and, of course, royally appointed bishops, which he had always seen as absolutely necessary to an Erastian state. His dedication to this spiritual mode resulted in those who saw no future for the Church in England decamping firstly to Holland and on to the New World aboard the *Mayflower* in 1620. It was equally anathema to those more reformist Kirk elders who had, in the king's absence, become as entrenched in their desire for Presbyterianism. During his visit, James pushed his 'Five Articles of Perth', designed to move the Kirk closer to English forms of worship. These provoked a mixed reaction, though they were passed by the General Assembly the following year and ratified by the Scottish Parliament in 1621. James was, however, politically astute. He knew his home nation was a political and religious powder-keg and did not look too closely into whether individual parishes were following his commands.

For the moment, however, the king was keen on enjoying his hunting and lecturing the Scots. In his mind, he claimed, was the desire 'to reduce their barbarity [by this he meant their lack of obedience] . . . to the sweet civility of their neighbours [the English]: and if the Scots would be as docible [docile] to learn the goodness of the English, as they were teachable to limp after their ill, then he should not doubt of success; for they had already learnt of [from] the English to drink healths, to wear coaches and gay clothes, to take tobacco, and to speak a language that was neither English nor Scottish'.[1] The devil, evidently, was still at work in Scotland – though thankfully, under the moderating hand of Alexander Seton, 1st Earl of Dunfermline and Lord Chancellor of Scotland, no purges had been attempted (this despite the law still being in force).

Rather, the by-now standard cases had come to litter the records: Isobel Grierson, for example, had been strangled and burned for turning herself into a cat and invading the home of a neighbour with a cluster of others; for causing the devil, 'like a black man', to drag a servant around by the hair; for 'pissing' on one Margaret Miller; and for causing disease. This was probably the result of a private dispute against a woman long reputed querulous, and it did not light any great fire of persecution, cruel as it was to Isobel. The same was true of Margaret Barclay, of Irvine, who, following a dispute with her brother-in-law in 1618, found herself accused of storm-raising alongside a supposed seer, John Stewart, who produced the usual confession of wax images being used. The pair, under torture, implicated Isobel Insh and Isobel Crawford, and all four were damned by Insh's young daughter, who supplied the requisite demonic dog story. Insh tried to escape and fell to her death; John committed suicide; Margaret's legs were broken with iron bars until she confessed fully (whereupon she was strangled and burned, denying her confession at the last); Isobel Crawford was likewise executed after having suffered the strappado (and she too recanted her confession).

As ever, confession, however it could be drawn out of the accused, was the key – this satisfied even strict standards of evidence. This did not, of course, make them true. Family disputes were eternal, people undoubtedly did try and curse one another, and witchcraft remained a means of ridding people of unwanted relatives and unpopular members of the community. James, to his credit, did not attempt to restart any great hunts – his goal now, despite his fiery language, was to encourage Scots to incline naturally towards the English, and in any case he was in the country only for the summer, returning to England later in 1617. Afterwards, from the safety of England, he increased the power and visibility of his Scottish bishops; from 1624, they were granted a key role in witchcraft trials, with all information presented to diocesan bishops before being passed to the Privy Council. Even remotely, James had no intention of letting Scotland lose the centralisation he had long laboured to institute.

The king had, by 1617, achieved one of his dreams: a loving family, with Queen Anna (by now suffering recurrent illness) in lock-step with his new lover, George Villiers, who had been elevated to the Earldom of Buckingham at the beginning of the year. In time, James took to wearing an image of Buckingham – whom he nicknamed 'Steenie', after an image of the angelic St Stephen – on 'a blue ribbon under my waistcoat next to my heart'. It was the king's family, however, which was to cause the last great crisis of his reign and see the undoing of his long, successful peace policy. In 1619, Anna died: a crushing blow to a man who was by his nature deeply sentimental. That same year, his son-in-law, Frederick, Elector Palatine, accepted the Bohemian crown from that state's Protestant elite, this despite the crown being a hereditary Habsburg possession. In retaliation, the Austrian Habsburgs invaded the Lower Palatinate, Frederick's hereditary land, before driving Elizabeth and Frederick from Bohemia. James, appalled at this subversion of heredity, was caught in the middle: either he could go to war – and this conflict would erupt into the hideously bloody Thirty Years' War – on behalf of his family, or he could side with the Catholic Habsburgs, thereby alienating his own fiercely Protestant people. His strategy was diplomacy – an almost Elizabethan attempt to prevaricate and delay. His larger solution involved seeking a Catholic Spanish Habsburg bride (the Spanish Habsburgs being natural allies to the Austrian branch vengeful over Bohemia) to inject British royal blood into the European dynasty and thereby reduce matters to a solvable family dispute.

Europe was to be James's battleground, much against his will, in his final years. As the king focused on diplomacy, the continent was, however, being riven by strategic alliances and religious division. The latter had proved invaluable in fuelling witch hunts, as both Catholics and Protestants sought to demonstrate their godliness against the common enemy. The elderly Julius Echter von Mespelbrunn, ferociously Catholic Prince-Bishop of Würzburg, had set his stamp on the town of Freudenburg with a mass trial in 1612.[2] Hundreds more went to the flames for witchcraft in Würzburg in 1616 and 1617. In Bamberg, Prince-Bishop Johann Gottfried von Anschausen and later Prince-Bishop Johann Georg Fuchs von Dornheim each instituted reigns of terror, the last ending in 1632 when the diocese came under external threat in the form of a Protestant army.

The evil genius coordinating many of the purges was Dr Friedrich Förner, a long-time demonologist and Counter-Reformation author who would pen his *Panoplia Armaturae Dei* (*Armour of God*) in 1626. This most Catholic of witch-hunters viewed witchcraft as not only real but linked to the heretical bent of medieval theorists. He would find opposite numbers throughout the seventeenth century, across the Old and New Worlds, in Protestant witch-hunters. They would have much the same reason for eliminating the influence of Satan and every intention of proving they were better qualified in doing so. In 1618, English barrister Michael Dalton provided, in his *The Countrey Justice*, the correct means of identifying and punishing witches: this emphasised the importance of the demonic pact, which could be proven by physical evidence in the form of devil's marks. He had almost certainly been influenced by his sovereign's insistence on educated, stringent standards of evidence.

In James's southern kingdom, however, large trials remained scattered, newsworthy events. This was certainly the case in 1619, when readers could find copies of *The Wonderful Discoverie of the Witchcrafts of Margaret and Phillip Flower, Daughters of Joan Flower neere Beuer castle*. This case was particularly attention-grabbing not due to the characters of the witches accused – a mother, Joan Flower, and her daughters, Phillipa and Margaret – but for their alleged victim. The women had been servants of Francis Manners, 6th Earl of Rutland at Belvoir Castle, an opulent Lincolnshire stronghold previously visited by King James (the additional staff needed due to the 1612 royal visit being the reason for their employment). They had not, however, been popular figures – something like the Devices in Pendle, they had a reputation as troublemakers. It was thus not long before all three were dismissed from service, following which the earl and Countess Cecily began suffering from fits. So too did the earl's heir, Henry, baron de Ros, who succumbed in the autumn of 1613, leaving his troubled family to continue their ongoing suffering. The new heir (who took his deceased brother's title of baron de Ros), Francis, was soon similarly afflicted by a wasting illness – though the Rutland daughter, Katherine, improved after a brief spell. In desperation at the thought of losing the remaining heir, in 1616 Cecily sought the advice of the esteemed royal physician, Dr Henry Atkins, who had stood at the deathbed of the late Prince Henry. Advising from a distance, Atkins was reluctant to directly identify witchcraft as the cause, confining himself to recognising the curious illness as bearing the symptoms of what we would now call epilepsy. This was not satisfactory to the family. At the height of Francis's sickness, the Rutlands allegedly called upon Joan Flower, either due to her reputed healing abilities or because they suspected that, having bewitched him, she could remove the curse. Whatever her involvement at this stage, she failed, and the boy's illness grew worse.

This sickness, running rampant through the noble family and having caused one death, looked increasingly suspicious. The obvious suspects were the Flower women. They were brought in for interrogation in late 1618 and examined by, among others, the Earl of Rutland. In the process, a test was undertaken: Joan, supposedly, was offered and refused the Eucharist, asking instead for plain bread. On receiving instead the hated Eucharist, she dropped dead: proof positive that she was a witch. This, at any rate, is the story told by the *The Wonderful Discoverie*. In reality, she probably died of poor treatment. Her daughter Philippa confessed to witchcraft whilst

Margaret attempted to blame her late mother – but both eventually admitted to having made a pact with the devil and having kept a familiar: a cat named Rutterkin. After having stolen the late Henry, baron de Ros's glove, they had given it to Joan to be rubbed on the demonic feline. Additionally, they had stolen feathers from the Rutland marital bed and used sorcery and incantations to cause the earl impotence. Only their attempts to kill the Rutland daughter had failed.

It is probable that these confessions were extracted under some form of torture, whether direct or indirect. At any rate, the Flowers went further than necessary – they named names: Anne Baker, Ellen Greene, and Joan Willimot. On being arrested, this trio made their own confessions (in reality probably identifying more healers or cunning folk). Joan Willimot, however, provided her own devilish admission – she had, she claimed, kept a familiar called Pretty, who first appeared in the form of a fairy, and she claimed Joan Flower had, indeed, attacked the sickly Francis and his deceased elder brother (in addition to keeping a rat and an owl as familiars). She accused one Gamaliel Greete, too, of being a witch, keeping a mouse, and having the power of the evil eye. Anne, a spinster, claimed to have kept a white dog and confessed to 'hearing voices in the air', and Ellen to have sent familiars (called Puffe and Hisse, conjured for her by Joan Willimot) in the form of a mole and a kitten to kill multiple people who had offended her. All gave various accounts of having let their demonic pets bite them or having seen others allow theirs to do the same. From this concoction of old folk beliefs and newer ideas about the demonic pact, a conspiracy was proved (this despite Ellen drawing no connection to the Flowers).

Margaret and Phillipa Flower were thus tried in Lincoln Castle before Sir Edward Bromley (of the Pendle witch trials) and Sir Henry Hobart of Blickling Hall, then Chief Justice of the Common Pleas. On the basis of their confessions, both women were found guilty, sentenced to death, and hanged on 11 March 1619. If the Rutlands thought the deaths of those they believed had bewitched their remaining son might relieve him, they were to be disappointed; Francis died in 1620. Probably, neither he nor his family had ever been directly harmed by anyone, even if the Flowers had attempted some harmless witchcraft in revenge at having been sacked (and their confessions are hardly reliable proof of even that). Any manner of illness might have run in the family and found scapegoats in the unpopular Flowers, who in turn appear to have tried to give their interrogators what it was by now clear they wanted: devilish antics, witchcraft, and the names of other folk, likewise marginal and probably engaged in charms and attempts at sorcery, who could do the same.

Once again, the sensational nature of English witchcraft was apparent. It recurred in 1621, following the execution of Elizabeth Sawyer, an old woman of, again, historically dark reputation (being known for her foul mouth), who had apparently made a pact with Satan via a demonic dog named Tom, and thereafter bewitched Agnes Ratcleife to death following a quarrel. Unsurprisingly, the devil's mark was found on her – apparently on her buttocks – and she went to the gallows. Her tale was told in *The wonderful discovery of Elizabeth Sawyer, Witch* and immortalised onstage in Thomas Dekker, William Rowley, and John Ford's *The Witch of Edmonton*.

Nor were dramatists the only ones to see the cash value in selling demonic tales. It was in 1621 that the Star Chamber interrogated Thomas Saunders and Katherine Malpas for, allegedly, having devised and carried out a scheme whereby Katherine would feign diabolical possession – counterfeiting 'certain strange fits and trances . . . to practice and use divers strange & unusual tricks & deceits in the manner and fashion or her behaviour and gesture' – in order to charge people to 'come to see her, in pity & commiseration of so strange a sight'.[3] As ever, the real had to be sorted from the fake – and now commercial and artistic interests were further muddying the waters of what precisely was real.

One man was in no doubt. In York, the poet Edward Fairfax (whose half-brother, Thomas, had been a go-between of James and Elizabeth I from the 1580s, and who had been amongst the first to greet the Scottish monarch as England's sovereign) suspected his children of having been genuinely bewitched. One infant daughter,

Ann, died, and the others, Elizabeth and Helen, showed signs of possession, detailing the visions that came to them in their trances. Five local women of historically 'evil report' were charged in 1622 with casting spells, making images, and feasting with Satan – though thankfully the case against them collapsed (to Edward's disappointment). The grieving and concerned father had, though, penned his *Daemonologia: A Discourse on Witchcraft* (1621), which recounted his afflicted daughters' visions of 'strange and deformed things', 'a terrible monster with three heads', fighting cats, and 'glorious apparitions' which, on the girls' refusal to join with them, grew horns and took on frightful shapes.[4] Though far from a disinterested observer, Fairfax claimed that King James himself was dissatisfied with England's laws, stating that his monarch had complained that the only witches punished in England were those 'who by that means killed, so that such were executed rather as murderers than as witches'. In this he was half-right; James had indeed updated the law, though he remained unconvinced that there was a profusion of witches at work in England. Nevertheless, with each new piece of media (whether pamphlet, play, or treatise) came increased public knowledge of witchcraft. If the Scots were being educated in the ungodliness of demonism, the English were being instructed in its sensational horrors (and frauds). More people would see their misfortunes as being due to it, and more discontented or vengeful people might try it.

King James himself appears to have taken something of an interest in the Belvoir case at least – which was inevitable, given the involvement of his nobility. He would, despite her Catholicism (from which he encouraged her to make a show of conversion), make the surviving Rutland child, Katherine Manners, now a significant heiress, the wife of Buckingham (with Buckingham's mother also encouraging the match, in the teeth of Rutland's opposition). This has led, recently, to speculation that Buckingham had engineered the deaths of the Rutland male heirs via poison, framing the Flower women – but this is unlikely. By this stage, the great favourite was ambitious, vainglorious, and in need of a plain, rich bride who would not arouse the king's jealousy, but he was not a murderer. The only real crime of which he was capable would be peculation, of which he was fast becoming a master. At any rate, James Howell noted in the aftermath that his sovereign 'was loath to believe there were witches, but that which happened to my lord Francis of Rutland's children convinced him'.[5] What he might have more accurately said was that James was loath to believe that devilry was so active or effective in England; as we have seen, the king did not necessarily repudiate his views on what he considered true demonic witchcraft. Certainly, he made no attempts to intervene in Scotland when, in 1622, six women were investigated and tried in Aberdour by the proper procedure of royal commission. Their alleged crime had been murderous witchcraft, and the devil had loomed large in their confessions. More commissions were granted the following year, and in 1624 seven alleged witches were tried (in Culross and Torryburn).

In truth, James's attentions were focused elsewhere as his reign drew to a close. His days as a witch-hunter were in the past. His goal now was to see his heir, Prince Charles, wed to a Catholic Spanish Habsburg, still with a view to preventing Europe's collapse into war and ensuring British influence abroad. This was dealt a blow in 1623, when his lover, Buckingham (whom he would raise to the only non-royal dukedom in England, the Norfolk dukedom having lapsed by the attainder passed by Elizabeth against the 4th Duke of Norfolk in 1572) convinced him to grant Charles licence to travel incognito into Spain to woo the Infanta Maria Anna. James was, as Henry VIII had done via his will, attempting to engineer governance beyond the grave; by adopting his lover as a member of the royal family and fostering a relationship between this protégé and his son, he was setting up a future monarch and chief minister in the image of his own rule.

Yet Buckingham, who could see in the ageing, paunchy, semi-toothed king a setting sun, was already turning fully to the coming man. After a rocky start, he had won over Charles and become his chief adviser (Charles either not knowing or not caring about

Buckingham's sexual relationship with the king, however withered). The pair's jaunt to Spain, however, was a disaster, and both men returned boiling over with hatred of the perfidious Spaniards. For their part, the Spanish had no desire to see one of their royal house wed to a heretic. If the visit of Charles and Buckingham (in the unlikely guises of Jack and Tom Smith) was intended to cut the Gordian knot of diplomacy, it succeeded only in pouring oil on it. The English Parliament, horrified, animated, and belligerent at the prospect of a Catholic match, then struck a match. The Spanish marriage was a dead letter; this much was clear in 1624. Worse, from James's perspective, his son and his lover (whom he had, since his sexual attraction had been replaced with deep affection, come to consider a surrogate son himself) had combined against him. Charles and Buckingham now turned themselves into Parliament's darlings, waxing militantly against the Spanish and encouraging English hopes of returning the realm to a state of Protestant jingoism. James's much-vaunted Spanish match was thus, under Buckingham's guiding hand – and by now the duke had come into his own as a seasoned if overly ambitious politician – replaced with a French one. Charles's marriage to the Princess Henriette Marie (or Henrietta Maria to the English) was grudgingly approved by the king in late 1624. He accepted, too, the need to send English soldiers, under Buckingham, to the continent in defence of his daughter and son-in-law's Lower Palatinate.

This was one of James's final acts. In the spring of 1625, his declining health took a turn for the worse. He had been plagued for some years now with bad legs and feet (probably as a result of frequent riding accidents, given the amount of time he spent avoiding London and decamping to his hunting lodges). After a series of mini-strokes, he suffered a final, fatal one. Buckingham's attempts to cure him, which later took on a sinister complexion, did not help. King James died, surrounded by divines, on 27 March. He was fifty-eight.

James's legacy in England was of peace (broken only by the outbreak of the Thirty Years' War). Although he had been at loggerheads with his English Parliaments on multiple occasions, he had been able always to avert any outright conflict (which neither monarch nor members of either House wanted). In terms of witch-craft, though he had overseen a widening of the law to allow the death penalty for crimes which had previously escaped it, he had also used his understanding of elite, modern conceptions of demonology to encourage high standards of evidence. In this, his natural bent for scholasticism had been a boon. On the other hand, confessions, often claimed as freely given (but probably extracted by hideous treat-ment), remained the gold standard, whilst evidence of demonic pacts in the form of devil's marks took on ever greater significance.

In time, his 1604 Witchcraft Act and his own writings were wielded by others who had very different motivations from the king, who had always been a believer in 'genuine' witchcraft, if only it could be proven to his satisfaction. The legal machinery existed, and it only awaited someone to really turn the crank. As a result, England would, soon enough, endure persecutions which would have left James reeling. Accusations of political sorcery, which might in some cases have been based on genuine consultations between notable figures and charlatans, remained lively – and though these had not been to the king's taste, they would continue. During James's last year, indeed, reports had reached the government that the late Queen Elizabeth was being slandered as 'a whore and a witch' and it was being said of the much-lamented Prince Henry that 'before his body was cold on earth, his soul was frying on a gridiron in hell'.[6] Soon political allegations of sorcery would engulf the seemingly untouchable Buckingham.

James's legacy in Scotland, a country he had had a curious mix of affection for and suspicion of, was equally complicated. He left behind a working legal system whereby a complainant might raise a witchcraft accusation locally, generally to Kirk Sessions, with local authorities investigating (perhaps via illegal torture) before sending for a commission – vetted by the diocesan bishop – to try those named (or occasionally sending the accused to Edinburgh for trial). Central authorities – the Privy Council – might issue the commis-sion and the matter could be dealt with: the witch or witches would either be convicted or acquitted. But James had demonstrated the power of these central authorities to escalate matters: to turn isolated cases, sometimes of multiple people, into hunts, either local or national, and depending on the enthusiasm of authorities or the names of those the alleged witches accused. To both nations, he bequeathed a firm belief in elite attitudes to witchcraft: the reality of the phenomenon, the centrality of the devil's role, and the necessity of finding reliable proof of that role. The latter would see ever more grotesque means of evidence-gathering as witch fever gripped Britain, and this was a result of the king's drive to educate his people in new continental ideas.

Yet the idea that James had been an evil persecutor or malicious monster, however tempting, should be resisted as unfair and ahistorical. He was, by the standards of contemporary educated opinion, in the vanguard of the fight against evil. Those who denied the reality of witchcraft were dangerous at worst and the equivalent of modern flat earth enthusiasts at best. James was, however, prey to extreme biases, both in his differing attitudes to Scotland and England and in his increased credulity when accusations of witchcraft tended towards conspiracy against himself. As this complex, idealistic, flawed, well-meaning king was laid to rest in Westminster Abbey, the worst was yet to come in Scotland as well as England.

PART IV

Possession

'These are the statutes and judgments which ye shall observe to do in the land, which the Lord God of thy fathers giveth thee to possess it, all the days that ye live upon the earth'

– Deuteronomy 12:1–7
King James Version (KJV) 1611

15

Lambs to the Slaughter

In 1628, the late King James's physician-in-extraordinary (that is, a physician over and above the usual complement), William Harvey, published his *de Motu Cordis*: a treatise which put forward a revolutionary conception of the circulation of the blood. It was not immediately accepted but rather greeted with scorn. It went against ancient beliefs, drawn from Galen and Aristotle, about blood being produced in the liver via food digestion and flowing centrifugally through the veins to nourish the body. In time, of course, Harvey was proven a pioneer of the circulatory system. In time, too, his views on witchcraft – reached via his usual method of experimentation and observation – inclined towards the sceptical, not least when in 1634 he discovered a woman who truly believed herself a witch, possessed of a familiar: a toad.[1] This animal he confiscated, dissected (causing the woman to attempt to assault him), and found to be a perfectly normal toad. He thus proved two things, albeit, once again, to no great immediate notice: witchcraft was nonsense, and people really were attempting to practise it (or to fool others into believing they were, presumably for financial gain).

For the moment, 1628 was to prove a year of death as well as discovery. The new king, Charles I, was on the throne but he was not finding the English system, which required the consent of an increasingly outspoken Parliament in granting subsidies, any easier to accept than his father had done. From his days as a sickly child, Charles had grown into a vigorous, active young man, but he had inherited James's views on the divinity of monarchy, as well as a co-terminous preference for absolutism and the Duke of Buckingham.

Buckingham, who crested a wave of popularity in the late king's reign thanks to his support for English involvement in a godly Protestant war, had lost his lustre. This was due to his inept handling of naval affairs, which had been his due as Lord High Admiral and which he had intended to be the jewel in his ducal coronet. Instead, his military blunders had mounted up and, in 1626, he was being openly denounced for 'intermeddling with the great affairs of state'.[2] Parliament would give the king no money until the duke was removed, much to Charles's disgust. More dangerously, that same Parliament, the second of Charles's reign (the first having achieved the unhappy moniker of the 'Useless Parliament'), began the process of impeaching Buckingham: a medieval method of removing an unpopular royal servant which, ironically, Charles and Buckingham had revived under James (who had, at the time, presciently warned them, 'You are making a rod with which you will be scourged yourself').[3] Buckingham had cause to panic. Not was only his military reputation in tatters, but his godly reputation was in jeopardy.

This he seems to have realised even before James's death. In February 1625, he had launched a campaign against his sister-in-law, Viscountess Purbeck (the daughter of Sir Edward Coke, who had been forcibly married to Buckingham's mentally unstable brother). Lady Purbeck had, understandably, begun an affair (with Sir Robert Howard), which had resulted in a child. Buckingham had been keen in early 1625 to see her tried by the High Commission (the English Church's highest court) not only for adultery but for witchcraft, alleging that she had used sorcery on both him and his brother. This was pure deflection. Buckingham himself had been consulting with magicians of the Simon Forman variety, probably seeking magical protection for himself and his family (but possibly also seeking to destroy the careers of his many enemies). In doing so, he suggested that a pair of notorious wizards, John Lambe and Humphrey Frodsham, might be called to give evidence against his sister-in-law; they admitted she had hired them in her evildoing. This was revealing. Buckingham was supplying the names of men with whom he himself had had dealings.

It was information such as this which was to feed into the duke's downfall. In 1626 there appeared a pamphlet titled *The Fore-Runner of Revenge*, written by one of James's physicians, George Eglinton, which alleged that Buckingham had poisoned his sovereign. This was untrue, although the duke's actions – and those of his mother, who had been made Countess of Buckingham in her own right – certainly looked suspicious. The pair had inserted their own unqualified medic into the royal bedchamber and had him brew up dubious plasters and syrups which had appeared to cause the king to decline. These allegations added heat to the anti-Buckingham air, which only grew more febrile throughout the year. On 15 June, Charles dissolved the Parliament before it, and Buckingham's archenemy the ornery Earl of Bristol, could touch his adviser. The king had failed to ensure that his second summoning of the institution would be less hostile than the first.

What he had achieved, however, was a momentary pause. Charles was in an unenviable position. His new wife, Henrietta Maria, had arrived in England in 1625 and, though they would eventually form a remarkably deep and loving bond, frostiness at first marked their relationship. Despite the queen's initial popularity, her ardent Catholicism soon made her a target for invective, and thus the king had both a wife and a chief adviser under fire. On top of this, the war with Spain, which his father had resisted but which he and Buckingham had championed, was still ongoing, still expensive, and still costing lives and money – and war with France beckoned, to the queen's horror. He had also inherited the late king's financial woes and the English reliance on Parliament to alleviate them. Thus it was that he was induced to call the third sitting of the new reign in January 1628. By this time, verses against Buckingham were endemic, with the most famous reading, 'Who rules the kingdom? The king. Who rules the king? The duke. Who rules the duke? The devil!' Further, Charles had made himself deeply unpopular in the wake of the previous failed Parliament by raising a forced loan, thus bypassing MPs entirely for the sake of a single, admittedly necessary, cash injection into the war chest.

The 1628 Parliament made no bones about its intentions, tabling a Petition of Right, which would make clear the institution's rights and liberties and defang the king's evident desire to rule as an absolutist. Charles prevaricated, refusing to grace the Petition with any more than his royal word (which MPs were loath to accept). When the attacks on Buckingham grew hotter, he eventually gave in, assenting to the Petition of Right. If direct assaults on the duke were constantly stymied by the king, however, there were other means available to his enemies. In June, one was found: the taking of his magician, Dr John Lambe.

Lambe was, by repute, a conjurer, a wizard or a mountebank. He boasted of having the power to undo the effects of witchcraft, to find lost or stolen property, and to summon spirits. The last two were in themselves illegal, but he, like a good many others, seems to have been hedged by elite support of and belief in his powers. It was this that protected him when he was accused of raping a child, Joan Seager, in 1627; despite being convicted and sentenced to death, a stay of execution gave him his liberty and allowed him to continue practising. Like any magician, Lambe also inspired fear, and popular report held him responsible for storm-raising: he had, allegedly, raised a whirlwind which whistled up and down the Thames in 1626. During this time, in the reign of Charles I, witchcraft, sorcery, and prophecy had begun to occupy a place in the popular imagination, which moved as easily from terror to macabre fascination. This was the era in which, for example, the legendary Ursula Southeil (circa 1488–1561) was resurrected as 'Mother Shipton', with embroidered tales of her terrifying appearance, soothsaying, and prophecies first appearing in print in 1641.

The repellent doctor – who was almost certainly a charlatan taking advantage of others' beliefs – left the Fortune Theatre in June 1628 and, as he picked his way through the streets of St-Giles-without-Cripplegate, he heard cries at his back: 'The duke's devil! The duke's devil!' The voices rose in pitch, volume, and number. A mob was forming. Lambe began to move more quickly, hopping over cobbles, sewer channels, and muck until he reached a cookshop. Here, he imperiously commanded a guard of sailors – no doubt his master,

Buckingham's – to protect him. He settled down to eat. Outside, the clamour rose. The mob thronged the shop, banging on walls and crying for justice against this devil who had escaped it in his avoidance of punishment for rape. Plucking up his courage, Lambe attempted to brazen it out, stepping out with his guard and fleeing southeast to Lothbury. A hail of dirt and stones rained down on his back. As he neared the Windmill Tavern, the pursuers reached him, thrust aside his guard, and beat him to the ground. Lambe was punched, crushed, and kicked until one of his eyes burst. The mob retreated, leaving the supposed magician bleeding on the ground. He died within hours.

Buckingham's wizard was dead – and the royal adviser, who was busily preparing for his next military venture, soon followed. Rumours and prophecies swirled in the days leading up to it. In August, he was planning an expedition to La Rochelle and staying in the Greyhound in Portsmouth with his wife, Katherine (formerly Katherine Manners, whose family had accused the Flower women of witchcraft and saw them to the gallows). There, a former officer called John Felton followed him, armed with a hastily bought dagger. On the 23rd, as Buckingham rose from his breakfast, Felton walked up and stabbed him in the chest, uttering the words, 'God have mercy on thy soul!' Blood gushed from the duke's mouth and panic rose – amongst it could be heard the duchess's screams – as an unashamed Felton volunteered himself as the assassin.

Charles, at his prayers when the news reached him, took the news calmly, finishing his orisons before retiring to his bedchamber to weep. To him, it seemed a brother had been murdered. Felton would be tried and executed, protesting that he had acted independently. King Charles, however, was convinced that, despite the outpouring of rejoicing the duke's death had caused, the assassin had been part of a tight-knit political conspiracy; it was inconceivable to him that any private man might simply have hated Buckingham and all he stood for enough to kill him. In this, the king misunderstood his people, as he not infrequently would.

*

If Charles could not understand the universal English hatred for Buckingham, he could also not understand his Scottish subjects. Despite being a Dunfermline lad, he had been raised as an Englishman and shared his father's Anglophilia and belief in High Church aesthetics, being if anything more episcopalian. This extended to following James in attempting to anglicise Scotland, but he did this without much skill and with unintended results. It was in 1628 that he introduced circuit courts in his northern kingdom. In theory, these revived the old justice ayres which had been held under earlier Stuarts (including not just Mary Queen of Scots but the Regent Moray); in practice, the new courts were modelled on English travelling courts, with judges on the move, presiding over courtrooms in groups of sheriffdoms.[4] Indictments (or dittays) would be invited from local notables in the sheriffdoms and, the Scots being thoroughly educated in the dangers of witchcraft by the old king, flurries of complaints arrived – so many, in fact, that the episcopal screening process was overwhelmed. Further, King Charles had removed Court of Session judges from their *ex officio* seats on the Privy Council (which thus lost measured, legally minded heads) in favour of bishops. The bishops, naturally, were fewer in number than judges. This resulted in a leaner and, as it turned out, meaner Council, in addition to stoking religious and political tensions. In debates on the matter, which took place at Whitehall with Scottish councillors, the king remained stiff-necked, ill-at-ease, and rigid in his demands.

These changes had unexpected and certainly unintended results. As the circuit courts offered a new forum for complaint, so complaints rose – including complaints about witchcraft. This was first evident in East Lothian, where applications were made for three commissions, granted to local notables, to try thirteen women from Prestonpans (though only one, Janet Boyd, was definitely executed). Two more commissions, to try four more women, followed. Thus far, these must have appeared relatively normal: complaints were being raised and dealt with. Yet the applications for commissions did not stop.

In September, bailies Alexander Turnbull and Archibald Weddel sought and were granted the right to try two women, and in December they were given a commission to try two more. Yet another pair of accused witches, in Borthwick and Newbattle, were tried for murderous witchcraft for allegedly having caused the 2nd Earl of Lothian to commit suicide. This would ruffle feathers in the gilded ministerial cage in Edinburgh; the women not only confessed to the requisite demonism but were under suspicion of causing the deaths of their betters. In Scotland, the names and quality of those involved, whether accused of being witches or alleged victims, mattered – and, as on the continent, anyone might be caught up in the widening circles of a hunt. In November, the Catholic George Seton, 3rd Earl of Winton, was granted a general commission to examine suspects (though not to try them), probably as part of his effort to demonstrate he was as conscientious in combating the imagined and imaginary common enemy as his Calvinist peers. It was, evidently, time for a crackdown.

A purge, of the type recently begun in Würzburg under Catholic Prince-Bishop Philipp Adolf von Ehrenberg, was underway, and it extended over a fairly widespread eastern area. Although it must have started with individual complaints, much depended on the enthusiasm of those seeking the commissions and those in the Privy Council granting them. Accusation by upright citizens or other witches could lead to arrest – with confession, as in England, remaining the goal of hunters. Searches for the devil's mark might then provide fool-proof evidence.

The women (and some men) brought in were, undoubtedly, treated inhumanely, probably denied sleep, and possibly tortured more directly. The results were confessions of demonic activity (in some cases with the devil appearing as a 'black dog' or a 'black man', and who always sought pacts when he appeared), murder, enchantment, and lists of names, which in turn brought in more accused. This was certainly the case in Dalkeith, from which accusations spread to embrace Haddington and on to Berwick. It is impossible to say how much was entirely produced via torture and how much had any basis in truth (of attempts at magic and witchcraft, that is), but occasionally there are telling glimpses.

Sara Keith, for example, was a beggar tried on 17 February 1629, following an earlier commission to examine her. She confessed to occasional healing and harming and a great deal of demonic activity, having sold her soul to the devil in the pursuit of revenge against a man who had deprived her of her late father's fortune. She admitted meeting with Satan at Michaelmas in 1628, whereupon she asked him what would happen if a hunt should occur (this betraying contemporary knowledge that occasionally the government would crack down, and an acknowledgement that when it happened it was unusual); he told her to deny everything. Sara further confessed that later the devil had raped her and requested a gift. She had promised him her six-month-old son. Satan then returned months later and whisked the child away, leaving a sickly, deformed changeling in his place. In this unusual (in confessions) story, we see what was probably the truth of Sara's history: she had been desperately poor and possibly felt she'd been defrauded, had possibly been raped (she mentions Satan appearing to her on one occasion as a 'fine gentleman'), and had had a child with some form of deformity or illness. It is perforce speculation, but these might have been the nuggets of truth in an otherwise fanciful tale born of fear or agony.

The 1628 hunt lasted, in various areas, until 1631, with varying degrees of scepticism. Some Kirk Sessions either declined to pursue accusations or punished false ones, whilst some members of the Privy Council – effectively Scotland's governing body in the time of an absentee king who had little knowledge of the country and extensive problems in his southern realm – actively promoted persecution. Although councillors might only personally examine a minority of accused (as King James had done), their willingness to be involved, and to grant commissions, betrays an active interest at the top. As Julian Goodare notes, 'The fact that there were far more cases during the panic, and that the commissions were duly granted, shows that the local elites and the Privy Council were *both* caught up in [it].'⁵ As in King James's time, wide-scale purges resulted when there came a perfect storm of elites, legal machinery, and common people (whether genuinely suspicious, eager to please authorities or display their obedience to the law, terrified lest they might be accused themselves, malicious, or acting for personal gain) able to feed names to investigators. It would be an exposure of the cynically opportunistic that fed into the petering out of the panic, albeit it arose from abuse of the system amongst witch-hunters at the local elite level.

James Mowat, Berwick's Sheriff-Clerk, drew out depositions from a vagabond called Alexander Hamilton, charged with using witchcraft to kill Lady Ormiston, wife to Sir George Cockburn of Ormiston, who had supposedly turned him away from Penkaet Castle. Hamilton had then fled into northern England before being recovered, after which he confessed to Mowat that he had been in the devil's service for five years but had not received the tell-tale mark. He admitted, too, to raising a flood to drown Mowat, and in this he had been assisted by a slew of named accomplices. Further, he confessed that there were designs against Sir George Home of Manderston (who had been curiously active in gaining the Privy Council's permission in recovering and seizing Hamilton). According to Hamilton, Home's wife had hired an English witch, John Neil, to kill her husband, as well as consulting Satan herself.

Hamilton's infamy had already drawn attention, and the alleged witch was ordered to be dealt with more centrally – indeed, Home had waylaid him so that Mowat could interrogate him privately. In the course of the ensuing investigation, it emerged that his confessions had been tampered with by Mowat, acting on the behalf of the avaricious Home of Manderston, who wished to be rid of his wealthy wife (with whom he was engaged in a property dispute). Tellingly, the Council remained more interested in the veracity of Hamilton's mass accusations of having conspired with other witches than his having been forced to make false confessions. Alexander Hamilton claimed again, at the last, that all his confessions save those touching Lady Manderston had been true, and he received the death penalty. The Manderstons continued in their unhappy marriage, and Home continued making witchcraft accusations against others. John Neil was captured and investigated in the course of events, whilst Mowat was briefly imprisoned, his reputation as a local hunter in ruins. Amid a welter of complaints about treatment by men like Mowat, the Privy Council cut back on its granting of commissions, returning to routine issuances for discrete cases, which had continued throughout the purge (with Jonet Rendall, for example, being strangled and burned in Kirkwall in 1629 for confessing to keeping a familiar called Walliman after making a pact with Satan).

King Charles did not understand Scotland as his father had (even if James's understanding had been hopelessly jaundiced), though in his defence he did insist on having his much-delayed Scottish coronation in 1633, at which he received a lavish reception rich in pageantry, including a celebration of the New World in the form of a woman in 'Olive coloured maske, long blacke Locks waving over her backe, her attyre . . . of divers coloured feathers, which shew her to bee an American, and to represent new Scotland'.[6] Nevertheless, within four years the country was in uproar – not over witches, but over the new Prayer Book which the king had his resolutely High Church Archbishop of Canterbury, William Laud, draw up, and which he tried to enforce in Scotland. Orchestrated opposition followed across the nation, resulting in the National Covenant of 1638, which was framed as a contract between the Scottish people and God, the former pledging to lead virtuous, godly – and very much reformist – lives. If there were lessons to be learned from the unexpected witchcraft panic – about not meddling in Scottish affairs without sound knowledge of them – Charles I had failed to notice.

If Scotland had experienced its early Caroline witch panic, England was soon to gain an injection of scepticism. The new monarch's southern kingdom was already showing itself to be experiencing an age of decorum over exuberant excess, graceful falling bands over cartwheel ruffs, and conflict over peace. And Charles had resolved, following the 1628 Parliament's dissolution in 1629, to rule without the ancient body, finding cash by whatever alternative means the constitution allowed (or could be interpreted to allow).

In 1634, William Harvey, of the radical thinking on blood circulation, was called in by Charles to investigate cases arising in Lancashire. That county, as it had in 1612, was proving problematic; twenty people were accused of witchcraft at the Lancaster assizes in March. As in 1612, the star witness was a child, eleven-year-old Edmund Robinson, and seventeen were found guilty. Unsure of whether to have the sentences carried out, the judges appealed to the king, who had the child sent to London for examination. Evidently, English legal authorities were not using confessions and accusations to fuel hunts, the system of justice being different from Scotland; they were referring matters to their resident monarch when they felt them serious enough. It was swiftly established that Edward was a fraud. Further, four of the accused women were brought south to be examined by an expert panel led by William Harvey in his role as royal physician. He found no evidence of any devil's mark and the quartet was quickly pardoned. However, the charges against the alleged witches (which included the murder of one Isabel Nutter) were evidently too strong to overturn their convictions, and those found guilty were kept in gaol (including the four pardoned women, who were to remain locked up until they had repaid the cost of their imprisonment). Among them was listed one Jennet Device: very probably the same Jennet Device who had helped send her brother, James, and sister, Alizon, to the gallows in 1612. Thomas Heywood and Richard Brome found fit material for their *The Late Lancashire Witches*, which incorporated shapeshifting into cats and the feeding of familiars with blood.

James VI and I had been an autocrat, but he'd had the wit and political instinct to match imperiousness to the moment and, when the situation called for it, to present himself as an avuncular patriarch. Charles I, though a gentle, loving family man, appeared by contrast a cold fish. Worse, his rigidity could scarcely be masked, and his attempts at political guile and duplicity were not camouflaged by public charm. His statecraft thus appeared to his enemies, who sought any political capital against him, like transparent double-dealing. His reign was shortly to descend into chaos, as he was forced to summon Parliament after eleven years of personal rule (which, admittedly, had been stable and certainly artistically vibrant), partly to fund the struggles against his rebellious Scottish kingdom.

Conflict erupted immediately, leading to dissolution after three weeks. Further armed victories by the Scottish Covenanters forced him to summon a second Parliament in 1640. The outlook was no better. Staunch English Protestants were disgusted at their monarch's war on fellow Protestants north of the border and no more in favour of Charles's Catholic-looking High Church leanings than the Scots. The king found himself pressured to lose another chief adviser, this time the 1st Earl of Strafford, whose death warrant Charles was forced to sign.

The following year, in 1641, Ireland, which Strafford had once brutalised, broke out in revolt, whilst the king made a show of acceding to Scottish Covenanter demands (something he did not intend to make good on in the long term). On a roll, Parliament presented its famous Grand Remonstrance, first proposed by MP John Pym: it listed grievances relating to the king's financial, religious, and foreign policies, demanded the expulsion of bishops from Parliament, and gave the institution the right to veto Crown appointments. Charles refused it, astutely attempting to win less radical parliamentarians to his side. There was, however, no hope of reconciliation; king and Parliament were headed for collision. Although, to his credit, Charles attempted to make concessions, the truth was that his political enemies were prepared to make none – and on the fundamental issues of sovereignty there could be no lasting rapprochement. The point of no return came when Charles attempted to swoop on the House of Commons to arrest Pym and four other radical leaders. Forewarned, the men had already left. The king left too, departing London to raise an army and leaving Parliament to declare its own authority. The first English Civil War was about to be added to the Bishops' Wars (which the Scottish conflicts had become known as) and the Irish Confederate Wars in the ongoing, politico-religious Wars of the Three Kingdoms.

By anyone's measure, Charles had proven a perfectly nice man –
at least to his friends and family – but an incompetent king, which
three kingdoms in religious turmoil could not afford. It was his great
misfortune that, in attempting to negotiate a settlement with
Parliament, he met an institution controlled by men even more
inflexible and unwilling to make concessions than he was. In his
defence, he had not been an ardent witch-hunter, albeit his ill-
considered handling of Scottish affairs had inadvertently helped
along a hunt. In the tumultuous decade that followed his calling of
his last Parliament – a decade of conflict – England would see its
first witch panic. At its heart was a man greatly inspired by the theological reasoning and evidentiary methods of the old king but,
unlike James, entirely cynical and self-seeking. The Witch-Finder
General was about to leave his own devil's mark on history.

16

The Witch-Finder General

In March 1645, a young man in his twenties was busy listening in on conversations in the little town of Manningtree, Essex.[1] Suspicion rose, as it rose easily in everyone at the time. These were unsettled days. Great Britain and Ireland had been plunged into war. Religion – the future of England's soul – lay at the mercy of crossed swords: only King Charles's or those of the English Parliament could be victorious. God looked, at present, to be on the side of Parliament. The beleaguered King Charles kept a court in exile at Oxford and fought for control of his kingdoms and his genuinely felt faith and method of worship, but his enemies were combining against him. Scotland's National Covenant of 1638 had been replaced, by radicals, with 1643's Solemn League and Covenant, which pressed for the institution of a perfectly reformed Presbyterian system of ecclesiastical and civil government across Britain – a system which appealed to Puritanical English minds. The Scottish Covenanters, natural allies to the Parliamentarians, had ended the Royalists' Siege of Newcastle in August 1644. Parliamentarians had scored a victory, rich in symbolic if not strategic value, at Newbury in October of that year, and this itself had followed the loss to the Royalists of much of southeast England in the battle of Cheriton. With Scots and Parliamentarians in league, the smart money was on ultimate Parliamentarian victory – and if there was one thing Matthew Hopkins knew, as he eavesdropped in Essex, it was money.

But the woman Hopkins listened in on – and, in truth, we have only his word that he did any such thing – was not talking about money or war. She was supposedly talking to her familiars, sending them to meet a fellow witch. Hopkins had read King James's *Daemonologie* and, living as he did in prime Parliamentarian country, he could see the financial opportunities inherent in helping to produce a godly society. This was an apt time: soon enough, the newssheet *The Parliaments Post* would be reporting that 'there is an infection in wickedness; and the spirit of the Cavillers because it could not prevaile with our men, hath met with some of our women, and it hath turned them into Witches'.[2] In 1643, the publication of *A most certain, strange, and true discovery of a witch* told the tale of a woman, probably a suspected Royalist, summarily shot by foraging Parliamentarians on being discovered dancing and walking across a river at Newbury on a plank of wood.

Hopkins was, like many of his time, a rank opportunist. He had been born to a clergyman of Puritan leanings, James Hopkins, of Great Wenham in Suffolk, and had possibly spent time in Amsterdam, where he learned a little maritime law whilst articled to a Mistley ship-owner. This allowed him to return to England with a veneer of learning and polish, and to set up as a minor legal clerk in Mistley. In this role, he crossed paths with an Essex landowner in his thirties, John Stearne, who also had an interest in witchcraft. Stearne took Hopkins on and together they tested a new business venture. Hiring staff – including Goodwife (then a courtesy title below the higher-status Mistress or Mrs) Mary Philips – they offered their services in investigating accusations of witchcraft made in Manningtree and, for a fee, would prove or disprove the veracity of the allegations.

In this they were not lucky but, again, opportunistic. The eighty-year-old, one-legged Elizabeth Clarke (alias Bedinfield), generally known as 'Mother Clark', had been accused by a neighbour, John Rivet, of cursing his wife. She had subsequently been taken up by the people of the town, who insisted that Sir Harbottle Grimstone, 1st Baronet, an MP in the 'Long Parliament' (called by Charles in 1640 and never dissolved), investigate her. He accepted the need for a trial – but if it were to go in the accusers' favour, a confession would be needed. Stearne seized upon the case, with Hopkins as his aide. Their aim was not to disprove the allegation – quite the opposite.

By studying the methods by which various witch-hunters had drawn confessions from accused people across the decades, and by studying such texts as *Daemonologie*, they were able to refine their own methods of torture. Chief amongst these was sleep deprivation, which had probably been in use unofficially, in England and Scotland, for many years. To further push the old woman, she was continually watched and her body searched for the devil's mark (which yielded three 'teats') which Stearne and Hopkins's assistants, known as 'prickers', could jab to test their sensitivity. This had, after all, been one of King James's definitive sources of evidence, and interest in spirituality and the body remained lively, thanks to the runaway success of *Religio Medici* (1642), in English *The Religion of a Doctor*. But new methods were also pioneered: the suspect would be forced to sit in an uncomfortable position on a stool for hours, bound with cords if necessary. This would be done in a small room with only one opening allowed; if those watching her spotted any insects which then dared evade them, these were construed as familiars. Used also was the process of walking the witch. This involved forcing a suspect to walk ceaselessly until her feet blistered.

Elizabeth could not endure this barbarous treatment for long. She not only confessed to possessing a menagerie of familiars: Holt (a white kitten), Jarmara (a fat spaniel with no legs); Vinegar Tom (a grey-hound with an ox's head, who could transform into a headless four-year-old child); Sack-and-Sugar (a black rabbit); and Newes (a polecat). Some of these Hopkins claimed to have actually seen conjured up. Additionally, the old woman admitted she knew sundry other witches, who kept similar rosters of imps: 'Elemanzer, Pyewacket, Peckin the Crown, Grizzel, Greedigut,' which, he boasted, 'no mortall could invent'.[3] Dozens of women were named, some from Manningtree and some from other nearby villages, with the town's Anne West accused of being the one who had inducted Elizabeth into witchcraft. Thereafter, she and her fellow witches had supposedly attended weekly conventicles, always on Friday nights:

this was Hopkins's own twist on the night-time assembly so much feared by earlier authorities.

The litany of names was exactly what the witch-hunters had hoped for. Their net had widened and their services – torture, essentially, carried out by experts – was in greater demand. Those arrested on the strength of Elizabeth's confessions were probably subjected to the swimming ordeal (which Stearne alleged, perhaps honestly, that the witches preferred to detention) in addition to sleep deprivation and the cruel searches, watches (undertaken by what were now known as the hunters' professional 'watchers'), and pricking. It might have been this particular treatment that led one accused, Bridget Mayers, to admit to keeping a familiar in the form of a mouse called Prick-ears. Corroborating evidence was found in the form of neighbours' memories of odd or tragic experiences (one man, the wealthy gentle-man Richard Edwards, recalling he had heard a polecat cry before falling from his horse – which would become evidence of a familiar's demonic activity at the behest of his mistress; another decided that his infant daughter's death had been suspicious).

Here, the genius of the witch-finders is evident: Hopkins and Stearne knew how to exploit personal disputes and local prejudices to drive up accusations, encouraging memories back years and decades to turn up any bits of recalled potential devilry or witch-craft. Clergymen, too, would be brought in and invited to provide their own testimony against the witches. Rebecca West, accused by old Elizabeth along with her mother, Anne (who had a historically poor reputation), confessed to Hopkins that she had been wed to Satan, and, to save her own life, she offered to become a witness for the prosecution. To buttress their evidence, the witch-hunters called in a panel of female experts (including Frances Mills and Grace Norman) to verify their discoveries. The accused women went to trial in Chelmsford in July 1645, with most women accused of having murdered via witchcraft, others having admitted, under the hunters' horrific treatment, to causing injury to property or death to people and livestock (in the Wests' case, as part of a feud with a rival family, the Harts) or to have kept familiar spirits.

In all, fifty indictments against thirty-six suspects were prepared for Robert Rich, 2nd Earl of Warwick, who presided at the trial. Nine people, however, died as a result of their treatment. Nineteen were found guilty and executed on the basis of their confessions: garbled accounts of consorting with animal familiars, copulation with Satan, and, in at least one case, flying. Two, including Rebecca West, escaped the horror – Rebecca probably due to her youth. In the course of their first hunt, the witch-hunters had faced opposition: Stearne, for example, noted that they had been opposed by a man (sadly unidentified) who laboured to keep one alleged witch 'from her legal trial'.[4] This fellow had also apparently threatened the hunters 'and all that had given evidence against her'. Yet, on the whole, the venture had been a success.

At this stage, it is worth giving a charitable interpretation of the hunters' behaviour. As Alan Macfarlane pointed out in his invaluable *Witchcraft in Tudor and Stuart England*, 'The usual motive ascribed to them is greed . . . but the suggestion that they started looking for witches because they were impecunious . . . appears to have no factual basis.'[5] This is true. It is true also that no evidence of any particular religious fervour on either man's part exists. Macfarlane's suggestion that they were motivated by 'curiosity, bewilderment, and anxiety, with a desire to exercise power and perform a useful public duty' is, even if it can be accepted as the motivation of their early ventures, undermined by their subsequent willingness to sell their self-taught professional services. Hopkins and Stearne did not accuse witches, to be sure, but, like certain authorities in Scotland, they turned the handle of the legal machinery (to its limits, in their use of torture) and thereby escalated local accusations into mass trials. As Hopkins later claimed to have seen things – magical familiars – he could not possibly have seen in order to justify his actions, we can dispense with the idea that he was acting wholly in good faith. England's most infamous local purge, whatever the motives behind the initial accusations around East Anglia, cannot be called an unreservedly godly pursuit in terms of the celebrated witch-hunter's involvement.

It was after the Chelmsford assizes that Hopkins appears to have begun presenting himself to the world as an authorised and commissioned witch-finder, which role poet Samuel Butler would say he claimed (though no evidence survives to prove anything of the sort) to have procured from Parliament. His business had certainly reached the institution, however; Parliament convened a special commission of oyer and terminer (managed by jurist John Godbolt) to examine the confessions produced by Hopkins's methods and oversee proceedings. One of its first acts was to condemn, probably fruitlessly, the use of swimming as a trial, probably not only for its barbarity but because some influential believers, like the author William Perkins, had questioned its efficacy.[6] Nevertheless, the association with officialdom, played up by Hopkins, rather smacks of what would now be called a branding exercise (even if his best-known title, 'The Witch-Finder General', seems to have attached itself to him only via the frontispiece of his later book). Even before the assizes had concluded, Hopkins was off. His fame – and it was certainly fame at first, rather than infamy – preceded him as he toured. There was, quite simply, demand for his services, which were billed as being what the late king had demanded: the production of material evidence which would uncover genuine witches. His journey took him and Stearne, by now the junior partner, to Bury St Edmunds in Suffolk.

Here, the Witch-Finder General assisted in investigating over a hundred suspects already rounded up. The most famous amongst them was the unpopular clergyman John Lowes, a suspected Royalist disliked in his community for long, bromidic sermons. Hopkins's team, now six-strong, intended to make him talk. The seventy-year-old John did, having been kept awake for days and forced not just to walk but to run up and down a room for hours at a time. In a fog of pain and delirium, he duly confessed to having made a pact with Satan, suckled familiars (Tom, Flo, Bess, and Mary), maimed cattle, and raised a storm to sink a ship of Harwich (with the authorities apparently making no effort to discover whether any such ship had been lost). Though he retracted his confession, John hanged.

Hopkins also induced one woman to confess to murdering her husband – a crime of petty treason which resulted in her burning rather than hanging. In all, eighteen people were hanged for witchcraft, sixteen of them women. The next sitting of the court, delayed by Royalist troop movements, featured dozens more condemnations (although it is less clear how many were hanged, with around seventy being a contemporary estimate).

Hopkins thereafter travelled to Great Yarmouth (at the invitation of the local authorities). In September, eleven people were tried, with some (including a man named Mark Prynne, accused of causing death by bewitchment in addition to using magic to find the lost hat of another accused, John Sparke) going free. One of those acquitted, Maria Verey, was accused – in language very close to Hopkins's preferred wording – of entertaining and feeding devils. Five women were hanged.

By this time, the activities of the Witch-Finder General were as lucrative as they were popular. He and his team concentrated their work in Norfolk and Suffolk, visiting such towns as Aldeburgh where, again, local demand to sort the guilty from the innocent was high. From a purely business perspective, there was greater capital in ensuring a mix of both: too many guilty bred fear, whilst too many innocent threatened future business, as non-believers might begin to proliferate. Thus far, although there had been voices of doubt and eyebrows raised about the activities of the witch-hunters (particularly in the Suffolk mass trials), Hopkins had been able to point to local demand – good Protestants wanted a godly society – as justification.

Yet the real threat to the Witch-Finder General came in the spring of 1646, when Hopkins took his team into Huntingdonshire. There, an Oxford- and Cambridge-educated local clergyman, John Gaule, who resented the professional witch-hunters, preached openly against them. Hopkins was able to force him to retract his potentially inflammatory sermon, but Gaule then renewed his efforts, publishing his *Select Cases of Conscience touching Witches and Witchcraft*. Provocatively, he dedicated it to MP Valentine Wauton, one of the regicides of Charles I and a significant figure in the Parliamentarian movement (whose name could therefore lend authority to the anti-Hopkins tract).

Gaule was, however, not a non-believer; indeed, he believed wholeheartedly in witchcraft. What he objected to were the standards of evidence Hopkins and his ilk were producing. In this, he fell somewhere between King James and the new hunters. He shared the late king's beliefs about superstitious, silly beliefs not being witchcraft (in addition to dividing high magic from low), yet denied James's acceptance of swimming witches; he shared Hopkins's claim that circumstantial evidence was permissible but denied his methods of interrogating every unfortunate old person who fell in his path. In every parish, he wrote in disgust, 'every old woman with a wrinkled face, a furr'd brow, a hairy lip, a gobber tooth, a squint eye, a squeaking voyce, or a scolding tongue, having a rugged coate on her back, a skullcap on her head, a spindle in her hand, and a Dog or Cat by her side; is not only suspected, but pronounced for a witch'.[7] This he could not tolerate. Though he accepted that devil's marks existed, he was sceptical, finding that those identified by the hunters 'are more false then [than] true' – true devil's marks, he argued, faded. On the subject of punishment, he hedged: 'True and reall Witches,' he argued, 'should bee truly and really punished, to true and real intents.' Like James, he thought confessions sufficient; but might not 'non-operative' witches be treated differently? As for witch-hunters, though he found the calling potentially godly and laudable, he left no doubt as to his feelings towards Hopkins and his clique: 'For I am not satisfied: that such an office ought to be taken upon them by any privat persons, as a Calling, Profession, occupation or Trade of Life.' If historians might doubt Hopkins's financial motives, at least one contemporary did not.

This heralded the beginning of the end of the Witch-Finder General's brief but bloody career. Doubting voices had turned him from a wandering hero into a sinister figure eager to inflict cruel and unusual punishment. He left his trade in the summer of 1646, his pockets bulging with gold extracted from numerous local authorities. Stearne, too, retired to publish his rejoinder to Gaule: *A Confirmation and Discovery of Witchcraft* (1648). Although legends – entirely untrue – emerged that Hopkins was himself accused of witchcraft and forced to endure the swimming test, in reality he died of illness in his home in Manningtree – the same home from which he'd claimed to have first overheard a witch speaking to her familiars – the following year. Although he had been active he had, thankfully, never had the cachet – or of course the power – in England that King James had had in Scotland, and so the southern kingdom, though it continued to have ill-reputed hotspots where people, not surprisingly, kept accusing one another, never saw quite the same level of widespread viciousness as those nations or territories which had been led from the top by avid hunters.

England's most famous witch-hunter, whose posthumous reputation was darker than it had ever been in his lifetime, was dead. Within two years, England's king – having lost the wars even after engaging with more moderate Scottish Covenanters (thereafter derisively known as the Engagers), whom he disingenuously promised he would help to enforce the Scottish faith south of the border – followed him to the grave. The English Parliament tried him for treason without recourse to the Scots, and Charles would leave his kingdoms to produce their own version of a godly society. No such society, as Scotland would soon demonstrate, could tolerate witches.

17

The Godly Society

On 30 January 1649, King Charles I of England, Scotland, and Ireland stepped out from a tall window at Whitehall and onto a scaffold. He was dressed, at his own request, in two shirts: a guard against the bitter cold, intended to stop him shivering and thus risk encouraging the silent, overawed crowds to think him fearful. The twin experiences of attempting to govern multiple nations, none of which seemed to accept his brand of religion (this despite it having been England's religion since the dawn of the Elizabethan era), and of waging war against his rebels had aged him: his fair hair and beard had greyed. With the dignity of his grandmother, Mary Queen of Scots, he accepted his fate even if he could not accept the legality of his death penalty. Unlike his grandmother, his head was severed with one blow of the axe. King Charles's nations, for the first time since the system had begun in them, was no longer a monarchy. But what they were, exactly, was still uncertain.

Rather than a time of despondency and gloom, this was a period of optimism and hope. Democrats hoped for a fairer system of representative government. Various shades of Puritan hoped that England might achieve what Scotland was tilting at: a theocracy. Royalists pinned their hopes on Charles's son, whom they recognised as Charles II, albeit that he was in exile on the continent. Indeed, the northern realm, whose alliance with England had broken down, took the step of proclaiming Charles II King of Great Britain (James's favoured name for the mainland), Ireland, and France in February 1649, on the condition that he do as his late father had promised and establish Presbyterianism as the official faith of all his kingdoms. Irish Royalists followed suit. The Rump

Parliament (composed of those remaining from Charles I's motheaten Long Parliament), by contrast, voted to abolish the monarchy, opting instead for an English Council of State.

Scotland was, at this time, ploughing on with its desire to design and enact a truly godly state. The country was firmly under the control of the radical Covenanters, the more moderate voices having disgraced themselves by engaging with the late King Charles, and all efforts were aimed at preserving and spreading the Covenant, which remained a means of spiritually and legally contracting those who lived under it to God. This meant that witches, who by now were accepted as having contracted themselves to Satan, were the natural enemy. On 1 February 1649, Scotland thus enacted a new Witchcraft Act. In essence, this affirmed the 1563 Act and sought to widen it to condemn to death any who 'doe yet dreame to themselffis impunity because consulters are not expresslie mentionat' in that Act (when, in truth, 'consulters' were indeed mentioned in the old Act – it had simply been the case that they'd rarely been targeted by authorities).[1] It was a muddled piece of legalese, written in response to pressure from the Kirk's General Assembly; the governing party – the Kirk Party – had its hands full at the time in trying to modulate all aspects of morality, from fornication to blasphemy to drunkenness to incest to sympathy with the Engagers (thought to have betrayed the Covenant). It was well placed to do so. Though it's a cliché to say religion and politics were intertwined, there is a great deal of truth in it – particularly in seventeenth-century Scotland. Religion played a greater role in people's everyday lives than did the secular government. Aside from confessional matters of belief, it had long been the Church that dictated hours for prayer and pleasure, that restricted or allowed certain diets. The Church, too, chose or rejected holidays and festivals; it provided social spaces and ejected from them – and thus shamed – those who failed to conform; it codified morality and immorality and wielded extensive legal powers over language and behaviour. It had long provided jobs for many, in local and national administrative and government posts. In the post-Reformation period, it also championed – or often claimed to champion – the rights and truth-based religious freedom of the people. Popular preachers, therefore, were not likely to be viewed as mad-eyed fanatics but as figures of trust and community gatekeepers.

Witchcraft was one aspect of life among several which were recognised as being a problem in the creation of the ideal society. In its efforts, the Scottish Parliament took on greater significance than ever before (as had England's Parliament), but it was joined in its activities by the General Assembly, which, when not sitting, retained power through the Kirk Commission. As the king's Privy Council no longer existed in any meaningful sense, a Committee of Estates appointed by Parliament was the new body tasked with issuing commissions for witchcraft trials. In all, the machinery of state was in evidence, and its goal was to purge Scotland of the ungodly.

Yet, in 1649, the government was evidently not doing enough. In June, a minister of the Presbytery of Stranraer, John Crookes, complained that the commissioners appointed to deal with multiple accused witches – Marion Shenon, Jeneat McKenon, Africt Blam, Marion Russell, and Isabel Biggam – were not showing themselves active. This was not Parliament's fault. Already, demands for commissions were becoming numerous. In January, cases were recorded in Cupar, Dunfermline, and Haddington. In February, one had been granted to try a Dunfermline brewer (who was acquitted) for witchcraft. Two more had been granted in March, and fifteen – a major jump – in May. Clearly, something had shifted the usual isolated cases into a higher gear.

The initial driver, this time, was Inverkeithing's Walter Bruce, a Kirk minister. Like Matthew Hopkins, he was a zealous witch-hunter who did not make accusations but determined to investigate them – but quite unlike Hopkins, Bruce was almost certainly motivated by religious zeal, albeit it spiced with a strong dose of ambition. Bruce's involvement stemmed from a complaint made against him in March, regarding the rectitude of his reciting prayers and delivering a sermon at the execution of an accused witch. The Presbytery informed him that all that was required of him was the securing of confessions. This was enough to motivate him. Soon, those confessions began naming other witches, who named other witches – in short, the snowball effect had begun; by July, Bruce had procured accusations against twenty-three people, who in turn named another nineteen. This inspired the usual anxiety from central authorities when one of those named was high profile: Margaret Henderson, Lady Pittadro, a daughter of one of the late King James's favourite courtiers, James Henderson of Fordell. Lady Pittadro had, supposedly, been the leader of a local group of witches, and she had complained directly to Satan about Walter Bruce, soliciting devilish vengeance on him for buying a house she had hoped to have.

Lady Pittadro, sensibly, fled. Unfortunately, she got only as far as Edinburgh, where she was promptly captured, arrested, and imprisoned in the Tolbooth. There, she died, either due to her treatment or by her own hand, in December 1649. The former is certainly possible. By this time, professional witch-prickers, such as Matthew Hopkins had employed, were setting up their businesses in Scotland (where they were sometimes known as 'brodders'), and Walter Bruce was happy to employ them. Sleep deprivation, too, was by now endemic in the interrogation process, and Bruce remained assiduous in his desire for results: in July 1649 he had complained to the Committee that the purge – and by now it was a purge – might be stalled, as in the past certain magistrates had objected to their wives being accused and interrogated. His complaint was upheld, to the chagrin of Robert Brown, who himself went to the Committee in defence of his wife, Marjorie Durie, who was being kept in Inverkeithing under suspicion and daily threatened with branding, whilst being denied visits from her family. Mercifully, this was acted on, and Marjorie was ordered to be removed from her squalid conditions and warded elsewhere. The querulous Bruce responded by escalating matters, until both he and Robert were brought before the Committee in September. The minister asserted, with aggrieved righteousness, that the devil's mark had been found on Marjorie and demanded that Robert pay for the cost of keeping her. Bruce won – although the Committee did order that torture be stopped in the Presbytery (an order that was probably not obeyed).

Professional prickers could certainly ply their trade in Scotland, and in their movements around the Central Belt they helped increase the number of accusations. From Inverkeithing, allegations spread across the Lowlands: from Fife and Lothian down into the Borders and even northern England. As ever, they began with complaints made at the local level (where personal suspicions, dislikes, jealousies, and disputes were involved), with ministers then seeking commissions, now from Parliament or the Committee of Estates, to proceed. Affairs in between these stages, however, were critical. It was here that matters could be stemmed. Instead, brutal interrogations kept up the multiplication of names as frightened, tortured victims offered up people they knew or had heard of as their fellow witches. At this stage, the professional witch-pricker might offer his – or, as it might turn out, her – services.

John Kincaid is the most infamous: a man who first appeared in Tranent, East Lothian, offering – for a fee – to sort the innocent from the guilty by the usual method of piercing unusual physical marks. Some time before June, he was in Dirleton, where he performed his operation on Bess Hog, Marion Meik, Patrick Watson, and Patrick's wife Manie Haliburton, all of whom were in ward at the castle on suspicion of witchcraft. The first three at least were definitely strangled and burned in Haddington in June. With such experts, witches had no need to confess to the pact with Satan (which, to the frustration of authorities, who otherwise had to assume the devil's presence and role in trials, they did not always do): physical defects proved it. Applications for commissions to hold trials could then follow.

Occasionally, as in December, the commissions would be general: then, one Janet Coutts had accused several people of witchcraft. The Committee granted a commission to try anyone she might name, provided she was confronted with them. This was a take on James's belief in witches not only identifying other witches but being able to sort the guilty from the innocent. Janet named up to eighty-eight people. Thankfully, this was the only such commission granted. Otherwise, the authorities in Edinburgh, though they granted commissions to try named individuals, proved themselves actively interested (as those in charge had in the 1628–31 purge) in the course of events. The problem was that a great many names were being produced. Between 1649 and 1650, it seems that about 800 people were accused, not all of whose names survive. One witch-pricker alone claimed to have sent 200 people to the gallows.[2]

The purge of 1649–50 saw significant peaks in the late summer and early autumn of 1649, followed by another, smaller outbreak in the early summer of 1650. It had been driven by a combination of factors, not least of which was the willingness of central authorities to encourage it, the zeal of local authorities to use the legal processes available (in Walter Bruce's case, brazenly), and the publicity aroused by the new professional breed of witch-finders travelling throughout areas in which accusations were high in order to produce more names. The role of ministers, particularly, can be felt in the number of confessions involving dancing at conventicles, dancing remaining a particularly abhorrent practice to upstanding Protestants. It ended only when international politics intervened.

Scotland's Kirk Party was in control, and it had set up a working state machinery. It was, however, still nominally affected towards Charles II (if he would accede to its demands) whilst also attempting to work with England. The latter relationship broke down when James Graham, 1st Marquess of Montrose, Charles's man, landed in Scotland and attempted to raise support for the exiled king. Though beaten at the battle of Carbisdale, he survived and was taken to Edinburgh, where he was sentenced to death by Parliament and hanged. This activity curtailed the Scottish government's ability to dispense commissions and commissioners to try witches, and the number issued receded (though, of course, it did not cease entirely). Charles, in response to losing Montrose, opted to journey to Scotland himself, where he signed the Solemn League and Covenant in June 1650. The stolid Oliver Cromwell, by now the Commonwealth of England's leading figure and top general, had already begun preparations for invasion. The Scots, knowing what was coming, focused their attention on doing the same, their concern now being to produce a godly army rather than a godly society.

*

Oliver Cromwell, for all his many and varied faults, was not an inveterate witch-hunter. He seems, in fact, to have had no particularly strong opinions on the matter at all, even if he passively believed in the reality of the phenomenon and the need for the occasional, individual, murderous witch to be tried. This meant the usual scattering of hangings, with those that took place being notable – including, in 1652, Joan Peterson, an alleged witch tried and executed at Tyburn, accused of murderous witchcraft, causing fits, and keeping a talking squirrel as a familiar (though she bravely refused to denounce anyone else). Joan's story was told in *The Witch of Wapping: the life and devilish practices of Joan Peterson*, but this led to a curious counter-narrative, *A declaration in answer to several lying pamphlets concerning the witch of Wapping*, which suggested Joan had been framed.

More infamous still was Anne Bodenham, formerly an assistant to Buckingham's Dr Lambe, whose tale was told in *Doctor Lambs Darling* (1653). Indeed, the lack of official interest resulted, in Malmesbury, in locals attacking a suspected witch, Alice Elgar, themselves; Alice subsequently took her own life. This prompted the Salisbury authorities to be more proactive, trying and executing Goody Orchard, known locally as a witch, in 1645. In 1658 Jane Brooks was executed for bewitching a boy, after the scratching test – he scratched her and drew blood, stopping the bewitchment – had been applied, and after the lad, Richard Jones, claimed to have seen her spectre tormenting him. This spectre, apparently, had been slashed, which caused injury to the real Jane, in her house some distance away. This type of evidence would have huge significance in the future.

Cromwell's aim in invading Scotland was not religious but political; he was attempting to cut off the northern nation's ability to provide Charles II with a springboard to England. In this he was successful. Though Charles – still a vigorous young man, years away from the lugubrious, lanky, dissipated figure of his later years

– agreed to Scottish terms, he found the Covenant and Covenanters deplorable. His return further divided the Covenanters, with the Engagers (to whom the king inclined) seemingly vindicated, to the disgust of the radicals. Though Charles was crowned at Scone Palace in January 1651, it proved, in the short term, a small matter. Cromwell was, as he had during the war, showing himself a fearsome military commander. As the Anglo-Scottish war intensified, the king attempted to take the initiative, moving south with his army of Scots in the hope of gaining English Royalist support. This dream ended at the battle of Worcester and he fled to France in September.

In the meantime, Cromwell had continued his outright conquest of Scotland, which was made inevitable at Worcester. The Scottish government was dissolved in October 1651, having failed to drive Charles to power in England, and Scotland was annexed to the Commonwealth of England via the Declaration of the Parliament of the Commonwealth of England, concerning the Settlement of Scotland. This was later formalised, once Cromwell had been given the role and title of Lord Protector, by the Ordinance for uniting Scotland into one Commonwealth with England, which was itself ratified by the English Parliament (in which thirty Scottish MPs were allowed to sit). Although the Kirk would continue, criminal justice would be overseen and executed by appointed commissioners. King James's dream of a union by which England swallowed up Scotland had come to pass, albeit in circumstances that would have set him spinning in his tomb. It also would not last, and neither would the moratorium on witch-hunting brought about by the irruption of Cromwell (and his military man in Scotland, General George Monck) and the union he enforced at the point of a sword. Scotland might be subdued, but belief in witches and witchcraft would prove too resilient even for Oliver Cromwell.

18

The Devil in the Detail

Cromwell's Protectorate has, historically, been viewed as a time of repression: a theocracy enforced with the backing of military power. This is not entirely accurate. Cromwell, to be sure, was a soldier (and, particularly in Ireland, a merciless tyrant), but in England he was more akin to a king. He and his family moved into the former royal palaces, held court like royals, and, though he refused the crown, he nominated his son to succeed him on his death in 1658. He was, further, no democrat, intent as he was on keeping the franchise limited in the teeth of those with more radical views.

In his attempt at instituting a hereditary Protectorate he failed, as Richard Cromwell lacked the support or inclination needed to rule as his father had done. In the spring of 1660, the political elite invited Charles II to England to, at last, take the throne he had failed to win by Scottish-backed conquest. The second Lord Protector, whose government had collapsed in April 1659, was deposed, though he was allowed to live out his long life freely, and at the beginning of 1660 General Monck and his army of occupation left Scotland. The union between Scotland and England was likewise undone, and a separate Scottish Privy Council restored (in July), as the king attempted to turn the clock back to a time before the manifold wars that engulfed the British Isles. King Cromwell was to be erased – or demonised; indeed, a pamphlet soon denounced him as *The English devil: or, Cromwel and his monstrous witch discover'd at White-Hall* (1660). Lurid stories emerged of him having sold his soul to Satan on the eve of the battle of Worcester (gaining seven years of success in return). All legislation enacted after the early 1630s was revoked, including Scotland's 1649 Witchcraft Act – but that didn't matter greatly; it had done little more than pay lip service to Kirk demands. This, unfortunately, meant a return to witch-hunting, in Scotland at least – and in its wake came one of the most elaborate confessions ever seen in Britain.

Witchcraft accusations had, admittedly, not entirely disappeared from Scotland during the period of the Protectorates. In 1659, for example, Marion Wilson of Inversesk claimed to have seen Agnes Adamson sitting with the devil. The Kirk, however, whose Sessions had continued virtually unimpeded and unrecognised by the union, had focused its attention on charmers: those 'daft wives' who had, historically, not been criminalised in Scotland and who continued to be more in need of spiritual correction than secular punishment. Yet only scattered cases of witchcraft – where the prickers attempted to continue their trade – appeared, with the demonic aspect more prevalent in those closer to Edinburgh.

It was closer to Edinburgh, in the Lothians, where the first rumblings of another panic were heard. This followed, tellingly, the reconstitution of the old Scottish government – Parliament, headed by ex-Engager John Middleton, 1st Earl of Middleton, and the Privy Council – and with it, in what radicals vituperatively labelled 'the Drunken Parliament', the looming threat of restored episcopacy and an end to Kirk governance as it had been practised. It is not surprising to note that the usual pattern was followed: local complaints were made and local authorities sought commissions to deal with them. The Privy Council, headed by Chancellor William Cunningham, 9th Earl of Glencairn, and John Leslie, Earl of Rothes, then complied. In a renewed cold war between episcopalian Royalists (who egged on the distant king) and radical Kirk ministers, neither side wished to be seen as being ungodly (or soft on witchcraft).

The question is why so many people were caught up in the ensuing purge, which lasted some seventeen months, in 1661–62: and the answer seems to lie in an outpouring of pent-up suspicions, and possibly resentments, that only found its voice when the new system (or the revived old system) stabilised in early 1661. This is not surprising. Since James VI and I's reign, people had been steadily educated into believing in the reality of demonic witchcraft. Then politics – and an army of occupation – had intervened. No one, however, had attempted to educate them out of those beliefs. What caused large numbers to inflate still higher was the willingness of the new central authorities to grant these commissions across a wide geographical area, and, once again, the rise of professional witch-prickers, whose trade relied on generating accusations.

John Kincaid, again, was active, and by now he had, like Matthew Hopkins, hired assistants. One of these might have been Christian Caldwell, a remarkable figure who disguised herself as a man (calling herself John Dickson) in order to set up on her own. She thereafter travelled extensively throughout Scotland, offering her services to local authorities who had already found and often imprisoned suspects. In some cases at least, the accused were actually offered the service, as John Stearne had claimed English suspects were offered the swimming test: Isobel Ferguson, in Newbottle, in July 1661 responded boldly that she would welcome a pricking and to send for Kincaid, the better to prove her innocence. Isobel, typically, also accused others, notably one Geillis Charters, who also requested to be searched and pricked. Unfortunately, in her case, the marks were apparently found. Another accused, John MacMillan, behaved in much the same manner; on being pricked himself and confessing to be a warlock, he claimed that Janet Wilson and Janet Watt were not only his fellow witches but he had personally seen them with the devil. These women also apparently offered to be pricked.

In this climate, it is understandable why the likes of John Kincaid and Christian Caldwell, who got as far as Moray in the north of Scotland, found rich pickings. This, like the cost of keeping witches imprisoned, was a necessary irritant to local authorities, who routinely, as they always had, attempted to recoup expenses from the suspects' families (as they would charge the same families for such costs as the rope with which to execute those found guilty and the fuel to burn the bodies). This could be difficult, given there was not often much money to be had from witches, many of whom were poor. The only consistent money to be made was from the service industry of pricking or torture-for-hire.

In this, the last and one of the largest purges in Scotland, hundreds went to the gallows and flames. Their crimes were typical. Margaret Cant, who had a historically bad reputation and one previous arrest, was tried in 1661. Janet Clark, in Edinburgh, was another repeat offender. Margaret Porteous and Margaret Grieve were tried by the High Court of Justiciary for charming – evidence of attention given to this widespread low magic as a criminal activity – and released on condition they refrain from repeating their offences. The Kirk Session at Stow investigated Margaret Cooper for consulting with witches – another misdemeanour which generally was overlooked. Janet Cock, in Dalkeith, was strangled and burned in September 1661, with her daughters claiming she had been accused maliciously by a land-hungry bailie.

Christian Wilson, also of Dalkeith, was held in great suspicion by the minister and bailies over the strange death of her brother, Alexander: she was forced (apparently whilst showing understandable reluctance) to touch his corpse, which subsequently bled, this being constituted proof of her being his killer (the ancient theory of 'bier right', as this phenomenon was known, having been noted by such learned men as Sir Francis Bacon). The devil's marks on her confirmed her witchery. Christian was tried alongside Elspeth Graham, Beatrix Leslie, Isobel Ferguson, Marjorie Wilson, and Christian Paterson.

The devil had certainly not been forgotten, even if his presence sometimes had to be inferred, as it was probably always inferred by those recording confessions (Beatrix Leslie, for example, confessed only to sending cats out to kill, without identifying the devil as her master). Satan's appearances, as Stuart MacDonald has noted, seemed to figure most prominently in cases in the Dunfermline Presbytery, whilst he was largely only explicitly identified in those which went through the central courts (implying that confessions were fashioned to be, or interpreted as, demonic the closer one was to Edinburgh, where elite beliefs and elite power had historically met). Close to the heart of government – the Privy Council – authorities were keen to be seen to be acting conscientiously and responsibly, with demonic witchcraft their primary concern. The clock had indeed been turned back, to a time when King James had lived, Scotland had been viewed, at least by the government, as the devil's playground, and England by contrast was affected only sporadically by old, unpopular, or vulnerable people being tried. This made sense. If the late James VI and I had held his home nation in disdain and distrust, the 'merry monarch' (a sobriquet which masks his perpetual inner melancholy), Charles II, positively loathed it. On leaving Britain after his failed attempt to take the throne in 1650, he had declared he would rather be hanged than return to Scotland; later, he recalled the country as unnatural, his father having supposedly seen his hawk attacked by docile partridges there.

The central authorities' interest in devilry continued and confessions duly met it. Janet Blaikie, in August 1661, confessed that she had lain three times with a man, whom she called 'Henry Beat', but who was cold to the touch on the first two occasions. Evidently, she had had illicit sex – but in her confession this became garbled with theories (seen in Scotland at least since James's 1590–91 purge of treasonous witchcraft) of the icy-cold devil. In Duddingston, John Scott confessed that he had met Satan multiple times, the devil appearing 'in the likeness of a black man with black clothes'.[1] David Johnston, in July 1661, gave a similar description: he had sold his soul to a 'large, grim man in black clothes'.[2] Isobel Ferguson, curiously, reported a 'woman in a black gown' who could transform into a black cat.[3] Janet Howitt claimed that she and her mistress, Isobel Syrie, who made the introductions, had danced with him, feasted with him, and been nipped by him. Isobel found herself denounced also by another Forfar witch, Joanet Huit, who also claimed to have been introduced to the devil by her (and it is here one wonders whether Isobel Syrie might have been procuring women for rendezvouses with a distinctly nonmagical man). Three Dunfermline women admitted to making the baptism-renouncing demonic pact.

Agnes Williamson was accused not only of having sex with Satan but making a child disappear, setting fires, raising storms, and being rechristened Nancy Luckyfoot by her demonic master. Agnes, thankfully, could afford a prolocutor (defence counsel) who had most of the charges dismissed, and she was acquitted. Again, evidence of beliefs which had long been drummed into the Scottish people were emerging as confessions, just as England had sensationalised, repeated, and seen parroted back tales of mysterious dogs and oddly named familiars.

Notable, too, was the number of witches accused in separate cases. In England, by contrast, any witchcraft trial remained aberrant and newsworthy. In 1662, Bury St Edmunds, one of Matthew Hopkins's old stomping grounds, witnessed another trial – this of two elderly widows, the wealthy Rose Cullender and comparatively poor Amy Duny, who faced thirteen charges of witchcraft against children, one of which was of the murderous variety. The misogynist Sir Matthew Hale presided, inviting the jury to consider only whether the children afflicted had been bewitched and, if so, whether it had been done by Rose and Amy. The two women went to the gallows, their fate taking two decades to reach the obligatory pamphlet, *A Tryal of Witches* (1682), when it became a weapon in the battle between witchcraft-denying men of science and witchcraft-affirming ones. As the reality and efficacy of witchcraft had provoked academic debates across Europe a century before, so did it again, albeit now the momentum was less with the godly than with the doubters.

On the continental mainland, the dark age of great purges was over everywhere except in Sweden. Instead, as in England, executions had become scattered affairs, and so they would remain. In Germany, for example, Brunswick-Lüneburg saw probably its last death – officially at least – when the widowed Anna Roleffes was decapitated and burned in 1663. France saw the end of intermittent horrors in the late 1670s, with Peronne Goguillon and her daughter, Marie-Anne Dufosset, burned – although a brief discrete revival took place in 1745 when the priest Louis Debaraz was executed for alleged demonism.

In Scotland in the early 1660s, however, in the midst of a major outbreak of accusations and trials, commissions were sought to try groups with alarming frequency: a clutch of people in Spott; a group from Musselburgh; in Forfar, Helen Guthrie, who was apparently known for bad behaviour, openly boasted about her powers and named multiple others as her accomplices, claiming, as Margaret Aitken had back in 1597, that she had the ability to identify other witches. Not only this, but she and some of them had apparently disinterred an unbaptised infant and baked it into a pie, the eating of which was intended to keep their evil secrets safe. For good measure, Helen added that she had also murdered her half-sister. In her revelation of names, as Julian Goodare has pointed out, she conspicuously omitted any reference to her daughter – and so her naming of names (as in, most likely, numerous cases) might have been an attempt to divert attention from her loved ones and thereby assert some control over the direction of events.[4]

The amount of time, energy, and paper needed to deal with all these cases – and these were a fraction of the whole – is considerable, especially when one takes into account the complaints prisoners and their families had also issued, and which also required attention. Neither the Privy Council nor the commissioners were inclined to wave through executions or acquittals: courts, courtrooms, and judges took time, money, and space to organise, and the personnel were generally eager to do thorough jobs (even if the standards of evidence they accepted remain baffling to modern eyes). This resulted, in late 1661, in a special committee being formed to act as a screening body whilst the backlog was dealt with.

Although cases spilled over into the next year and more applications for commissions arrived in Edinburgh in 1662, ranging from Largs and Bute in the west to Jedburgh in the southeast to Ross in the northeast (the entirely reversed L-shape of the Lowlands), the Council, finally, considered applying some restraint. This came in the form of increasing demands from the centre that pre-trial interrogators cease applying torture. A warrant was issued in early 1661 for the arrest of John Kincaid, and he was released only on bond and with a promise extracted that he cease his business. Similarly, the pricker 'John Dickson' was arrested for causing trouble – specifically issuing false allegations, illegally torturing people, and causing deaths – in and around Inverness and Moray, and, to her interrogators' surprise, found to be a woman; she was exiled to Barbados the following year.

In September 1662, this hardline attitude against freelancers took on a more concrete form: a proclamation went out noting that 'a great many persons in several parts of the kingdom have been apprehended and hurried to prisons, pricked, tortured, and abused, as being suspect[ed] of the horrid crime of witchcraft: and that by persons as have no warrant or authority to do so'.[5] This was a late response to a problem of long standing – and an attempt by authorities to rein in what they had allowed to get out of hand (as had happened, to King James's disappointment, in 1597). Henceforth, the Council wanted restrictions on torture, restrictions on punishment for magic which did no harm, and only voluntary confessions and devil's marks – not pricked by tradespeople – to stand as evidence.

One confession arising from the panic, which itself petered out late in 1662, had apparently been extracted without the use of torture. This came from Isobel Gowdie, a married woman who came before the minister of Auldearn, Harry Forbes, in April. She then issued the first of four confessions given over a six-week period, during which she was imprisoned (though, apparently, without the usual depredations). She alleged that she'd met the devil in the form of a black, hairy man on the road and immediately formed a covenant with him, renouncing her baptism. She then met with him in the kirk at night, where he held forth at the pulpit with a black book. Her ritual that night involved touching her feet and head, promising that the body in between was his. Satan then stepped down and came to her, biting her on the shoulder and sucking blood, which he spat into his hand before sprinkling it on her head, thereby rebaptising her as one of his slaves. On their third meeting, they had sex; she claimed to have found his body and private parts cold, and though he sometimes wore boots, his feet were cloven. On later occasions, at conventicles, he would show himself violent if any witch disobeyed him or was insolent, beating them with cords, and he would always prefer copulating with the younger members than the older ones. He could, further, shapeshift into the form of a deer.

Isobel then confessed to having been part of a coven (an early use of the word in the context of witchcraft) of thirteen, herself included, with one John Young as its 'officer' (though in the course of her confessions, around forty people were named). She volunteered not only the names of her fellows, but the demonic sobriquets of several of them: her mother, Isobel 'Bessie Rule' Nicoll; Margaret 'Pickle-nearest-the-wind' Wilson; Bessie 'Through the corn-yard' Wilson (who would on occasion stand up to the devil); Elspeth 'Bessie Bald' Nishe; Bessie 'Able and stout' Hay; and Jane 'Ower-the-dike-with-it' Mairtin.[6] A veritable zoo of familiar spirits was attendant upon them, each wearing coloured coats and bearing names like Robert the Jakis, Thief of Hell, Roaring Lion, and Saunders the Red Reaver. The coven would meet in the kirkyard at Nairn (about three miles away from Auldearn), where they had disinterred an unbaptised child and used the body to spoil a cornfield. They had, too, ploughed a field using frogs and a plough formed from the horn of a wether (ram). Her confessions grew only more colourful and folkloric, as she admitted to having feasted with fairies clothed in white linen; having been frightened by elf-bulls; and having seen Satan (whom they nicknamed Black John) make arrowheads for elves to fashion and then pass to the witches, who would flick them from their thumbnails to kill people. She could name some of these victims – David Black, James Dick, and one Dunbar – whilst others, men and women, she simply recalled having murdered without noting their names. Other acts of demonic *maleficia* involved making clay figures to strike down the children of a local laird.

Unfortunately, there is no record of what became of Isobel Gowdie, though she was recorded as being penitent. Her colourful confessions, have, though, given rise to numerous theories as to why she provided such detail. Was she suffering a mental disorder? It is possible, though she was evidently lucid enough throughout her imprisonment to deliver eloquent speeches. Was she suffering from ergotism – a type of poisoning which arises from consuming the fungus *C. purpurea*, which can be found in rye and cause hallucinations? This theory has been advanced to account for numerous witch confessions, and attempts have been made to associate Scottish panics with the importation of rye bread in times of dearth. There is, however, no proof, and there is no reason to look for psychotropic causes when the human mind is capable of producing all manner of fanciful claims. It stretches credulity, further, to imagine that outbreaks of ergotism could or would produce broadly similar accounts.

Nowadays, we would be inclined to think of what happened as an outbreak of mass hysteria – a not uncommon phenomenon when a society is infected at various levels by insidious beliefs and the framework exists to express those beliefs. Isobel's claims were detailed and contained some unusual elements, but many of them were similar to previous accounts, some from confessions of other accused witches and some from folklore. She produced nothing that a good storyteller couldn't manage: a synthesis of existing information woven into a narrative. If an actor from Stratford could turn Arthur Brooke's lightweight *The Tragical History of Romeus and Juliet* into *Romeo and Juliet*, a cottar's wife from Auldearn could take folk tales and a wealth of decades-old (and still popular) notions of demonic Scottish witchcraft to produce 'Pickle-nearest-the-wind' and elven arrows. Whether she came forward for attention, infamy, or due to delusions, we cannot know. Isobel's case is therefore less interesting in terms of finding a concrete material cause than for what it reveals about where attitudes were in the 1660s. James VI and I's absolute belief in the devil had become entrenched enough that witches would, in various ways, incorporate it into their confessions, but old beliefs about witches (which the late king had denounced as fantasies produced by Satan) remained lively.

The 1660–61 purge, which cost so many lives, itself died out as the reconstituted Privy Council clamped down on wandering witch-hunters and the new king's reign really made its aims – not least a desire to stamp an episcopalian system on Scotland and remove hardline Presbyterian ministers from office – clear. Scotland underwent further religious and political convulsions over the coming decades, but there were no more large-scale purges initiated from the bottom, the middle, or the top – though certainly accusations, trials, and executions would continue as long as the law allowed. A limit had been reached, with the wide-scale, spreading horrors inviting an understandable backlash: a pattern noticeable across Europe, as Sweden, which had hitherto suffered only scattered cases, featuring the typical accusations of flying and devilry and encouraged initially by Charles IX and Gustav Vasa early in the century, experienced an intense explosion of panic under Charles XI between 1668 and 1676 (of which the infamous 1675 Torsåker trials were part) – this when a clergyman, Lars Elvius, led a crusade against supposed demonic assemblies. This was, as in Scotland, exacerbated by the legitimacy granted by a centrally authorised commission – and it was only when the commission reached an accommodation with the clergy and agreed an end to the hunt (and to the commission itself) that the legal machinery was broken (though it was not removed until 1779, decades after the last torture-backed trial was begun and thankfully cancelled in the 1750s).

Times were changing in Europe. They were certainly changing in Scotland, which followed the trend of a decline in witchcraft prosecutions, as the scientific method gradually made converts of those who needed reassurance that science would not kill God. Thanks to this rather slow process, and the even slower wheels of justice, the collapse of witchcraft as a crime happened as a managed decline rather than with a swift and definitive end.

The worst aspect of King James's Scottish legacy, at least, was at an end. However, in another of those territories over which he had had held dominion – in his role as coloniser – witchcraft would see possibly its most infamous manifestation.

19

New World, Old Problems

The English colonisation of North America, after several false starts dating to the reign of Elizabeth I, had seen its first real foothold under King James, when the appropriately named Jamestown colony finally managed to retain a permanent settlement. By 1692, the equally appropriately named New England was well established, resolutely Puritanical, and firmly English in the administration of its laws.

England, by this time, had matured – or at least certain influential attitudes amongst certain influential thinkers had. Even during the reign of Oliver Cromwell, a new atmosphere had been brewing – not of disbelief, necessarily, but of faith in a new scientific method: as Miranda Malins notes, the members of what would, under Charles II in 1660, become the Royal Society had begun to meet during the Protectorate.[1] For some time, the heirs to James VI and I's bête noire, the witchcraft-doubter Reginald Scot, and the doubting William Harvey, had voiced their own criticisms of belief in the phenomenon. These included Thomas Hobbes, who found the confessions of his day uncredible and thus bemusing. Others, like Henry More – author of *An Antidote against Atheism, or an Appeal to the Natural Faculties of the Minde of Man, whether there be not a God* (1653) – found in witchcraft beliefs a remedy to the lurking threat of non-belief.

Joseph Glanvill, who became a Fellow of the Royal Society in 1664, believed a way could be found through this apparent impasse. His solution was to subject witchcraft to the emerging scientific method – empiricism – pioneered by James VI and I's former Lord Chancellor, the exceptional polymath Sir Francis Bacon, who had died in 1626. His first contribution to the debate was *A philosophical endeavour towards the defence of the being of vvitches and apparitions* (1666). Dr John Webster, a physician and alchemist, hit back a decade later with his *The displaying of supposed witchcraft* (1677), which mocked believers in low magic. Clearly, something was happening amongst England's intelligentsia. Witchcraft was now a matter for debate; no longer was it the case that education meant being taught to believe unquestioningly in the reality of the phenomenon.

What was happening, slowly, was this: educated men – we would now call them early scientists – were attempting to rationalise witchcraft. Some found it wanting; others found it a matter of faith which honest religion could uphold. These debates became live issues when witchcraft reports emerged from Somerset, where Richard Hill claimed his daughter had been bewitched by Elizabeth Style. The girl confirmed this, claiming Style's spectral form was attacking her during convulsions. Attempts were made to compare the child's description of Elizabeth with the clothes the real woman – who was elsewhere – was wearing, and they were found to match. Neighbours then came forward to also accuse Elizabeth of murderous witchcraft. Elizabeth confessed in January 1665: to having made a pact with the devil (who could appear in human or animal form) in return for twelve years of comfort; to allowing him to suck blood from her ring finger; to receiving a mark on her head; and to using a wax image to torment Richard Hill's daughter. Moreover, she named Alice Duke, Anne Bishop, and Mary Penny as her associates. On repeat interrogation, her story varied, until eventually she claimed to have been part of a coven fifteen-strong, including men as well as women.

Elizabeth died in custody, but this local case spread into Brewham, where the death the previous year of the local overseer of the parish's poor had sparked rumours. In March 1655, Margaret Agar was accused of causing the death by witchcraft, and she was further denounced by other suspects when they too were brought in for questioning. Similar confessions were read: of deals with the devil, the sucking of blood from the ring finger, murderous sorcery, and familiars (in one case, a hedgehog). So similar were they, in fact, that they were almost certainly provided for those accused to agree with. Yet this was evidence to believer Joseph Glanvill of the reality of the phenomenon.

Another Royal Society member, Sir James Long, served as a magistrate in the 1672 trial of several women in Malmesbury accused of flying on sticks. This made its way to print a decade later, the year after the 1682 trial in Bideford of Temperance Lloyd (who had previously been acquitted of witchcraft). Temperance confessed to having to do with the devil, turning herself into a cat, and using a doll to cause convulsions. With her were tried Mary Trembles and Susanna Edwards, who were accused of having sex with the devil (in the form of a black man) and causing injury and convulsions. The devil's marks were searched for and found. Witnesses were called who claimed to have heard the women confess whilst they were imprisoned (when they had evidently become something of a local sideshow). All three women were hanged – and have gone down in history as the last witches known to have definitely been hanged in England (although trials would continue, with one Mother Munning being tried and acquitted in Bury St Edmunds in 1694).

The Bideford case provoked something of an outcry, at least in academic circles, due to the nature of evidence: the confessions were scarcely plausible – and flew in the face of materialist demands for proof – and the witnesses could produce only hearsay. This was nothing new, but the criticism of it by active, learned men with strong social and political connections and genuine interest in whether witchcraft was real or not was. It was, indeed, this burst of debate which caused Sir James Long, a believer, to produce his little work on the Malmesbury case, his goal being to reconcile belief in the demonic pact with emerging scientific thinking – this following Glanvill's *Saducismus Triumphatus* (1681), another compilation of cases affirming the reality of demonic witchcraft in the modern, increasingly enlightened world.

There was no wholesale, overnight rejection of magic. Rather, old ideas about scepticism towards the confessions made by common folk – of using curses, charms, images, and sorcery – began to revive. High magic was again separated by academics from low magic, not in the way King James had separated them (both high conjurers and necromancy and low curses and witchcraft being provided by an active Satan), but in a way that someone like John Dee might have recognised: high magic was being reclaimed in the form of the occult, with its impossible practices taken up by modern thinkers who intended to pass them through the sieve of empiricist thinking to sift the false ones out, and the extraordinary claims of low witches were now subject to scrutiny and demands for higher standards of evidence. Now, witchcraft was open to intellectual curiosity and exposed to rational experimentation. This was not, however, a triumph of intellectualism over hoary superstition. As authors like the old king had shown, demonology had always been an intellectual pursuit. What was changing was the academic approach to it, thanks to the emergence of the scientific method. Old ideas – Galen's theory of the body and Ptolemaic notions of a geocentric universe – were slowly being abandoned as erroneous. Reliance on, or the refining of, existing, generally ancient beliefs, which were James's academic standard, no longer sufficed.

This was enough to give authorities pause, at least in England. Confessions extracted via torture had been recognised as dubious (even in Scotland). Professional prickers were, and had been, tainted by their making the process a trade, demonstrable abuses of power, and unreliable claims: this meant the devil's mark, so long considered a reliable source of evidence, was open to doubt. The things witches were confessing to were – and always had been – untestable and unprovable. Many of James's key tenets of belief were breaking down.

Religion and the law, however, lagged behind academic thinking (and it is worth noting that it was far from all academics who disputed witchcraft), and so the Witchcraft Acts remained in force and fears about the devil remained lively. James had found it difficult to teach people about what he believed was genuine demonic witchcraft, but he had largely managed to do so (witness the quality and character of confessions and the rise of professional hunters in his kingdoms). The new, more radical intellectuals would find it even harder to teach people a less palatable new idea: that they, the people, had been taught to be too credulous for nearly a century. They would find an even frostier reception – and even slower recognition of the need for rational scepticism – across the Atlantic.

*

The New World was in many ways as ripe for serious witch-hunting as Scotland had been: it had been populated, after all, by a number of people who wished to establish a godly society free of what they perceived as the errors riddling the established churches of Europe. Indeed, when people think of Puritans, they probably do not think of English (or even Scottish) reformists, but rather of American colonists in austere black and white. They likely think, too, of the Salem witch trials – no other case in history has received so much attention. They are now so much a part of American history and culture – and an iconic, chilling part – that it is easy to forget how much the trials were influenced and shaped by English custom, English precedent, and English law. To this was added a desire on the part of the colonial government for Biblical codes of conduct to be enforced amongst the residents – particularly in Massachusetts.

This became a particularly ardent desire following the Restoration and Charles II's concomitant brand of Anglicanism (itself tinged with the king's deep attraction to Catholicism), when the godly American colonists developed their own strain of aggrieved self-righteousness. Though Charles died without legitimate issue in 1685, his brother, James VII and II, proved himself inclined to Catholicism, which to Puritans was simply the natural result of affection towards middle-ground Anglicanism. His reign ended in deposition and military failure and, despite having issue (which would form the Jacobite line), he was replaced in the so-called

Glorious Revolution with his daughter, Mary II, and her husband, William of Orange. Catholicism was banished from the British Crown and, in Scotland, both Catholics and Episcopalians were brutally restrained. This was, though, neither what would now be thought of as constitutional monarchy nor was it the establishment of a godly, Puritanical England. The latter was what the deeply reformist Massachusetts theocrats, who could easily imagine the devil to be lurking in the vast, Native-populated unknown areas of the continent, wanted.

In 1692, Increase Mather, a Puritan clergyman who had already made a name for himself in America (having become President of Harvard in 1685), travelled to England to make his case for godly governance, the Massachusetts Bay Colony's charter having expired in 1684, leaving the colony in a state of legal uncertainty. In doing so he was buoyed by his studies into the occult, published as *An Essay for the Recording of Illustrious Providences* (1684), which drew on examples he'd gathered and such texts as the *Malleus Maleficarum* to prove the existence of spirits and witches. In this, the colonies kept on providing; in 1688, Ann Glover, an elderly Irish Catholic servant, was hanged in Boston for bewitching the Goodwin children – the episode was included in Increase's son Cotton Mather's *Memorable Providences* (1689).[2]

What Increase and his ilk perceived was that emerging scientific scepticism was a threat to godliness and a threat to God. The devil, to Increase, was as real and active as he had been to James VI and I. What the Mathers, father and son, sought was a means of balancing scientific beliefs alongside religious belief in the absolute reality of the devil and his doings. Further proof of that proposition soon emerged in the town of Salem – and Satan was increasingly thought not just to be making slaves of locals but trying to destroy the godly colony and its governance.

The trouble started in February 1692 in the reasonably well-to-do Parris household. There, eleven-year-old Elizabeth ('Betty') Parris and her nine-year-old cousin, Abigail Williams, stopped what they were doing – later claimed to have been folk fortune-telling techniques, such as the use of a 'Venus glass' to glimpse future husbands' occupations – and began shaking. The shakes became convulsions. The convulsions gave way to screeches and shrieks and sobs. This would have been alarming to any normal parent, but Samuel Parris was not any normal parent: he was the fiery Reverend Parris, and there was potentially something dangerously wrong with his daughter and niece. Worse – it showed no sign of stopping. Abigail seems to have been particularly affected: she would hurl herself at the fireplace and toss firewood about the house.

Elizabeth was sent away to live with Stephen Sewall, a legal clerk, but her fits continued; in the course of them, she would throw Bibles about the room. A fast was ordered in the Parris household, combined with prayer readings. During these, Abigail began screaming. The physicians (including, probably, the newly arrived Dr William Griggs, whose niece, Elizabeth Hubbard, soon started showing symptoms) could find no bodily infirmities in these young people and so their behaviour was, understandably, construed as bewitchment. This led a neighbour of the Parrises, Mary Sibley, to suggest fighting witchcraft with witchcraft. In this she let her superstition carry her, turning her attention to a slave in the Parris household named Tituba, who had supposedly regaled those girls first afflicted with stories of her native Barbados. Mary Sibley instructed Tituba's Caribbean husband, John Indian, to bake a 'witch cake': a cake infused with the afflicted girls' urine, which, when fed to a dog, was thought to remove the bewitchment. The result was increased attention: the seventeen-year-old Elizabeth Hubbard (niece of Dr Griggs) began her convulsions, and she was joined by another girl, the twelve-year-old Ann Putnam. Suddenly, witchcraft being the cause had gained legitimacy and the easiest targets were those in no position to fight back.

At first, Betty Parris and Abigail Williams could not name their tormenters, but this was not an insoluble problem. Salem was host to a number of women deemed undesirable by the godly, not least Tituba – and, fed leading questions, the girls made useful accusations. Tituba was thus arrested; as was the beggar Sarah Goode (accused by Ann Putnam and Elizabeth Hubbard and brought in at the demand of Ann's father, John); and the disabled widow Sarah Osborne, a woman who had married a servant and was involved in local property disputes. All three were searched and found to have the devil's marks. These were Salem's disenfranchised: the people who did not fit the mould of the godly.

Tituba confessed, naming the other two women and claiming she had sent her spectral image to do the devil's work. This was key. The idea of a witch sending a spectre in her own image to cause trouble had already been seen in England (where it had undoubtedly been pioneered by authorities hoping to explain why accusers claimed to have been assaulted when the accused was provably elsewhere) and subjected to scrutiny. It had, further, been hinted at by King James decades before; his *Daemonologie* noted that witches might lie insensible whilst their spirits attended devilish conventicles. Indeed, the Salem authorities could even point to precedent in English common law: Sir Matthew Hale's sentence against the elderly Bury St Edmunds witches for bewitching multiple children. The girls – and Tituba – thus provided a means of validating the phenomenon before American doubters.

Sarah Goode was interrogated in Nathaniel Ingersoll's tavern as to her alleged demonic dealings. These she denied, insisting on her innocence. One of her examiners, Judge John Hathorne (the other being Jonathan Corwin), thus turned to the girls Sarah was accused of bewitching: Ann Putnam and Elizabeth Hubbard. The young people obliged. They were brought before Sarah Goode and immediately began claiming they were being pinched, bitten, and otherwise tormented by her. This was considered proof, and the woman's interrogation continued, though she would maintain her innocence. By contrast, Sarah Osborne admitted that the others arrested were witches but that she herself was innocent. This looked less than likely when she briefly escaped captivity, and more so when Elizabeth Hubbard claimed Sarah had visited her spectrally again and once more tormented her.

The questioning continued, and more names began to emerge. Ann Putnam, for example, accused Elizabeth Proctor, wife to a wealthy local businessman and landowner, John. John Proctor's servant, Mary Warren, suddenly began experiencing fits herself – and she blamed them on an elderly local farmer, Giles Corey. For her troubles, Mary was threatened with a thrashing by John Proctor, which seemed – for a day at least – to mysteriously relieve her symptoms. Martha Corey, Giles's wife, was likewise accused, again by Ann Putnam. The real shock came, however, when Abigail Williams named Rebecca Nurse, a seventy-one-year-old woman and upstanding member of the community. This prompted Salem's minister, Deodat Lawson, to launch his own investigation. He saw for himself, as he went from wooden house to wooden house, the troubled atmosphere in the town. He saw, too, Abigail Williams shrieking that the spectre of old Rebecca was trying to make her sign the devil's book. Williams wasn't done there – she shouted over Reverend Lawson in church that she could see Martha Corey's spectre leaving her body. This caused an uproar – but it might have demonstrated, to the less credulous, that the girls were colluding.

Martha was arrested and examined, with a party of men attending Rebecca Nurse to see for themselves whether she was a witch. She denied it, leading to an arrest warrant being issued against her. More troublingly, a warrant was also issued to arrest Dorcas Goode, Sarah's daughter, who was about four years old. The child, so her interrogators thought, implicated her mother.

By now, Salem was turning on itself and gaining attention; the nearby town of Ipswich had its own outbreak of accusation. Others in Salem, probably due to the news being everywhere in the town, also involved themselves. The afflicted girls were joined by other friends: Mary Walcott (niece of Mary Sibley), Mercy Lewis, and Susan Sheldon. John Proctor, one of the few voices of reason, called the girls out publicly for their behaviour. In turn, his wife was again accused, this time by Mercy Lewis. Abigail Williams soon added that not only had she seen Elizabeth Proctor's spectre but John's too. In late March, the Reverend Parris would preach that Satan could only manipulate the forms of the guilty: spectres, therefore, if seen, were proof of witchcraft. Rebecca Nurse's sister, Sarah Cloyce, took understandable offence at this presumption of guilt and stormed from the church. She later publicly defended her sister and was accused of witchcraft herself.

The issue of spectral torments had by now become a hot one. The town of Ipswich, itself undergoing a panic, produced a petition declaring itself against such tales, particularly with regard to John and Elizabeth Proctor. This did little to save the latter, who was arrested in April (alongside Sarah Cloyce, whose spectre was now, according to the girls, disrupting church services). In April, Elizabeth and Sarah came under interrogation, this being held before Thomas Danforth, the Deputy Governor of the Massachusetts Bay Colony. John Proctor had little luck defending his wife; Mary Warren, his troublesome servant, simply accused him of witchcraft and he, too, was arrested and jailed. Within days, Warren admitted to having lied (and accused the other girls of lying), but this potential means of de-escalating affairs was itself defanged when she was encouraged to recant her admission.

By now, the Salem witch panic was fast becoming a *cause célèbre*; on it rested the proposition, being queried by some scientifically minded Englishmen and affirmed by others, that demonic witch-craft was real (or, rather, that it was really effective). Names and accusations were now flying as quickly as authorities could deal with them. Giles Corey, the farmer, was again accused, as was Mary English. So too were Abigail Hobbs, Deliverance Hobbs, Bridget Bishop, and Mary Warren, whom the other girls had turned on since she had denounced them as liars. Some confessed, others accused one another. Giles Corey, however, remained resolute in his innocence.

As a result of confessions and accusations, further arrest warrants were issued: dozens of people would be denounced, arrested, or flee throughout April and May. No one was safe. From its humble begin-nings – an attack on the weak – the hunt had deepened and threat-ened everyone and anyone. A former constable, John Willard, who found himself accused, attempted to flee but was swiftly captured. Philip English, the prosperous husband of the accused Mary, was taken to join his wife in Boston (the gaol of which had to purchase new shackles). Thankfully, both escaped, probably with the help of their social connections.

Already, Salem could not hold all these people – some accused had to be held in Boston (albeit that one space was freed up in Salem by the death in custody of Sarah Osborne). Still names poured in, with Sarah Proctor (daughter of Elizabeth and John) and Sarah Bassett, Elizabeth's sister-in-law, accused. The Proctors' son, Benjamin, followed (and it should now have been obvious that someone amongst or connected to the girls had an especial issue with the Proctor family).

At this point, Sir William Phips arrived in the company of Increase Mather – and with them came the new charter for Massachusetts Bay which, to the chagrin of some, did not reaffirm the old one but began afresh, and named William Stoughton as Lieutenant Governor. Local tensions were only raised further. The Governor was, however, immediately alerted to the extraordinary goings-on in Salem.

In late May, Governor Phips appointed seven judges to a special court of oyer and terminer (empowered to try specific criminal cases), amongst whom were Lieutenant Governor Stoughton (soon to be Chief Justice) and John Hathorne, who had already been deeply involved in interrogations. Still, the snowball of accused was by now reaching the proportions of a snow-boulder. Yet more people stepped forward to provide accusations and claim to have experienced torments by, or to have seen, spectres: Sarah Churchill, Sarah Trask, Margaret Reddington, Phoebe Chandler, Martha Sprague, and Sarah Bibber (known locally as an attention-seeking trouble-maker). Still the Proctor family was harassed, with son William Proctor joining his family in gaol.

Court proceedings began in June, with searches made for the devil's mark (by a male doctor and female assistants) on the first arraigned for trial (including Elizabeth Proctor). This was deemed necessary as spectral evidence was clearly problematic: it could not be proved and thus could not stand alone. Nothing was found on those searched. Indictments were, however, still made for Rebecca Nurse and the former constable, John Willard, with Abigail Williams providing her last piece of testimony (before, unfortunately for historians, disappearing from the records, her motives thus giving rise to all manner of fictional treatments). Even without Abigail, accusations were made: Elizabeth Booth, for example, began convulsing.

In the face of this evidence, the first executions began, with Bridget Bishop sent to the gallows, this requiring a resurrection of the death penalty (which had fallen into abeyance). Bridget died on 10 June. She did not die, however, because she confessed to being a witch; no one, in fact, was executed in Salem for having admitted to bewitching anyone – rather, every judicial death resulted from the accused refusing to confess and thus being found guilty. Strenuous efforts were made in the infamous trials not to condemn the effects of witchcraft (though these certainly could be used to prove its existence) but to condemn the demonic pact. Authorities were concerned predominantly with what they believed to be a mass outbreak of sin in the community, and hanged only those who denied their demonism and thus denied themselves the chance of being shriven.

At this point, Governor Phips, exasperated by the arguments of clergymen, the number of names pouring in (many of which probably arose from personal disputes or fear of being named first), and the paranoia of Salem, made preparations to leave the area (having probably not taken an active part in proceedings) to see to military affairs (England's colonies being under threat from the French).

Thus it was that the subsequent trials became an infamous parody of justice. Sarah Goode and multiple others refused to confess, were found guilty, and hanged at Gallows Hill (now Proctor's Ledge) on 19 July. Included amongst their number were Rebecca Nurse, who had had such a good reputation, and who had at first been found not guilty by the jury; this, however, had provoked an outcry, and the jury had been forced to reconsider its verdict. Rebecca had thus been found guilty and sentenced to death, with Governor Phips's reprieve being swiftly rescinded due to its unpopularity. In the wake of these terrible deaths, more accusations were made and more interrogations held.

Still in a state of rightful defiance, John Proctor attempted, from gaol, to have the ongoing proceedings halted or at least moved to a different jurisdiction with different judges. This was in vain, though his would not be the only voice to rise in opposition to what was going on. Rising scepticism – and John's request – reached the eyes and ears of Increase Mather, with Mather's real interest being, as his son Cotton's was, to determine the validity of spectral evidence.

The result was a meeting of ministers in August which reasoned that Satan could, in fact, take on innocent forms, gulling people into believing the innocent were guilty. These men were believers, but they were neither blind nor immune to empirical thinking – and they did not want what they considered genuine witchcraft to be muddied by false accusations, weak evidence, and hysterical superstition (any more than had King James during his English enquiries into alleged witchcraft cases). This sense of scepticism was strengthened when members of the Mather family and Governor Phips's wife were 'cried out upon', and solidified when the wife of a prosecutor, Reverend John Hale, was arrested.[3] It is tempting to scoff at what looks like being naked nepotism in the attitudes of these men, who seemed to shift their opinions when their own loved ones were threatened, but these accusations probably really did lead to genuine doubts about spectral evidence; Mather, Phips, and Hale knew their families were innocent and so, when the accusers began their claims, it was axiomatic that they were and perhaps always had been lying.

John and Elizabeth Proctor had been tried, along with others (including John Willard), in June. They were convicted and sentenced to hang. Most were executed in mid August, with Elizabeth thankfully being granted a reprieve until her coming child had been born. September saw the by-now usual arrests, confessions, accusations, and examinations – but so too did it see some of the afflicted girls, by now local celebrities (or objects of terror) carried to nearby Andover to find witches there. This was, at it had nearly a century before in King James's Scotland, thought to be a surefire method of detection. It resulted in a slew of new people being carried back to Salem for investigation – and it proved almost as much of a debacle when the terrified multitude accused in the town recanted all that, under the pressure of the moment, they had admitted to.

That same month, the redoubtable Giles Corey refused to plead, having just seen his wife, Martha, found guilty and sentenced to hang. Under English law, refusal to plead allowed for authorities to mete out the ghastly punishment of pressing: Giles, however, knew that a guilty verdict would lead to his property being forfeited, whilst false confession would imperil his soul. He submitted to being pressed. He was accordingly taken outside, lain flat on the ground, probably on jagged stones, and a board was placed over his body. On to this were set rocks of increasing weight. Courageous to the end, he famously requested 'more weights', both to end the agony and in defiance of his tormenters. He lived through this assault, his body gradually more shattered, for two days. Martha and those convicted alongside her were hanged later in the month. Amongst them was Samuel Wardell, who had confessed but recanted, denying as he did the reality of witchcraft. This saw him fit for the gallows, in one of the more terrifying aspects of witchcraft nodded to by the *Malleus Maleficarum* and further suggested by King James's *Daemonologie*: denying the reality of witchcraft might constitute proof that, as James had put it, one was 'of that profession'.

The court stopped dealing death in October, and Increase Mather, again, reiterated the unreliability of spectral evidence. Governor Phips, returning from his military venture, accepted this and wrote to England's Privy Council on the matter (foregrounding his own sense of scepticism): 'I hereby declare that as soon as I came from fighting . . . and understood what danger some of their innocent subjects might be exposed to, if the evidence of the afflicted persons only did prevail either to the committing or trying any of them, I did before any application was made unto me about it put a stop to the proceedings of the Court and they are now stopt till their Majesties pleasure be known.'⁴

A halt was called, too, to the avalanche of arrests, with the court of oyer and terminer formally closed at the end of October. This came in time to save the reprieved Elizabeth Proctor, thankfully – and though she lost her husband, the rest of her family survived (albeit that legal battles would ensue over the restitution of forfeited Proctor property). Phips thereafter washed his hands of witchcraft, referring it to a superior court of judicature in November. Thereafter came releases, pardons and recriminations. Nineteen people had been hanged, five had died in custody, and Giles Corey had met his terrible end under the weight of legal torture for refusing to plead. This had been done on the word of children, their imaginations having turned what might otherwise have been a minor matter into a testing ground for theories about the reality or unreality of demonic witchcraft and the evidence on which it could be proven or disproven. What no one seems to have considered is that children, then as now, are magnetically drawn to spooky stories and magical tales of witches and monsters; further, they have always had active imaginations, can be possessed of marvellous acting skills, and thrive on attention and validation. It was the convicted of Salem whose misfortune it was that these children's theatrics were encouraged by authorities with a vested interest in discovering whether or not the devil could or did make slaves on earth and empower them to produce tormenting spectres. To this had been added hysteria and the usual welter of interpersonal grievances and concerns for personal safety.

There continued to be trials in what would become the United States, including another attempt at passing off possession as the result of witchcraft when young Margaret Rule attracted the attention of Cotton Mather, who investigated her in his house. Mather himself retained the position of the scientific believer, as set out in his *The Wonders of the Invisible World* (1693): a text which found refutation and examination in Robert Calef's critical *More Wonders of the Invisible World* (1700), which pleaded for a Christian rejection of superstition in favour of scriptural study.

Witchcraft was taken seriously by authorities until at least 1706, when in Virginia Grace Sherwood was forced to undergo the swimming test after being accused. She was found guilty, but mercifully not hanged, the government having learned to be wary of issuing the death penalty following the disturbances and infamy resulting from Salem. Back in Britain, however, both the problem of what constituted evidence and the reliability of children as accusers was about to be tested during the final act of the age of the witches.

20

Gallows Green

In the late summer of 1696, eleven-year-old Christian Shaw, daughter of the wealthy laird John Shaw of Bargarran in Renfrewshire, was busy snooping. What she saw alarmed her. One of the servants, Catherine Campbell, apparently stole a cup of milk belonging to the family. Christian did her duty; she told her mother what she'd seen. As a result, Catherine allegedly cursed her by wishing Satan would drag her to hell. This took on even more frightening proportions when, four days later, Christian encountered a mysterious old woman, Agnes Naismith, known in Renfrewshire for her bad reputation. The next day, Christian began manifesting all the symptoms of possession-caused-by-witchcraft: convulsions, sobbing fits, and shrieking. In the course of these, she claimed that Catherine and Agnes were spectrally tormenting her.

As this behaviour dragged on for weeks, Christian's parents naturally decided to seek professional help, taking her to a physician in Glasgow, Dr Matthew Brisbane. He noted that, when out of her episodes, she was 'in every way healthful' – and Christian appeared to recover, being sent home with her parents.[1] After eight days, however, she began again: arguing with invisible spectres and vomiting scraps of rag, broken pins, gravel, hair, feathers, and fragments of eggshell (over a century later it would be alleged that these had been passed to her through a hole in the wall by an accomplice). She could point also to scratches allegedly laid on her by her invisible tormenters. The family returned to Dr Brisbane, who consulted another physician, Dr Henry Marshall. This was all looking very much like witchcraft might be a cause – though, to modern eyes, it is clear that Christian's behaviour was drawn from previous frauds dating back at least as far as King James's Anne Gunter.

Scotland, however, was in the same position as many other European countries – and North America – in terms of the accepted reality of witchcraft. Deeply religious men of science believed in the devil's ability to grant demonic powers of affliction to witches, even if they were growing wary of what constituted proof; other, more materialist thinkers doubted almost everything that had arisen from confessions which could not be demonstrably proven. As had been the case so often, alleged witches became a bone to be fought over – not now between competitive Catholics and Protestants, nor even between Protestant sects, but between those who disagreed on what was acceptable as convincing evidence. Rather edifyingly, this suggested a positive trend in that those who demanded higher stand-ards of evidence, simply by virtue of being allowed to make the argu-ment (without being denounced as witches for it), appeared to have changed the terms of the debate in their favour.

Debate was, though, a matter of academic interest (although it obviously had far wider implications), with bewigged men in author-ity attempting to push their theories – orthodox, radical, or some-thing which sought to reconcile the two – into the mainstream. To the average person, of whatever degree, it didn't greatly matter whether the earth revolved around the sun or vice versa, or whether the blood was produced by the liver or pumped via the heart, or whether spectral evidence was or wasn't valid; God remained in charge and Satan was his enemy.

This had certainly been visible in Renfrewshire, when, in 1676, Sir George Maxwell of Pollok fell ill 'with a hot and fiery distemper' and a pain in his side.[2] On the advice of a 'young dumb girl', he came to believe he had been bewitched, and soon enough he accused a local widow, Janet Mathie. Janet apparently freely confessed, offer-ing to bring the wax image (which she'd hidden behind her fireplace and occasionally pricked in the side) to Maxwell provided she was given an armed escort. Instead, Maxwell's servants converged on the woman's house and searched it, finding the image with two pins protruding from it. The discovery caused some easing of the landowner's suffering. On being arrested and interrogated, Janet blamed the mysterious young 'dumb girl'. Maxwell, however, was convinced that Janet had done it – he had, after all, threatened her son for breaking into his orchard. She was thus searched for the devil's marks before the Sheriff-Depute of Renfrew, and 'there were very many found upon her'. Maxwell's illness then returned with a vengeance, and charges were also brought against Janet's son, John Stewart, who had apparently been storm-raising by means of a clay effigy. This was found and subjected to a pseudo-scientific test, which revealed pins lodged within it. John was also taken up, along with his thirteen-year-old sister, Annabil. Annabil confessed to dealings with the devil ('the black gentleman') and malice against the whole Maxwell family. She also named others, whilst John was searched and devil's marks found on him. He ratified his sister's confession, admitting also to his 'paction' with Satan. The women they named were arrested (all but three, including the resolute Janet, confessing) and, once again, a mysterious effigy was found – this time, curiously, in Janet's prison cell in Paisley.

A commission was sought from and issued by the Privy Council, which nevertheless insisted on rigorous due process. At the ensuing trial, Annabil claimed that her mother had inducted her into witchcraft and encouraged her to sell her soul to the devil with the promise of a new coat in return. She received also a familiar spirit called Enippa (or Anippy). The little coven composed of the Mathies and the women accused with them had, thereafter, been granted a bevy of familiars – Sopha, Rigerum, Landlady, and Locas – to aid them in their image-magic. John corroborated this, volunteering his own spirit's name: Jonas. Other confessions followed, along with witness depositions, with the obstinate Janet apparently being shackled to prevent her from taking her own life. All save Annabil – due to her age – were sentenced to death.

This had all come about not just from the credulity of Sir George Maxwell but due to the claims of the 'dumb girl', who soon enough attracted scholarly attention. Her name, Janet Douglas, was discovered, and it was claimed she had regained the power of speech and could speak Latin without having learnt the language. Professor of Philosophy George Sinclair of Glasgow interviewed her in the summer of 1677, whereupon she claimed to have visions and to know many things via what might later be called telepathy, though she denied any commerce with Satan. Janet Douglas attempted, apparently, to make a career out of accusing witches (leading one woman to drown herself in the River Clyde), but the interest accruing to her backfired; the *wunderkind* was taken to Edinburgh, imprisoned, whipped, and deported to a colonial plantation.

In the late 1670s, therefore, scepticism and by-now ingrained belief in the power of witches were colliding, with the accused being caught in the crossfire. This was again the case in Renfrewshire in 1696, when young Christian Shaw's bizarre behaviour spiked and her accusations grew to include more than just Catherine Campbell and Agnes Naismith. With the physicians at a loss, a commission was requested from the Privy Council not for a trial but for an investigation. This was granted in early 1697. By now, those accused include the seventeen-year-old Elizabeth Anderson and her father, a beggar called Alexander; Elizabeth's grandmother, Jean Fulton; two of Elizabeth's cousins, fourteen-year-old James and eleven-year-old Thomas Lindsay; and two local women of good repute, the midwife Margaret Lang and her seventeen-year-old daughter, Martha. Margaret, well respected locally, stood up as boldly to her denunciation as had Giles Corey in Salem, refusing to flee with the courageous words 'Let them quake that dread and fear that need'.[3] Others targeted by Christian were less bold – they named still more people in an attempt to deflect attention from themselves and their families or to give the investigating commissioners what they wanted. In all, twenty-one people were arrested in Renfrewshire. The local Presbytery became involved, ordering a fast to encourage Christian's release from bewitchment: the ministers were evidently keen to demonstrate their godliness, although the consequence was a public validation of the girl's claims.

A scientific approach was again taken; the commissioners were keen to prove or disprove the charges. This involved parading those accused before the afflicted little girl and forcing them to touch her, whereupon she launched into screaming fits and cried that she was being tormented. The devil's marks were searched for and apparently found. Additionally, they secured confessions from some of the young people arrested. James, Thomas, and Elizabeth confirmed Christian's accusations (stating they had spectrally tormented her with cords and evil touches) and admitted to having been inducted into witchcraft by their grandmother, Jean. According to Elizabeth, the devil was present at her induction in the form of a 'black grim man', and promises of new clothes had been given her if she made the pact. Though she resisted, she was taken to a moor in Kilmacolm, where several people were present (including Catherine Campbell and members of Elizabeth's family). On entering into the devil's service, she and her coven had therefore begun campaigns of torment against an Inverkip minister, William Fleeming. This had graduated to murder – of the child of one William Montgomerie, the slaying of another, and the upturning of a ferry.

Elizabeth claimed also to have flown on her father's back to conventicles, whereupon the coven engaged in pricking pins in images (of a Dumbarton minister) before roasting them. Young James Lindsay confessed to much the same, adding that he found Satan's hand 'exceeding cold'. Thomas, too young to provide valid legal evidence, nevertheless confirmed the 'black grim man' story, thereby revealing that the three youngsters had together concocted (or been provided with) a coherent tale they hoped would release them from their predicament. Moreover, those confessing claimed to have been provided with a 'piece of an un-christened child's liver to eat', which the duplicitous devil had told them would prevent their ever being apprehended or, if they somehow were, would prevent them confessing – a piece of religious interpolation probably provided by the clergymen involved in the investigation.

The commissioners' report satisfied the Privy Council, and a new warrant was issued allowing them to proceed to trial in Renfrew, Paisley, or Glasgow (key judicial arenas in the western Central Belt). The venue chosen was Paisley which, perhaps not coincidentally, had in 1692 punished six people (by forcing them to wear placards) for falsely accusing twelve local notables of witchcraft. The town was, thus, under scrutiny from true believers, with Reverend Blackwell thundering forth on the presence of the devil in the pulpit of the semi-ruined abbey (whose western section remained in use). By the time of the trial, two more confessions – from Margaret and Janet Roger – had been secured. Experts were called in to aid with the prosecution: the jurist (and believer) Francis Grant, assisted by James MacGilchrist, a solicitor who happened to be Christian's uncle. Grant presented the evidence against the accused as unassailable: some of those on trial had been previously accused; the devil's marks were abundant; none of those accused had shed tears (construed as a sign of witchcraft); and there were the physical scratches apparent on the little girl. Old, apparently still-sound arguments as to why confessing witches weren't simply mad were rehearsed: 'melancholians are lovers of solitude; witches of society and feasts'.[4] It was on the back of such specious beliefs that authorities had so often pressed their captives to name their colleagues.

Despite the judges also being in favour of guilt, the jury took nearly seven hours to return seven guilty verdicts: Catherine Campbell and Agnes Naismith, the original women accused, were guilty; three Lindsay men (another James, John, and John of Barloch), of longstanding bad reputation and previous accusations, were guilty; Margaret Lang, who had eventually admitted to having some knowledge of the devil but not to witchcraft, was guilty; and Margaret Fulton, another of Elizabeth Anderson's relatives, was guilty (Margaret having either lost her mind in terror or having attempted to please her interrogators with wild tales of magical horses and elves). All of them had been held in Paisley, a thriving burgh-in-barony spreading uphill from the ancient Abbey, save one accused, John Reid, who had been found mysteriously strangled in his cell in nearby Renfrew's tolbooth.

In the west end of the town, on Gallows Green, the guilty were led to their deaths. Catherine Campbell raged against her accusers before being silenced, as did Agnes Naismith. The executioners, charged with strangling the 'witches' before burning their bodies, did an incomplete job. So it would be that those who had come to watch reported the sight of still-living people thrown on the flames, their flailing limbs being beaten back with a borrowed walking stick. The judicial murders of the Paisley witches had been just one of the many horrific, heart-rending cruelties inflicted on people since the dark age of witchcraft persecution had begun. Thankfully, it was the last mass execution for what was now being openly questioned as a crime worthy of state punishment. As in Salem, no one who confessed openly to demonic witchcraft was executed. Also as in Salem, witches were not on trial; the reality of demonic witchcraft was.

Christian Shaw's torments ended as quickly, and she went on to lead a successful life, marrying a minister, Mr Miller of Kilmaurs, and later introducing Dutch sewing techniques and machinery to the area (in 1722 creating the Bargarran Thread Company). Her deceptions, however, were soon a source of debate; the jurist Francis Grant, who had helped prosecute the accused witches, presented the case in *A True Narrative of the Sufferings and Release of a Young Girle* (1698) and returned to it in a 1700 treatise on the law. In his attempts to prove the credibility of the evidence presented, he had, ironically, missed what might have been the truth: that Christian had been a fraud, coached and aided by her father in the pursuit of sparking a witchcraft panic capable of eliminating those against whom he had a grudge.[5] In the history of witchcraft, her name stands alongside those other children, from the Throckmorton girls who had accused Alice Samuels in the 1590s through to the fame-seeking Leicester Boy in 1616 to the girls of Salem, whose attempts at gaining attention were enabled and encouraged by those whose interest was in fighting the potential rise of atheism they perceived in the questioning of demonic witchcraft.

*

The British Isles – and Europe, as it turned out – had seen the end of witch panics, but old beliefs died hard. In Pittenweem in 1704, a sixteen-year-old named Patrick Morton exhibited signs of posses-sion-by-witchcraft and accused multiple women, including a local woman known as a charmer, Beatrix Laing (or Layng), of spectrally tormenting him. He was taken seriously by the local minister, a fanatical Calvinist named Patrick Cowper, and a commission was granted for investigation. Beatrix was tortured, searched for the devil's mark, and denied sleep. On breaking down, she confessed and named accomplices – Isobel Adam (who herself implicated Thomas Brown), Janet Cornfoot, Nicholas Lawson, and Lillie Wallace – who was likewise brought in and cruelly treated, with Patrick Cowper personally administering beatings.

Although Cowper was keen on securing immediate convictions and death sentences, the Privy Council intervened, insisting that the matter be referred to Edinburgh, where the High Court refused to indict them (to the anger of many locals, who believed whole-heartedly that the witches deserved condign punishment). The sceptical Council demanded also to examine Patrick Morton, whose symptoms had, apparently, ceased. In Pittenweem, the authorities, facing difficulties in housing the accused, were forced to free them on the security of fines. This did not come in time, however, to save one of the accused, Thomas Brown, who had starved to death in gaol. Beatrix Laing, too, was forced to flee the area due to hostility, and thus died penniless in St Andrews. Janet Cornfoot faced more direct extra-judicial punishment on her escape from captivity whilst under investigation. An enraged mob, encouraged by Cowper, lynched her, dragging her to the beach, stringing her up on a line drawn between a ship and the shore, and stoning her. When she was cut down, still living, they placed a board on her limp body and piled stones on it, before having a horse trample over her mangled corpse. Cowper then refused her a Christian burial. The central authorities, at this point, had begun exercising restraint – but belief in and fear of witches, which had begun in earnest at the centre, in the sixteenth century, had spread far too widely to be eradicated.

Scotland's Privy Council and its independence, however, could be. The country united with England to form the kingdom of Great Britain in 1707: a union probably more to the late James VI and I's tastes than had been Cromwell's, but still not quite as comprehensive as he would have liked (James's goal having been to unite the two countries' religious and legal systems as well as their secular governing bodies). Henceforth, Scotland had a select number of seats in the new Parliament of Great Britain, which procedurally operated according to the traditions of the English Parliament, until that itself became the Parliament of the United Kingdom of Great Britain and Ireland. Despite political restructuring, however, legal executions for witchcraft continued: the last in Scotland was Janet Horne in 1727, who was possibly suffering mental illness and appallingly treated by neighbours who accused her of riding her daughter, who had deformities in her hands and feet, to meet with the devil.

Ireland, in which the writ of central Anglo-British authorities had never run too strongly (despite the bloody efforts of those authorities), had largely escaped the panics in Great Britain. In 1661, an elderly beggar named Florence Newton was tried under the country's 1586 Witchcraft Act (in reality a copy of Elizabeth I's 1562 Act stamped on Ireland), apparently for mumbling curses, in Youghal – though she died in custody before she could face any other penalty. In 1711, eight women were tried at the Country Antrim assizes (for causing one Mary Dunbar to have fits and vomit the usual pins and other detritus), where the presiding judges were split on their guidance to the jury, despite locals apparently being violently in favour of execution. Mary Dunbar herself died during the course of the trial. The records are lost, though the women were almost certainly executed; the husband of one of them was subsequently tried and executed for murderous witchcraft at the Carrickfergus assizes. These were the last judicial executions – but, again, belief in the supernatural and the demonic did continue.

The age of witchcraft, however, was over as far as the authorities were concerned. In England, the last trials took place in Leicester in 1717; twenty-five witnesses were called to provide testimony against Jane Clarke and her children (the so-called 'Wigston Witches'), but the jury pronounced them not guilty. To freedom, too, had gone Jane Wenham in 1712, accusations that she could fly being treated with scorn by the presiding judge; Jane was convicted but that conviction was quashed, although popular feeling necessitated her removal from the parish. Old standards of evidence – King James's standards of evidence – were no longer fit for purpose in the courtroom. Due to the sluggish nature of the law and people's tendency to misunderstand, misuse or ignore it, trials for witchcraft, whether legal ones or hole-in-the-wall, *ad hoc* affairs, thus petered out rather than ending neatly – and the complex web of jurisdictions across Europe resulted in the last-known trials taking place in Poland in the late eighteenth century. Due to the messiness of records and legal systems, both Anna Göldi (executed in Switzerland in 1782) and Barbara Zdunk (executed in 1811 in Prussia) have been given the sad honour of being identified as the last women killed for having allegedly practised witchcraft, but in both cases their trials and sentences were based on different charges, witchcraft having ceased to be a crime where they lived and died.

In Great Britain, the Witchcraft Act of 1735 not only repealed existing legislation but achieved a complete reversal, making it illegal to argue in favour of the existence of supernatural powers. Educated opinion could now scorn, disavow, or studiously ignore what educated opinion had once endorsed. The people – and people of all ranks – might have continued to believe in the presence and power of the devil and his disciples, and certainly in the supernatural more broadly, but in the eighteenth century, an age of materialism and industry, these things could no longer be taken on trust. In fact, they were to be distrusted and denounced. This would only become more necessary as, freed from the prospect of torture and the gallows, increasing numbers of charlatans and deluded people began setting themselves up as magicians, wizards and sorcerers in succeeding generations. What could and had been proven during the era of belief was that miscarriages of justice had happened – and eventually it was accepted that all cases had been miscarriages of justice.

The witch, over time, ceased to be a direct threat and came to be, by turns, a fairytale monster, a figure of fun, and a literary trope. Language, iconography, and the popular imagination seem, if anything, to have embraced witchcraft once it was decoupled from the courtroom; the emergence of words like 'cantrips' (attested in Scots from the eighteenth century and meaning incantations or spells) and neo-rituals like the grotesque black mass indicate that witchery only grew in the cultural consciousness once the age of legal hunts and persecution was over. It is fitting that perhaps the earliest image of the storybook witch – flying on her broomstick, as she did in continental accusations, and wearing her pointed hat – comes from an antiquarian book, *The history of witches and wizards: giving a true account of all their tryals in England, Scotland, Swedeland, France, and New England*, published in 1720: after the dark age of witchcraft had passed.

In the ensuing centuries, Scotland, England, Europe, the New World, and beyond have seen memorials spring up to those sacrificed on the altar of false belief: in Paisley, a horseshoe embedded in the ground at a crossroads marks the spot where the awful judicial execution of innocents took place in 1697; in Dunning, a memorial stands to Maggie Wall, believed to have been executed in 1657; in Admirals Park in Chelmsford, an oak tree commemorates the dozens executed there; in Salem, granite benches are inscribed with the names of those put to death during the panic. These are only a few of the memorials amongst the hundreds raised to remind us of those once deemed criminals by the state, despite their crimes being, in essence, impossible (as the 1735 Act asserted). They are now recognised as victims.

We thus, rightly, remember those accused of witchcraft – those who were tried, those who were tortured, those who were executed, and those who escaped execution but were associated with imaginary demonism nonetheless. We must ask, though, given the length of time that witchcraft endured as a genuine fear and a crime punishable by death, why these terrible things happened. What drove them? What elicited major outbreaks, local and national, and widespread persecution? These are questions, fortunately, easy enough to answer.

21

The Devil's Decline

James VI and I has been rather a neglected monarch, despite his historical importance as the man who first united the crowns of England and Scotland. Though he is often respected for his contributions to the Protestant religion – namely, his commissioning of the Authorised Version of the Bible – his name has also been blackened by his association with witchcraft. One might ask, then, whether that stain upon his reputation is deserved.

The answer is, as is so often the case, perhaps – but with caveats. James did not construct his belief in witchcraft out of whole cloth, and he didn't invent the idea of legal proscription (which predated him in Britain), but he certainly did much to popularise the perceived dangers of the phenomenon in Scotland, just as he promoted the importance of sorting the false from what he considered the genuine in England. Further, he was inarguably a major driving force in leading the charge against devilry – and emphasising the role of Satan and his ostensible pacts – in his native realm. In this, however, he was not a deranged witch-hunter, nor was he acting against the grain. Indeed, the opposite is true: he was a cultured, educated leader whose beliefs reflected what was developing as enlightened opinion on demonology. It was hardly his fault that scholarship had got it wrong, any more than it was the fault of contemporary physicians and surgeons who killed patients when treating them according to erroneous beliefs about the human body. James was one of several leaders in the early modern period who took the threat of witchcraft seriously as a scholar-ruler. But he was also, during his time in Scotland, a deeply paranoid and suspicious man who could perceive threats against his throne lurking everywhere. In this era of intensely personal rule, personal obsessions could have national implications.

The sixteenth century is often recognised as the age of Reformation and early Counter-Reformation. It might be better thought of as the age of suspicion and paranoia, for the ructions of religious transformation resulted in a great deal of both. This was a time of treasonous plots and hidden fifth-columnists, of international conspiracies and assassinations. When people met in private, it was always possible they were planning something illicit and dangerous. No one could be sure whether their neighbours, family, friends, or fellow courtiers inwardly believed the right thing even if they seemed to be conforming outwardly. Witchcraft was simply another means by which any monarch's enemies might plan and enact an attempt on the sovereign's life or throne, and thus witches had to be rooted out, demonised, and their designs, however imaginary, validated. Only in this way could the people, who already had some idea of the phenomenon, see its truly dark potential. Hence, James could instigate hunts and mass trials aimed at ensuring his personal safety, and in so doing he could both secure his coveted position as his country's leading religious figure – Satan's greatest enemy – and educate his people in the dangers not just facing Christendom but facing Scotland particularly.

When he departed the country, he left behind a framework for how witchcraft should be viewed and how the legal machinery ought to deal with it: it thus only took the conjunction of interested (and active) authorities, laws with sufficient teeth, and credulous people to spark hunts. On succeeding to the English throne, the benevolent king felt assured in his new position and could thus continue his academic pursuits in more convivial surroundings; he taught the English how to separate true demonic witchcraft from the false accusations of attention-seeking counterfeits. In this way, although his standards of evidence were appallingly low to future generations, he left a means for later rationalists to deconstruct the phenomenon and thus demand higher standards of proof which witchcraft was, by its nature, incapable of providing.

The seventeenth century, born of its predecessor, was one of conflict and competition. The religious divisions of the Reformation and its sequels had not gone away; rather, positions were entrenched. Paranoia remained prevalent too: institutions such as the Scottish Kirk could reasonably fear for the souls and lives of the godly and, in so doing, panic about their opposite numbers, the ungodly. Supposed witches, again, would suffer. In this way, witches were perennially useful. What began in the medieval period as a means of attacking non-Catholics became also a means of attacking non-Protestants and grew to embrace attacks on any non-conformist beliefs, traditional folk beliefs and behaviour, the socially unpopular, and anyone who might be caught up in personal feuds or grudges. Europe and North America were, in the seventeenth century, battlegrounds, and battlegrounds have casualties.

Unfortunately, accused witches were equally useful to all orthodox religions, whether they were fighting other faiths or looking for enemies within. By this time, there existed the judicial machinery and a pool of distrustful people who believed in the phenomenon, both of which were required to fuel great hunts and mass trials. The more the early media – academic treatises and books as well as pamphlets, sermons, and oral transmission of confessions – promoted and legitimised demonic witchcraft, the more entrenched convictions about its reality became.

This, then, is the reason why James's beliefs in witchcraft proved so popular in Britain – even in England, where he sought to enforce his own idiosyncratic standards of proof in the face of obvious and recurring fakes. At root, witchcraft persecutions happened because people across the social spectrum wanted them to happen, having been educated – in part by men like King James, but his was only one expert voice – into accepting the phenomenon. In low-level cases even before James's reigns, people believed that witches existed and could cause harm, even if they did not think too deeply about the demonic sources of that power. The authorities – and the legal system – acknowledged effects but, like the people, identified the wrong causes and encouraged belief in demonic origins. Thus were ancient beliefs – in magic, superstition, cursing, and healing – rebranded as devil-sent, with new fears and terrors (such as spectral attack) added over the course of a bloody century. Individual motives, of course, could vary wildly, from the vengeful or suspicious villager to the self-righteous minister to the paranoid local dignitary or monarch: all were supporting one another in the belief that witchcraft was as real and threatening as murder or theft – more so, in fact, as it imperilled whole communities if they allowed it to continue without the occasional purge.

The horrific mass trials and hunts happened generally because those in power either actively drove them (as James had in 1590–91 and 1597, and numerous European leaders did throughout the period) or enabled those lower down the social hierarchy to keep purging. The witch, once she had been academically accepted as a genuine threat, was both durable and useful to just about everyone for over a century. In her lay a means of discovering potential mass treason. In her lay the reason one's cow had died or one's child was convulsing. In her was an enemy of God who could be purged in order to sanctify society. In her lay a means of besmirching the reputation of political enemies. As to why so many 'witches' confessed to things they couldn't possibly have done, again reasons were manifold: from delusion to terror to attempts to save family members to confabulation to embroidery of actual misdemeanours and futile attempts at magic.

Given all this, it is perhaps less worth asking 'why did this happen?' than 'why didn't this happen even more often?' The answer is that, throughout the period, there were more people across society *un*willing to believe the worst of others than otherwise. It is, at least, a vindication of humanity that mass hunts and trials were always the exception rather than the rule. Still, around 2,500 people (84 per cent of them women) lost their lives in Scotland, whilst in England the number is thought to be just over 100 (although, in both nations, many more people were tried and subjected to barbaric treatment before acquittal). It happened not just for the reasons social scientists might offer – for example, because social tensions arising from general anxieties about societal decline, as in the seventeenth century, caused people to look for easy enemies and to invest them with handy attributes of evil – but because leaders told people (in fact, taught people) that certain communities were being targeted by the devil. People in those areas, not surprisingly, believed them. Some saw manifestations of that demonic activity – or so they thought – and denounced it; still others might denounce friends, neighbours, and local undesirables for fear they might themselves be denounced.

The subsequent Enlightenment slowly began to subject witchcraft beliefs and claims to the new scientific methods; these didn't eliminate God or the devil but introduced new burdens of proof on those who claimed Satan was, indeed, stalking the earth and bestowing powers on his disciples. Gradually, the law (and therefore the state) was being dragged into a materialist position, with the courtroom a place where fact was intended to eradicate fiction. Confessions, ever more colourful thanks to the deep education in witchcraft that people had been given over the decades, no longer seemed enough – their content, clearly fanciful, was unverifiable. The devil's mark, too, was slowly discredited; it had been demonstrably abused by self-professed hunters and began looking decidedly unreliable as understanding of the human body increased and old ideas about medicine were discarded. The means by which witches had supposedly committed injuries and murders – effigies and curses – could not stand up to scrutiny as the medical sciences recognised new causes of illness and death. Accusations by accused witches against accused witches, which once King James had defended, had shown themselves utterly unjustifiable, as courtrooms found themselves overwhelmed by common complaints.

Thus, the dreadful period of witchcraft persecution took place, essentially, because people supported it. They believed, or the majority did, that witches existed and were possessed of supernatural powers derived from an active devil. But King James, in espousing and promoting this belief, had done his job too well. Although the 1735 Witchcraft Act attempted to deny the reality of the supernatural and criminalise anyone supporting it, the people were not so easily educated out of the ideas they had been educated into.

It is debatable whether this could have ever been done. If the legal system rejected its own previous position on supernatural powers (and with it the ability of Satan to bestow them on followers), then the people did not. So-called Satanic Panics certainly gripped the USA as recently as the 1980s. Across Britain, people had been thoroughly indoctrinated into believing in classical witchcraft: the demonic pact, cultish covens, and necromancy, to the extent that even in the 1970s writers were still theorising – unconvincingly – that many of those executed during the age of witchcraft had indeed formed a real cult of devil-worshippers.

Today, James's primary concern regarding witches' activity, the devil himself, looms less large in – though he has not entirely disappeared from – witchcraft, which is now an accepted form of spiritual practice that can take many forms, from esoteric Satanism to harmless neo-pagan Wiccan. The law might be largely uninterested in witchcraft unless it involves, as it almost never does, the carrying out of crimes, but public interest remains lively. Even those who have no interest in spiritual modern witchcraft can freely dabble in practices that James would have viewed as deriving power only from a demonic pact. One can easily, for example, buy a custom-made wax doll (complete with pins); visit a local spiritual medium with the aim of hearing from the dead or being foretold the future; buy books – ostensibly nonfiction – which promise guidance on raising demons; or join any number of online groups which share recipes for love potions. The allure of the supernatural remains strong. Despite a total lack of reliable evidence, people of all walks of life still believe in, and claim to see and experience, all manner of unorthodox things – mysterious terrestrial monsters and extraterrestrial visitations and abductions – which are not so different from the shaggy, frigid beasts, malign conspiracies, and fairy abductions claimed by our ancestors. Nowadays we might explain these unusual claims via psychological speculation, attributing them to misidentifications, hallucinations, or wishful thinking. In the past, the solution would have been devilry at work in the world.

Nor has the desire to hunt gone away, even if its targets have likewise shifted from devil-worshipping, demon-raising witches. Sadly, the term 'witch hunt' has had many afterlives. The human propensity to label certain beliefs anathema is as strong as ever; indeed, as societies rightly prohibit certain acts and proscribe certain categories of behaviour, it is inevitable that perfectly acceptable beliefs will sometimes be casualties – and not just in repressive societies. Perhaps more problematically, a great number of people (who need no longer be supported just by the printing press but have an array of new forms of media at their fingertips) can still be found claiming that certain groups – whether religious or ethnic, or based on sexual or gender identities – are inherently more likely to commit crimes.

In the true sense of the phrase – the paranoia-driven hunt for people alleged to have undertaken magical acts they couldn't possibly have undertaken, whether flying to conventicles or conjuring up Satan and making deals – there have been no modern witch hunts. In its metaphorical sense, however, witch-hunting remains a perennial human pursuit, and it will probably continue to be as long as significant numbers of people in any society are encouraged to inform against one another or to imagine grand conspiracies involving enemies hiding in plain sight and being responsible for society's ills. When Arthur Miller dramatised the Salem witch trials at the height of the McCarthy 'Red Scare' on the 1940s and '50s, the analogy was imperfect: communism certainly existed as a very real (if hardly threatening) ideology to which anyone could legitimately have subscribed, even if many of those accused had little or nothing to do with it. The hysterical fear and the tendency of people to accuse one another, however, was as lively when politicians were encouraging citizens to denounce each other as political dissidents as when they were encouraging subjects to denounce one another as witches.

So too can the term 'witch hunt' be incredibly useful when seeking to delegitimise opponents' arguments and actions. When US President Donald Trump accused those investigating his alleged criminal activities of engaging in a 'witch hunt', he was implying that they were acting out of paranoia and political motives alone, and that their accusations were no more valid than those who had once accused innocent women of being seduced by Satan.

The whole idea of hunting others who might be guilty of illicit activity, real or imagined, is as bound up in politics in the twenty-first century as it was in the sixteenth and seventeenth. Since the decline of the rallying-point hate figure of the stereotypical witch, human hatreds and fears have simply fragmented and found an array of other figures to cluster around. Those in charge have, accordingly, continued to find ways of taking advantage of those fears by stoking up hatred of the vulnerable or unpopular, or of masking their own misdeeds by comparing their accusers to blind, wild-eyed witch-hunters. As always, both witch and witch-hunter are useful figures, whether in their metaphorical or literal senses.

It is thus worth asking whether we have, then, been educated out of our belief in witches and witchcraft. As the people of the early modern period inherited ancient beliefs and had them filtered through the sieve of their educated classes and leaders (first ardent demonologists and later sceptical materialists), so have we inherited their beliefs and incorporated them into our own various world-views. Witches – and the occasional evangelical witch-hunter – still walk among us.

Notes

Introduction: That Old Black Magic

1 Alexander Leggatt, *William Shakespeare's* Macbeth*: A Sourcebook*, p. 95.
2 Jeffrey Burton Russell, *Witchcraft in the Middle Ages*, pp. 4–7.
3 Ibid, p. 23.
4 George Bagshawe Harrison, *Elizabethan and Jacobean Quartos, 10*, p. 28.
5 James VI and I, *Daemonologie*, p. 7.

1 The Origins of Evil

1 Henry Angsar Kelly, *Satan: A Biography*, p. 251.
2 Alan Charles Kors and Edward Peters, *Witchcraft in Europe: 400–1700*, p. 62.
3 Russell Hope Robbins, *The Encyclopaedia of Witchcraft & Demonology*, p. 77.
4 Michael D. Barbezat, *Burning Bodies*, p. 237.
5 Burton Russell, *Witchcraft in the Middle Ages*, p. 131.
6 Brian Paul Levack, *The Witch-Hunt in Early Modern Europe*, p. 204.
7 Julian Goodare, *The European Witch-hunt*, p. 40.
8 *Ecumenical Council of Florence, Session 9–23 March 1440.*
9 Goodare, *The European Witch-hunt*, p. 47.

2 This Twilight and Evening of the World

1 Jacobus Sprenger and Heinrich Kramer, *Malleus Maleficarum*, p. 90.
2 Ibid, p. 93.
3 Ibid, p. 217.
4 Ibid, p. 48.
5 Ibid, p. 32.
6 Ibid, p. 25.

3 A Continent Cursed

1 Heinz Schilling, *Martin Luther*, p. 446.
2 *Letters and Papers, Foreign and Domestic, Henry VIII, 2, 1515–18*, pp. 350–361.
3 Gilbert Burnet, *The History of the Reformation*, 1, p. 363.
4 *CSP, Spain, Henry VIII, 1536–1538, 5, 2*, p. 28.
5 *Letters and Papers, Foreign and Domestic, Henry VIII, 13, 2*, p. 560.
6 1541–2: 33 Henry 8 c.8: The Act against Conjurations, Witchcraft, Sorcery and Inchantments.
7 Maureen M. Meikle, *The Scottish People 1490–1625*, p. 177.
8 1563: Mary c.73: Anentis Witchcraft.
9 John Knox, *The History of the Reformation, 5*, p. 149.
10 *CSP, Foreign, Elizabeth, 7, 1564–1565*, pp. 378–394.
11 Frederik Schiern, *Life of James Hepburn, Earl of Bothwell*, p. 397.
12 Kirkcaldy of Grange, *Memoirs*, p. 245.
13 Michael Wasser, 'Scotland's First Witch-Hunt', p. 23.

4 Birth of a Mania

1 George Buchanan, *History of Scotland in Two Volumes*, p. 248.
2 Buchanan, *A Detection*, p. 31.
3 John Dalyell, *The Darker Superstitions of Scotland*, p. 372.
4 *Canongate Burgh Court Book 1574–77* SL150/1/2, pp. 370–3. See: https://witches.hca.ed.ac.uk/case/C/LA/3102 [accessed 06/03/2024].

5 Elizabeth's Witches

1 Luke Owen Pike, *A History of Crime in England*, 2, p. 23.
2 Lara Apps and Andrew Gow, *Male Witches in Early Modern Europe*, p. 49.
3 Joyce Gibson, *Hanged for Witchcraft*, p. 123.
4 1563: 5 Elizabeth 1 c.16: An Act against Conjurations, Inchantments and Witchcraft.
5 Tim Thornton, *Prophecy, Politics and the People in Early Modern England*, p. 26.
6 Ibid, p. 21.
7 Sprenger and Kramer, *Malleus Maleficarum*, p. 32.
8 John Phillips, *The Examination and confession of certaine wytches at Chensforde*.
9 R. H. Helmholz, *Select Cases*, p. 61.
10 Carole Levin, *The Reign and Life of Queen Elizabeth I*, p. 146.
11 Edward White, *A rehearsall both straung and true*.
12 Carole Levin, Anna Riehl Bertolet and Jo Eldridge Carney, *A Biographical Encyclopedia of Early Modern Englishwomen*, p. 322.
13 Doreen Valiente, *Where Witchcraft Lives*, p. 49.
14 Reginald Scot, *The Discoverie of Witchcraft*, p. 262.
15 Ibid, p. 208.
16 Ibid, p. 50.
17 Ibid, p. 209, 86.
18 Scot, *The Discoverie*, p. 192.

6 Denmark's a Prison

1 *CSP, Scotland, 10, 1589–1593*, pp. 151–162.
2 Andrew Lang, *The History of Scotland*, 2, p. 254.
3 *CSP, Scotland, 10, 1589–1593*, pp. 206–225.
4 Levack, *Demonology, Religion, and Witchcraft*, p. 67.
5 Robert Kolb, *Lutheran Ecclesiastical Culture*, p. 426.
6 Liv Helene Willumsen, 'Witchcraft Against Royal Danish Ships in 1589', p. 69.
7 Merry E. Wiesner, *Women and Gender in Early Modern Europe*, p. 277.
8 Willumsen, 'Witchcraft Against Royal Danish Ships', p. 70
9 *CSP, Scotland, 10*, p. 348.

7 The King's Evil

1 P. Hume-Brown, *History of Scotland*, p. 164.
2 Lawrence Normand and Gareth Roberts, *Witchcraft in Early Modern Scotland*, p. 95.
3 In April, one Meg Dow was accused, tried, found guilty, and executed, her case hinging on the claim that she had murdered a child via witchcraft. In July, Lady Foulis and Hector Munro were acquitted on witchcraft charges, and in August, in Aberdeenshire, Janet Grant and Janet Clark were executed for summoning the devil and causing death by witchcraft. In Stirling, Isobel Watson claimed to have been visited by Satan in the guise of an angel.
4 Normand and Roberts, *Witchcraft in Early Modern Scotland*, p. 254.
5 *CSP, Scotland, 10, 1589–1593*, pp. 456–480.
6 *CSP, Scotland, 10*, p. 524.
7 James Melville, *Memoirs*, p. 389.
8 *CSP, Scotland, 10, 1589–1593*, pp. 445–456.
9 *CSP, Scotland, 10, 1589–1593*, pp. 592–616.
10 Goodare, 'The Framework for Scottish Witch-Hunting in the 1590s', pp. 244–7.
11 *CSP, Scotland, 11, 1593–1595*, pp. 3–37.
12 *CSP, Scotland, 10, 1589–1593*, pp. 616–630.
13 Ibid.
14 *CSP, Scotland, 11, 1593–1595*, pp. 541–562.

8 These Detestable Slaves of the Devil

1 James VI and I, *Daemonologie*, p. 4.
2 Levack, *Witchcraft in Scotland*, p. 25.

9 Here Be Monsters Again

1 Patrick Fraser Tytler, *History of Scotland, 7*, p. 325.
2 See: https://witches.hca.ed.ac.uk/case/C/EGD/129 [accessed 15/03/2024].
3 Goodare, *The Scottish Witch-hunt in Context*, p. 55.
4 *CSP, Scotland, 13, 1597–1603*, p. 56.
5 Goodare, *The Scottish Witch-hunt in Context*, p. 61.

10 Let the Blood Run Free

1 Gareth Russell, *The Palace*, p. 149.
2 *CSP, Scottish Series, II*, p. 746.
3 Ibid.
4 Ibid, p. 748.
5 Ibid , p. 759.
6 Lang, *History of Scotland, 2*, p. 323.
7 *CSP, Scotland, 13 (1), 1547–1603*, p. 467.
8 James Scott, *A History of the Life and Death of John, Earl of Gowrie*, p. 293.
9 George Payne Rainsford James, *Gowrie*, p. 343.
10 James VI and I, *Basilikon Doron*.
11 Stanley Wells, *Shakespeare: For All Time*, p. 74.
12 James VI and I, *Correspondence with Sir Robert Cecil*, p. xlv.

11 Pins and Needles

1 George Lillie Craik, *The Pictorial History of England, 3*, p. 456.
2 John Hill Burton, *The History of Scotland, 5*, p. 222.
3 1604: 1 James 1 c.12: An Act against Conjuration, Witchcraft and dealing with evil and wicked Spirits.
4 Ivan Bunn and Gilbert Geis, *A Trial of Witches*, p. 64.
5 William Hawkins, *A Treatise of the Pleas of the Crown, 1*, p. 5.
6 *Cecil Papers, 17, 1605*, pp. 99–127.
7 Ibid, pp. 445–454.
8 Levack, *New Perspectives on Witchcraft, Magic, and Demonology*, p. 46.
9 Goodare, *The Scottish Witch-hunt in Context*, p. 68.

12 Out of the Mouths of Babes

1 Aikin, *Memoirs of the Court of King James*, p. 104.
2 Bodleian MS Tanner 299, fol. 11r.
3 NCRO MS IL 4304.
4 BL MS Harley 6947, fol. 211r.
5 Levack, *The Literature of Witchcraft*, p. 196.

6 Edward Baines, John Harland and William Robert Whatton, *The History of the County Palatine and Duchy of Lancaster*, p. 202.

7 Nicolas Rémy, *Demonolatry: An Account of the Historical Practice of Witchcraft*, p. 59.

8 Thomas Potts, *Discovery of Witches in the County of Lancaster*, p. 45.

13 The Cunning Countess

1 Anne Somerset, *Unnatural Murder*, p. 94.

2 Ibid, p. 115.

3 Thomas Bayly Howell, *A Collection of State Trials, 2*, p. 935.

4 Alastair Bellany, *The Politics of Court Scandal in Early Modern England*, p. 149.

14 The King Is Dead

1 John Lingard, *The History of England, 7*, p. 164.

2 William E. Burns, *Witch Hunts in Europe and America*, p. 327.

3 STAC 8/32/13.

4 Edward Fairfax, *Daemonologia*, p. 61.

5 James Granger, *A Biographical History of England, 1*, p. 30.

6 SP 14/175 f.90.

15 Lambs to the Slaughter

1 Gregory J. Durston, *Crimen Exceptum*, p. 74.

2 Samuel Rawson Gardiner, *History of England from the Accession of James I, 6*, p. 119.

3 Robert E. Ruigh, *The Parliament of 1624*, p. 336.

4 Goodare, *The Government of Scotland 1560–1625*, p. 198.

5 Goodare, *The Scottish Witch-hunt in Context*, p. 133.

6 William Drummond, *The Poetical Works of William Drummond of Hawthornden*, p. 118.

16 The Witch-Finder General

1 Hopkins's own book dates this as March 1644 – he was using the Old Style calendar.
2 Levack, *New Perspectives*, p. 277.
3 Matthew Hopkins, *A Discovery of Witches*, p. 4.
4 James Sharpe, *Witchcraft in Early Modern England*, p. 47.
5 Alan Macfarlane, *Witchcraft in Tudor and Stuart England*, p. 140.
6 Owen Davies, *Witchcraft, Magic and Culture, 1736-1951*, p. 89.
7 John Gaule, *Select cases of conscience touching vvitches and vvitchcrafts*.

17 The Godly Society

1 Goodare, *Scottish Witches and Witch-Hunters*, p. 86.
2 Hughes, 'Witch-Hunting', p. 91.

18 The Devil in the Detail

1 P. G. Maxwell-Stuart, *An Abundance of Witches*, p. 181.
2 Maxwell-Stuart, *An Abundance of Witches*, p. 198.
3 Ibid.
4 Goodare, *The European Witch-Hunt*, p. 210.
5 Maxwell-Stuart, *An Abundance of Witches*, p. 207.
6 Thomas Wright, *Narratives of Sorcery and Magic, from the Most Authentic Sources*, p. 352.

19 New World, Old Problems

1 Malins, 'Oliver Cromwell', p. 368.
2 Bernard Rosenthal, *Salem Story*, p. 2.
3 Abby Sage Richardson, *The History of Our Country*, p. 145.
4 Chadwick Hansen, *Witchcraft at Salem*, p. 165.

20 Gallows Green

1 Hope Robbins, *The Encyclopaedia Of Witchcraft & Demonology*, p. 39.

2 *A History of the Witches of Renfrewshire who were burned on the Gallowgreen of Paisley*, p. 36.

3 Hope Robbins, *The Encyclopaedia of Witchcraft & Demonology*, p. 39.

4 *A History of the Witches of Renfrewshire who were burned on the Gallowgreen of Paisley*, p. 161.

5 Tony McAleavy, *The Last Witch Craze*, pp. 208–10.

Bibliography

Abbreviations

BL Harley: British Library Harley manuscripts
Bodleian MS Tanner: Bodleian Library Tanner manuscripts
NCRO: Northamptonshire Record Office manuscripts
SP: Secretary of State's Papers at the National Archives
STAC: Star Chamber Records at the National Archives

Primary sources

1541–2: 33 Henry 8 c.8: The Bill against conjurations and wichecraftes and sorcery and enchantments. Available at: https://statutes.org.uk/site/the-statutes/sixteenth-century/1541-33-henry-8-c8-witchcraft/ [Accessed 14/09/2024]

1563: 5 Elizabeth 1 c.16: An Act agaynst Conjuracions Inchantmentes and Witchecraftes. Available at: https://statutes.org.uk/site/the-statutes/sixteenth-century/1563-5-elizabeth-1-c-16-an-act-against-conjurations-inchantments-and-witchcraft/ [Accessed 14/09/2024]

1563: Mary c.73: Anentis Witchcraft. Available at: https://statutes.org.uk/site/the-statutes/scottish-laws/1563-mary-c-73-anentis-witchcraft/ [Accessed 14/09/2024]

1604: 1 James 1 c.12: An Act against Conjuration, Witchcraft and dealing with evil and wicked Spirits. Available at: https://statutes.org.uk/site/the-statutes/seventeenth-century/1604-1-james-1-c-12-an-act-against-witchcraft/ [Accessed 14/09/2024]

BL MS Harley 6947, fol. 211r.

Bodleian MS Tanner 299, fol. 11r.

Buchanan, G. 1689. *A detection of the actions of Mary Queen of Scots concerning the murther of her husband, and her conspiracy, adultery, and pretended marriage with the Earl Bothwell and a defence of the true Lords, maintainers of the King's Majesties action and authority / written in Latin by G. Buchanan; translated into Scotch and now made English.* London: Richard Janeway.

Buchanan, G. 1722. *Buchanan's History of Scotland in Two Volumes.* London: J. Bettenham.

Burnet, G. 1837. *The History of the Reformation, 1.* London: Scott, Webster & Geary.

Calendar of the Cecil Papers in Hatfield House: Volume 17, 1605. 1938. Ed. M. S. Giuseppi. London: His Majesty's Stationery Office.

Calendar of State Papers Foreign: Elizabeth, Volume 7, 1564–1565. 1870. Ed. J. Stevenson. London: Public Record Office.

Calendar of State Papers, Scotland: Volume 10, 1589–1593. 1936. Ed. W. K. Boyd & H. W. Meikle. Edinburgh: General Register House.

Calendar of State Papers, Scotland: Volume 11, 1593–1595. 1936. Ed. A. I. Cameron. Edinburgh: General Register House.

Calendar Of State Papers Relating To Scotland And Mary, Queen Of Scots, Volume 13, Part 1, 1597–1603. 1969. Ed. J. D. Mackie. Edinburgh: Her Majesty's Stationery Office.

Calendar of State Papers, Spain, Volume 5, Part 2, 1536–1538. 1888. Ed. Pascual de Gayangos. London: His Majesty's Stationery Office.

Canongate Burgh Court Book 1574–77 SL150/1/2, pp. 370–3. Available at: https://witches.hca.ed.ac.uk/case/C/LA/3102 [accessed 06/03/2024]

Correspondence of King James VI of Scotland with Sir Robert Cecil and Others in England During the Reign of Queen Elizabeth. 1861. Ed. J. Bruce. Westminster: Camden Society.

Drummond, W. 1968 [1617]. 'The Entertainment' in L. E. Kastner (Ed.) *The Poetical Works of William Drummond of Hawthornden.* New York: Haskell House.

Ecumenical Council of Florence, Session 9–23 March 1440. Available at: https://www.ewtn.com/catholicism/library/ecumenical-council-of-florence-1438-1445-1461 [accessed 03/02/2024]

Fairfax, E. 1882 [1621]. *Daemonologia & Discourse on Witchcraft as it was Acted in the Family of Mr. Edward Fairfax of Fuyston in the Country of York in the Year 1621.* Ed. W. Grainge. Harrogate: R. Ackrill.

From authentic documents, a history of the witches of Renfrewshire, who were burned on the gallowgreen of Paisley. Publ. by the ed. of the Paisley repository (J. Millar). Paisley: J. Neilson.

Gaule, J. 1646. *Select cases of conscience touching vvitches and vvitchcrafts. By Iohn Gaule, preacher of the Word at Great Staughton in the county of Huntington.* London: W. Wilson.

Hopkins, M. 1647. *The discovery of vvitches: in answer to severall queries, lately delivered to the judges of the assize for the county of Norfolk. / And now published by Matthevv Hopkins, witch-finder. For the benefit of the whole kingdome.* London: R. Royston.

James VI and I. 1944 [1603]. *Basilikon Doron.* Edinburgh: William Blackwood.

James VI and I. 1924 [1597]. *Daemonologie.* London: The Bodley Head.

Kirkcaldy of Grange. 1849. *Memoirs and Adventures of Sir William Kirkaldy of Grange.* Ed. J. Grant. Edinburgh: William Blackwood & Sons.

Knox, J. 1816. *The history of the reformation of religion within the realm of Scotland, Volume 2, 5.* Edinburgh: Oliver & Boyd.

Letters and Papers, Foreign and Domestic, Henry VIII, Volume 2, 1515–1518. 1864. Ed. J. S. Brewer. London: Public Record Office.

Letters and Papers, Foreign and Domestic, Henry VIII, Volume 13 Part 2, August–December 1538. 1893. Ed. J. Gairdner. London: Public Record Office.

Melville, J. 1735. *The Memoirs of Sir J. Melville.* Edinburgh: George Scott.

NCRO MS IL 4304.

Phillips, J. 1566. *The Examination and confession of certaine wytches at Chensforde in the countie of Essex: before the Quenes Maiesties judges, the xxvi daye of July, anno 1566, at the assise holden there as then, and one of them put to death for the same offence, as their examination declareth more at large.* London: Willyam Powell.

Potts, T. 1845 [1613]. *Discovery of Witches in the County of Lancaster.* Ed. J. Crossley. Manchester: Charles Simms & Co.

Rémy, N. 2008. *Demonolatry: An Account of the Historical Practice of Witchcraft.* Ed. M. Summers. Mineola: Dover.

Scot, R. 1665. *The Discoverie of Witchcraft.* London: Andrew Clark.

The Scottish series of the reign of Queen Elizabeth, 1589–1603; an appendix to the Scottish series. 1543–1592; and the state papers relating to Mary Queen of Scots during her detention in England, 1568–1587. 1858. Ed. M. J. Thorpe. London: Longman, Brown, Green, Longmans.

SP 14/175 f.90.

Sprenger, J. & Kramer, H. 1968 [1486]. *Malleus Maleficarum*. London: Folio Society.

STAC 8/32/13.

The Survey of Scottish Witchcraft. Available at: https://witches.hca.ed.ac.uk/case/C/EGD/129 [Accessed 15/03/2024]

White, E. 1579. *A rehearsall both straung and true, of hainous and horrible actes committed by Elizabeth Stile alias Rockingham, Mother Dutten, Mother Deuell, Mother Margaret, fower notorious witches, apprehended at Winsore in the countie of Barks. and at Abbington arraigned, condemned, and executed, on the 26 daye of Februarie laste Anno. 1579*. London: Edward White.

Secondary sources

Aikin, L. 1822. *Memoirs of the Court of King James the First, I*. Boston: Wells & Lilly.

Angsar Kelly, H. 2006. *Satan: A Biography*. Cambridge: Cambridge University Press.

Apps, L. & Gow, A. 2018. *Males Witches in Early Modern Europe*. Manchester: Manchester University Press.

Bagshawe Harrison, G. 1966. *Elizabethan and Jacobean Quartos, 10*. Edinburgh: Edinburgh University Press.

Baines, E., Harland, J., & Whatton, W. R. 1870. *The History of the County Palatine and Duchy of Lancaster, Volume 1*. London: George Routledge & Sons.

Barbezat, M. D. 2018. *Burning Bodies: Communities, Eschatology, and the Punishment of Heresy in the Middle Ages*. Ithaca: Cornell University Press

Bayley Howell, T. 1816. *A Complete Collection of State Trials and Proceedings for High Treason and Other Crimes and Misdemeanours from the Earliest Period to the Year 1820, Volume 2*. London: T. C. Hansard.

Bellany, A. 2007. *The Politics of Court Scandal in Early Modern England: News Culture and the Overbury Affair, 1603–1660*. Cambridge: Cambridge University Press.

Bunn, I. & Geis, G. 2005. *A Trial of Witches: A Seventeenth Century Witchcraft Prosecution*. London: Routledge.

Burns, W. E. 2003. *Witch Hunts in Europe and America*. London: Bloomsbury.

Burton Russell, J. 1972. *Witchcraft in the Middle Ages*. Ithaca: Cornell University Press.

Dalyell, J. G. 1834. *The Darker Superstitions of Scotland*. Edinburgh: Waugh & Innes.

Davies, O. 1999. *Witchcraft, Magic and Culture, 1736–1951*. Manchester: Manchester University Press.

Durston, G. J. 2019. *Crimen Exceptum: The English Witch Prosecution in Context*. Hook: Waterside Press.

Gibson, J. 1988. *Hanged for Witchcraft: Elizabeth Lowys and her Successors*. Canberra: Tudor Press.

Goodare, J. 2002. 'The Framework for Scottish Witch-Hunting in the 1590s', *The Scottish Historical Review, 81, 212, 2*.

Goodare, J. 2002. *The Scottish Witch-hunt in Context*. Manchester: Manchester University Press.

Goodare, J. 2004. *The Government of Scotland 1560–1625*. Oxford: Oxford University Press.

Goodare, J. 2013. *Scottish Witches and Witch-Hunters*. Basingstoke: Palgrave Macmillan.

Goodare, J. 2016. *The European Witch-hunt*. London: Routledge.

Granger, J. 1824. *A biographical history of England, adapted to a methodical catalogue of engraved British heads, Volume 1*. London: William Baynes & Son.

Hansen, C. 1969. *Witchcraft at Salem*. New York: Braziller.

Hawkins, W. 1824. *A Treatise of the Pleas of the Crown Or a System of the Principal Matters Relating to that Subject, Digested Under Proper Heads*. London: S. Sweet.

Helmholz, R. H. 1985. *Select Cases on Defamation to 1600*. London: Selden Society.

Hill Burton, J. 1873. *The History of Scotland From Agricola's Invasion to the Extinction of the Last Jacobite Insurrection, Volume 6*. Edinburgh: William Blackwood.

Hope Robbins, R. 1970. *The Encyclopaedia of Witchcraft & Demonology*. London: Peter Nevill Ltd.

Hughes, P. 2013. 'Witch-Hunting in Scotland, 1649–1650' in J. Goodare (Ed.) *Scottish Witches and Witch-Hunters*. Basingstoke: Palgrave Macmillan.

Hume-Brown, P. 1911. *History of Scotland to the Present Time, Volume 2*. Cambridge: Cambridge University Press.

James, G. P. R. 2022 [1848]. *Gowrie, or the King's Plot*. London: Simpkin, Marshall & Co.

Kolb, R. 2008. *Lutheran Ecclesiastical Culture: 1550–1675*. Leiden: Brill.

Kors, A. C. & Peters, E. 2001. *Witchcraft in Europe, 400–1700: A Documentary History*. Philadelphia: University of Pennsylvania Press.

Lang, A. 2024. *The History of Scotland, Volume 2*. Loschberg: Jazzybee Verlag.

Leggatt, A. 2006. *William Shakespeare's* Macbeth*: A Sourcebook*. London: Routledge.

Levack, B. P. 1992. *The Literature of Witchcraft*. New York: Garland.

Levack, B. P. 1992. *Witchcraft in Scotland*. London: Garland.

Levack, B. P. 2001. *Demonology, Religion, and Witchcraft*. London: Routledge.

Levack, B. P. 2001. *New Perspectives on Witchcraft, Magic, and Demonology: Gender and Witchcraft*. London: Routledge.

Levack, B. P. 2013. *The Witch-Hunt in Early Modern Europe*. London: Routledge.

Levin, C., Bertolet, A. R., & Carney, J. E. 2017. *A Biographical Encyclopedia of Early Modern Englishwomen: Exemplary Lives and Memorable Acts, 1500–1650*. London: Routledge.

Levin, C. 2022. *The Reign and Life of Queen Elizabeth I*. Cham: Palgrave Macmillan.

Lillie Craik, G. 1840. *The Pictorial History of England, Volume 3*. London: Charles Knight & Co.

Lingard, J. 1883. *The History of England: From the First Invasion by the Romans to the Accession of William and Mary in 1688, Volume 7*. London: J. C. Nimmo & Bain.

Macfarlane, A. 1970. *Witchcraft in Tudor and Stuart England*. London: Routledge.

Malins, M. 2023. 'Oliver Cromwell' in I. Dale (Ed.) *Kings and Queens: 1200 Years of English and British Monarchy*. London: Hachette.

Maxwell-Stuart, P. G. 2005. *An Abundance of Witches: The Great Scottish Witch-Hunt*. Reading: Tempus.

McAleavy, T. 2022. *The Last Witch Craze: John Aubrey, the Royal Society and the Witches*. Stroud: Amberley.

Meikle, M. M. 2013. *The Scottish People 1490–1625*. UK: Lulu.

Normand, L. & Roberts, G. 2000. *Witchcraft in Early Modern Scotland: James VI's Demonology and the North Berwick Witches*. Exeter: University of Exeter Press.

Owen Pike, L. 1873. *A History of Crime in England, Volume 2*. London: Smith, Elder & Co.

Rawson Gardiner, S. 1896. *History of England from the Accession of James I. to the Outbreak of the Civil War, 1603–1642, Volume 6*. London: Longmans, Green & Co.

Rosenthal, B. 1993. *Salem Story: Reading the Witch Trials of 1692*. Cambridge: Cambridge University Press.

Ruigh, R. E. 1971. *The Parliament of 1624*. Cambridge: Harvard University Press.

Russell, G. 2023. *The Palace: From the Tudors to the Windsors*. London: HarperCollins.

Sage Richardson, A. 1875. *The History of Our Country from Its Discovery by Columbus to the Celebration of the Centennial Anniversary of Its Declaration of Independence*. Cambridge: The Riverside Press.

Schiern, F. E. A. 1880. *Life of James Hepburn, Earl of Bothwell*. Edinburgh: David Douglas.

Schilling, H. 2017. *Martin Luther: Rebel in an Age of Upheaval*. Oxford: Oxford University Press.

Scott, J. 1818. *A History of the Life and Death of John, Earl of Gowrie*. Edinburgh: William Blackwood.

Sharpe, J. 2014. *Witchcraft in Early Modern England*. London: Routledge.

Somerset, A. 1997. *Unnatural Murder: Poison at the Court of James I*. London: Weidenfeld & Nicolson.

Thornton, T. 2006. *Prophecy, Politics and the People in Early Modern England*. Woodbridge: Boydell.

Tytler, P. F. 1845. *History of Scotland, Volume 7*. Edinburgh: William Tait.

Wasser, M. 2013. 'Scotland's First Witch-Hunt: the eastern witch-hunt of 1568–1569' in J. Goodare (Ed.) *Scottish Witches and Witch-Hunters*. Basingstoke: Palgrave Macmillan.

Valiente, D. 2014. *Where Witchcraft Lives*. London: Aquarian Press.

Wells, S. 2002. *Shakespeare: For All Time*. Oxford: Oxford University Press.

Wiesner, M. E. 2019. *Women and Gender in Early Modern Europe*. Cambridge: Cambridge University Press.

Willumsen, L. H. 2020. 'Witchcraft against Royal Danish Ships in 1589 and the Transnational Transfer of Ideas', *The International Review of Scottish Studies, 45*.

Wright, T. 1852. *Narratives of Sorcery and Magic, from the Most Authentic Sources*. New York: Redfield.

Acknowledgements

In recent years, the study of witchcraft, witch-hunting and witch trials has exploded in all kinds of directions. I'm immensely grateful to those scholars who have helped refresh our understanding of this aspect of history – and to those, like Julian Goodare (and Joyce Miller and Louise Yeoman), who have not only written extensively on the subject but who have ensured that the surviving material has been catalogued and digitised in such resources as *The Survey of Scottish Witchcraft: 1563–1736*. I'm tremendously grateful also to those friends and colleagues in the history community who have supported me not just as I worked on this book but throughout my career so far: Erica Fudge, Sarah Gristwood, Lisa Hopkins, Elspeth Jajdelska, Leanda de Lisle, S.G. Maclean, Linda Porter, Melita Thomas, Alison Thorne, John Young – there are too many wonderful, kind, and supportive people to mention.

I would also like to thank the team at Birlinn, who have been endlessly enthusiastic about this project; Craig Hillsley for coming aboard (again!) to copy edit; and my agent, John Beaton, for having faith in both me and potential public interest in James VI and I and the alleged witches who suffered before, during, and after his reigns.

Index

ALSO BY STEVEN VEERAPEN

The Wisest Fool
The Lavish Life of King James VI and I

James VI and I has endured a mixed reputation. To many, the first monarch to reign over Scotland, England and Ireland is a stereotype: the loping, slobbering, colourless coward behind the authorised Bible bearing his name. For too long he has paled in comparison with his more celebrated Tudor and Stuart forebears.

But who was he really? To what extent have myth, anecdote and rumour obscured him? In this ground-breaking biography, James's story is laid bare and a welter of scurrilous assumptions put to rest. What emerges is a portrait of Elizabeth I's successor as his contemporaries knew him: a gregarious, idealistic man obsessed with the idea of family, whose personal and political goals could never match up to reality. With reference to many contemporary documents, this book casts fresh light on the personal, domestic, international and sexual politics of this misunderstood sovereign.

'A real page-turner'
Philippa Gregory

'A sensitive portrait . . . probing, well-rounded and very readable'
The Herald

'Highly accomplished and well written'
Country Life

'Balanced and minutely researched'
Tudor Times

Overlord
The Life of Henry VIII

Henry VIII is one of history's best-known characters and England's most famous monarch. He is simultaneously the virtuous Renaissance prince gone wrong, the psychopathic, paranoid tyrant and the much-married glutton.

Yet Henry didn't see himself as simply King of England. *Overlord* tells Henry's story as he saw it: the tale of a titan whose dominions embraced Scotland, Ireland, Wales, England and, if he could achieve his grandiose ambitions, swathes of France. Drawing on archival sources from across the British Isles, Steven Veerapen shows how Henry created an image of himself as a law-abiding and benevolent emperor, and thereby a rival to his European counterparts. By fair means and foul – murder plots, marriage negotiations and military ventures – he did all he could to realize a hitherto overlooked British dream.

By busting myths about the king – he was not particularly gluttonous, not particularly prudish, and not particularly messy in his religious changes – the real Henry can emerge: a blustering, self-aggrandising actor who swaggered about the stage of the British Isles in search of an imperial fantasy.